THE COMPLETE
BOOK OF
SOLITAIRE

Pierre Crépeau

FIREFLY BOOKS

A FIREFLY BOOK

Published by Firefly Books Ltd., 2001

First English language edition © Firefly Books Ltd. 2001

First published in Quebec by Les Éditions de l'Homme, 1999,
a division of the Sogides Group

First Printing

National Library of Canada Cataloguing in Publication Data

Crépeau, Pierre, 1927-
  The complete book of solitaire

Translation of: Le Grand Livre des Patiences.
Includes index.
ISBN 1-55209-597-5

1. Solitaire (Game).   I. Nguyen, My-Trang.   II. Title.

GV1261.C7413   2001   795.4'3   C2001-930408-0

U. S. Cataloguing in Publication Data
(Library of Congress Standards)

Crépeau, Pierre.
  The complete book of solitaire/Pierre Crépeau.
Originally published: Le Grand Livre des Patiences; Les Éditions de l'Homme, 1999.
[512] p.: col. ill.; cm.
Includes bibliographical references and index.
Summary: Rules and instructions to play 179 variations of the card game solitaire
ISBN 1-55209-597-5 (pbk)
1. Solitaire (Game).   2. Card games.   I. Title.
795.43   21   2001   CIP

Published in Canada in 2001 by
Firefly Books Ltd.
3680 Victoria Park Avenue
Willowdale, Ontario M2H 3K1

Published in the United States in 2001 by
Firefly Books (U.S.) Inc.
P.O. Box 1338, Ellicott Station
Buffalo, New York 14205

Translated by My-Trang Nguyen

Printed in Canada

This collection of my grandmother's solitaire games is a tribute to a great lady whose lively intelligence and noble heart filled me with admiration and affection as I was growing up. While compiling the material, I often thought about the scores of grandmothers who live alone in tiny apartments, completely cut off – save for their thoughts and memories – from their beloved families and familiar surroundings. I hope this book will bring them solace and amusement. May they find happiness in their forgotten world.

As the project slowly took shape, my thoughts turned to today's youth. These games of patience are eminently educational. Those who study them carefully will develop a capacity for concentration, a quick mind and a keen sense of observation and anticipation. Solitaire can also be a valuable tool for learning arithmetic and thinking with precision. And without being a course in moral virtue, the different versions of the game teach perseverance, honesty (note how easy it is to win a game if you cheat) and patience.

TABLE OF CONTENTS

INTRODUCTION

Grandmother and Her Playing Cards

My grandmother was one of those women who would terrify you at first sight, but then you'd adore her. Her bearing, patrician and aloof, invited respect and deference. She stood ramrod straight like a caryatid and yet glided fluidly about like a gently moving stream. Her face – smooth, unlined, handsomely tanned – radiated upper-class hauteur. But behind her dreamy eyes and raspy voice – the result of years of smoking – lurked a fragile soul.

There was a deep wound somewhere inside. I'll never know whether it was some personal tragedy or betrayal, for my grandmother was hardly one to confide in others. For her, acknowledging one's private pain in public was unacceptable, and she jealously guarded hers behind a veil of imagined diffidence. But the long, sleepless nights she endured spoke volumes about her inner turmoil.

Growing up, I never saw Grandmother sleep. Every evening, as we were getting ready for bed, she would stay by herself at the long kitchen table and absentmindedly shuffle her cards. In the morning, I'd find her in the same place, sitting in front of her cards, as though she'd hardly moved all night.

Intrigued by her "mania" – a word used by other members of the family to describe her behavior – I approached Grandmother one evening and quietly asked her why she always played cards alone. Instead of a direct answer, she taught me *Clairvoyance*, a children's game that involved predicting the color of the cards about to be turned up. It was love at first sight for both of us. Seeing my determination to beat the odds, Grandmother knew at once that I had what it took to be a persistent player. At last, she had found an avid student.

Soon the two of us played together almost daily. Grandmother taught me as many games as I could fathom and let me practice them with her, correcting my mistakes as they occurred and tapping on my fingers gently each time I attempted an "illegal" move.

One day she allowed me into her room. There, she lifted a little cedar box from a drawer, ceremoniously opened it and fished out an old deck of cards that were dog-eared and discolored. Yet, Grandmother held up the cards as if they were holy relics on display before an assembly of believers. She had inherited the cards from her own grandmother, she said, and had been preserving them as if they were sacred.

The Origin of Playing Cards

"Who invented playing cards?" I once asked her, and she treated me to a story. Hundreds of years ago in China, she said, most mandarins forbade their concubines to work lest it harm their physical beauty. The idle concubines, poor things, grew so desperately bored that the mandarins had to call upon a Chinese sage for help. The latter obliged by inventing playing cards as a pastime for the concubines. The great explorer Marco Polo eventually brought the cards back to Venice and, in time, the Venetians introduced them to Europe. Grandmother added that some people believed that playing cards had originated in India, where they were invented by a maharaja's wife to discourage her husband from playing with his beard.

I burst out laughing and told Grandmother I didn't believe a word of it. After a long silence, she said in that cigarette-strained rasp: "Ah! The things one invents just to counter boredom!"

Pictorial Symbols

One day, Grandmother decided to describe to me what playing cards actually represented. "They have always had four suits," she explained. "In the old days, these were a coin, a cup, a sword and a stick. The suits evolved as the cards gained popularity in Europe. The Germans opted for a leaf, a tassel, a bell and a heart. And it was the French who gave the cards their current suits, which originally symbolized the four social classes. Hearts represented the church; spades, the army; diamonds, the bourgeoisie; and clubs, the peasantry.

"For me, though, cards are a mirror of the human race," Grandmother added. "Hearts represent the lovers' race – people who are tall, attractive and impeccably groomed; they are happy, gregarious and generous. Spades represent sinister-looking criminals with black, bulging eyes and shaggy, grimy hair. Diamonds represent dreamers, like poets and artists – sensitive, whimsical people with slim, lithe and gracious bodies. Clubs represent the peasantry: narrow-minded, indolent and tenacious individuals. They are thick, heavy-set and muscular, with shiny, unkempt hair."

Watching Grandmother manipulate the cards, I sensed that she was also rearranging the story of her own life – the triumphs as well as the heartbreaks.

Playing Cards and the Calendar Year

Grandmother was so struck by the eerie affinity between a pack of cards and the calendar year that she often wondered whether or not some ancient astrologer had actually invented them. She pointed out that a deck contains 52 cards, just like a year has 52 weeks; the colors – red and black – correspond with the two yearly solstices; their 12 figures match the 12 zodiac signs; and there are four suits – hearts, spades, diamonds and clubs – just as there are four seasons. The 13 cards that make up each suit correspond with the 13 weeks in a season, or the 13 months – of 28 days each – in a lunar year. Since the ace is worth one point, the jack 11, the queen 12 and the king 13, the sum of all the cards in a suit is 91, which is also the number of days in a season. What's more, if you add up all four suits, you'll get a total of 364, which is the number of days in a year (52 weeks x 7 days, or, in the case of the lunar year, 13 months x 28 days).

Grandmother believed that the joker was added to the deck to fulfill the role of the 365th day in a leap year. Come to think of it, the joker does not really belong anywhere – not with the hearts, nor the spades, diamonds or clubs. He doesn't even have a figure – he is neither king, nor queen, nor jack – and has no rank. Withdraw the joker from the deck and it remains whole. Yet, introduce him in a game and at once he starts commanding it, dominating all the assets and out-classing all ranks. In Grandmother's mind, the advent of the joker must have been the work of a cheat.

Solitaire Games

There are two kinds of card games:
- the plastic game, or tarot, which originated in Italy and is based on images.
- the numerical game, which originated in Asia; it is based on rank and con-sists of one numerical sequence per suit.

Solitaire belongs in the numerical-game category, which can be broken down further into two categories: one is based on rank, such as in *Battle*, whereby the higher number prevails; the other is based on combination, whereby the player tries to put combinations together that will yield the greatest value. Poker is the best known of combination games.

According to Grandmother, solitaire is a game to be played alone and to say that it requires two or more players is utter nonsense. It is the most popular of all card games, and there are more varieties than all other forms of card games combined. Experts believe there are at least 350 different games of solitaire, and new ones are being invented all the time.

Blessed with an extraordinary intelligence and a fabulous memory, Grandmother was a high-caliber solitaire player. She knew more than a hundred games by heart. She had written out about 200 games in her notebook: some she had learned from her maternal grandmother and some from acquaintances; oth-ers she had picked up from old books or by corresponding with her parents and friends. Grandmother had even invented a few games. She was so proud of one particular game, *Germaine*, that she named it after herself. Unfortunately, I was unable to find her notebook; I assumed she burned it shortly before she died.

Most games of solitaire require a mixture of luck and skill. Rare are those that are designed to "come out" either through pure chance or by skill alone. They are mind games and as such require a good deal of mental effort, whether it be a children's game like *Clairvoyance* or *Announcement* or a complicated and subtle game like *Pascal* or *Germaine*, both of which call for finesse, a high degree of concentration and anticipation, complex calculations and a prodigious memory.

Solitaire demands time and perseverance in abundance. Some games, especially those based on anticipation and arithmetic, can come out only if the player is prepared to put in all the time it takes. Some games may last several hours. Grandmother once admitted she had spent two long nights trying to solve just one game.

There are people who mistake solitaire games for what the French call *réussite*, which is basically an exercise in fortune-telling. In fact, *réussite* is normally played with tarot rather than numerical cards and requires that you observe a rigid ritual – such as cutting the deck of cards heartside, that is, from the left-hand side – lest the entire exercise be deemed invalid. You then deal the cards face up, without manipulating them, into a tableau that will "tell" you what you want to know about, say, an affair, a relationship or an illness. *Réussite* is governed by a rather esoteric code of conduct, but, unlike solitaire, it leaves no room for maneuvers that could effect the final result.

Not all games of solitaire come out. A connoisseur can usually tell whether or not a game will come out as soon as the tableau is laid out, as is often the case with a game like *Mixed Pairs*. When faced with an unsolvable game, you should accept the inevitable right away, then start again.

You'll no doubt notice that some games of solitaire are governed by the same set of rules, and only their respective tableaux set them apart. This underlines the importance of the game's visual aspects. Solitaire must be as eye-pleasing as it is tempting for the mind. My grandmother, who was keen on stagecraft, loved games that had grand tableaux, such as *La Belle Lucie*, *Big Ben* and *Czarina*. For her, those tableaux were true works of art.

As to who actually invented the game of solitaire, Grandmother seemed to believe that it was Napoléon Bonaparte, while he lived in exile on the island of St. Helena. In fact, many versions bear his name. Some people, however, think the game was invented at least three centuries ago, but by whom no one knows. What we do know is that Napoléon used solitaire to keep boredom at bay during the long years on St. Helena; General Charles de Gaulle did his best to forget about the Algerian uprising by playing the game; President Franklin D. Roosevelt sometimes took a break from planning his New Deal policies for a game of *Spider*; General Dwight D. Eisenhower spent his longest day during World War II playing solitaire; the great Russian novelist, Leo Tolstoy, wrote about solitaire games in *War and Peace*; and the French writer, Stendhal, glorified the game *Salamander* in his own books.

"Games of solitaire are not just for the high and mighty," said Grandmother. "People from all walks of life have always enjoyed the game, even though there were times when both the church and the aristocracy vehemently condemned them for daring to play it. Ordinary people are just as entitled to savoring those delicious, solitary moments when all they have to deal with is the harmless tricks of a game of chance. It's a welcome break from the real-life, ugly tricks practiced by their bankers, lawyers or politicians."

About This Book

The 179 versions of solitaire and some 150 variants described in this book have been selected to suit all tastes. It is an assortment of both childish and serious games, simple and complex, easy and difficult, dull and flashy. An experienced player will find something pleasing, as will a beginner. My grandmother knew virtually all the games by heart. She practiced them religiously and passed them on to me. I, too, have played these games and their variants countless times. When I compare my grandmother's games with those I've come across in various books, I realize how much nicer my grandmother's look. And I still remember the clear and precise language she used to describe them.

I, too, went to great lengths to define as precisely and accurately as possible most of the words I use to describe these games: a sequence is neither a suit sequence nor a run; a pair is not a couple; a tierce is not a trio; a color is not a suit. Readers are invited to consult the glossary of card terms at the end of the book to ensure a thorough understanding of the games.

All the games are presented according to the same criteria, as follows:

- A brief introduction, often accompanied by a comment by or an appreciation of my grandmother
- Material (cards)
- Opening tableau (note the distinction between the maneuver zone and the foundation zone)
- Object
- Play
- Strategy tips (if available)
- Variants (if available)

In most books about solitaire, the games are presented sequentially in no apparent order. In this book, I classify them according to their object of play. Part I contains games whose object is either to eliminate cards or to gather them all back into one deck. Part II is for games that require either one or two decks of cards, and whose object is to achieve an ascending sequence. Part III includes games whose object is to achieve all other kinds of sequences – descending, mixed, circular or by intervals.

Ask someone to teach you a game of solitaire, and the person will likely start to explain the rules of play and show you how to lay the cards out. But ask him the name of that particular game and you'll probably draw a blank stare. This has happened to me so often that I can say with absolute confidence that most people don't even know what their favorite games are called. On the other hand, authors of books about solitaire often identify the games arbitrarily, which explains why so many of the same kinds bear a variety of names. My grandmother, too, gave her games whatever name she fancied, instead of relying on her own memory. "A name," she used to say, "is a poem. It should have a color, a fragrance or a mystique. Solitaire is only as beautiful as its name. And since most of the games are anonymous, I should have the freedom to call them whatever I want."

Rules

According to Grandmother, there are general rules that apply to all solitaire games, and to ignore them is, to put it crudely, to cheat. Using the joker, for example, is an absolute taboo. For another, one must shuffle the cards thoroughly before dealing. Exceptions to this rule – say, in cases where cards are to be gathered in a certain way so the player can earn extra maneuvers – are clearly indicated.

Where no tableau is provided, the general rule is to lay the cards out one by one, left to right, starting from the top left. In each case, I have indicated whether the cards are to be dealt face up or face down. Many solitaire games call for a face-down talon from which the player will draw the cards one by one, or three at a time (as the case may be), during play. Some players have the habit of glancing at the next card before deciding on a move, a habit my grandmother considered the rankest heresy.

Once a move is made, the player should stick with it no matter what. To go back on a maneuver is simply to cheat, Grandmother said. It's also against the rules to move a card from the foundation zone to the maneuver zone. Only on rare occasions is such a move allowed, as in the game of *Seven in a Row*. Such exceptions are indicated.

Generally speaking, a player must immediately fill a vacant space with a card drawn from the talon or the discard pile. In some cases, however, the player must wait until the next deal to fill the space, or has the option to do so or not. To avoid confusion, I'll indicate which rule prevails.

In general, one cannot break a sequence and move part of it into the maneuver zone. This is not a hard-and-fast rule, however, and exceptions will be indicated.

I take great care in differentiating between rules (marked by "must") and optional maneuvers (expressed by "may"). Solitaire practitioners generally admit

to changing the rules at will in order to render the game either easier or more difficult. This may be the reason why there are so many variants. My grandmother
believed that rules were there to be observed at all times; too much liberty, she
declared, would lead straight to anarchy.

GLOSSARY

Alternating colors: Red on black, black on red.

Ascending sequence: A sequence that runs from ace (low) to king (high), or from 2 to ace, in the case of a circular sequence.

Available card: A card that can be used in a maneuver. The top card of a discard pile is always available.

Back: The reverse side of a card, i.e., the side that doesn't bear its suit or rank. All 52 cards in a pack usually bear the same pattern on their backs.

Base card: See **Foundation card.**

Blocked card: A card that cannot be used in a maneuver, either because it is over-lapped by another or is unsuitable for play according to the rules of the game.

Blocked play: A game is said to be blocked when no further maneuver, as per-mitted by the rules of play, is available.

Chiasm: An intersection of two pairs or two couples.
1) Example of a pair chiasm:

$$A \diagdown \diagup 7$$
$$7 \diagup \diagdown A$$

2) Example of a couple chiasm:

$$10 \diagdown \diagup 6$$
$$8 \diagup \diagdown 4$$

Circular sequence: A sequence that starts from a foundation card other than an ace, a king or a 2 and, as a result, wraps around those three cards, like a snake swallowing its own tail. For example, an ascending sequence starting from the 8 will wrap around the king, the ace and the 2 on its way to the 7; a descending sequence starting from the 8 will run in the other direction, wrapping around the 2, the ace and the king on its way to the 9.

Color: Playing cards come in two colors: red (hearts and diamonds) and black (spades and clubs). In order to avoid confusion, the term "color" is not used to designate a suit in this book.

Column: The vertical alignment of cards.

Contact card: A card on which another card rests as a result of a compulsory maneuver.

Couple: Two cards whose respective ranks add up to a predetermined value, regardless of suit or color. For example, a 7 and a 3 form a couple with a total of 10; an 8 and a 6 form a couple with a total of 14.

Court card: The king, queen or jack.

Covered card: A card that is completely covered by one or several cards, constituting a packet.

Crenel: A confined gap (between two cards) created by the removal of a card.

Dead card: A card that figures in a tableau but plays no role in the game.

Deal: A maneuver used to unblock play. It consists in distributing – according to a predetermined order – a certain number of cards from the talon. A deal can usually be repeated until the talon is exhausted.

Descending sequence: A sequence that runs from king (high) to ace (low). A descending sequence may also be circular, running from any card other than the king, ace or 2.

Discard: To lay aside a card that may be used in a subsequent maneuver.

Discard pile: A pile of mostly face-up cards which are put on reserve temporarily for subsequent use. The top card of a discard pile is always available for play.

Double card: In two-deck solitaire games, a card of the same rank and suit. See also **Shadow card.**

Double suit sequence: In two-deck solitaire games, an ascending suit sequence from ace (low) to king (high), followed by a descending suit sequence from king (high) to ace (low) – the two suit sequences being joined by the *shadow* king card. A double suit sequence thus runs as follows: A, 2, 3, 4, 5, 6, 7, 8, 9, 10, J, Q, K, shadow K, Q, J, 10, 9, 8, 7, 6, 5, 4, 3, 2, A.

Draw a card: To take a card from the talon and introduce it into play.

End-of-sequence card: The last-wanted card in a run, sequence or suit sequence; for example, a king in an ascending sequence on the ace; an ace in a descending sequence on the king; or a 7 in an ascending sequence on the 8.

Ending tableau: The appearance of a tableau once the solitaire game has come out.

Face: The side of a card showing its rank and suit.

Face-down card: A card whose suit or rank is hidden from view.

Face-up card: A card whose face is visible.

Foundation card: A card that is put in the objective zone on which ascending or descending sequences are built. Also called a **base card.**

Foundation zone: An area, located at the top, to the side or even within the tableau itself, where results of card maneuvers, such as suit sequences, sequences or runs, are deposited.

Four-of-a-kind: Any group of four same-rank cards. Also called a **square.**

Game: A set of maneuvers ending in success or failure.

Interval of build: In skip sequences, the predetermined number of ranks between two cards. For example, an ascending sequence by twos is: A, 3, 5, 7, 9, J, K; a descending sequence by threes is: K, 10, 7, 4, A.

Junction: The meeting point between two sequences. For example, the ascending heart sequence 7, 8, 9 and the descending heart sequence Q, J, 10 meet at the 9 and 10 of hearts. At this junction, the player may reverse one sequence upon the other.

Lay out: To spread the cards – face up or face down – on the table according to a predetermined order.

Major card: A card of superior rank, usually one ranking from 7 and up.

Maneuver: The shifting of one or several cards during a turn of play.

Maneuver chamber: A section of the maneuver zone where sequences are being developed.

Maneuver zone: The area in the tableau where cards are being manipulated to build suit sequences, sequences or runs.

Match: To combine a group of cards according to a predetermined pattern.

Minor card: A card of inferior value, usually one between the ace (when it counts for one point) and the 6.

Mixed pair: Two cards of the same rank but different color; for example, a red 5 and a black 5.

Mixed suit sequences: The ascending and descending suit sequences that need to be built in a particular game.

Move: To modify the position of a card in the tableau according to the rules of play.

Moved card: A card that has been moved according to the rules of play.

Mutual impasse: An unsolvable situation in which two cards block each other – one occupying a space belonging to the other, and vice versa.

Opening move: The first maneuver to open the game.

Opening tableau: The arrangement of the cards, face up or face down, on the table according to a set of specific rules, at the beginning of the game. A tableau usually includes a foundation zone and a maneuver zone, as well as vacant spaces reserved for foundation cards.

Overlap: The position of a card that covers, entirely or partially, another card. Cards may overlap one another vertically or horizontally.

Pair: Two cards of the same rank, regardless of color. For example, two 8s or two kings.

Pairs-royal (or proil): Three cards of the same rank; for example, three 8s or three kings.

Pile: Contains face-up or face-down cards, entirely covered by the top card.

Quart: A four-card suit sequence that contains kings, queens, jacks and 10s.

Quincunx: A pyramid-shaped card disposition, according to which a card in a lower row overlaps two cards directly above it, with the exception of the two end cards of each row. See the opening tableau of *Pyramid* (no. 11) for an example.

Quint: Five same-suit cards, regardless of rank.

Rank: The order or position of a card in a suit or a sequence.

Release: To free up a card that has been blocked for subsequent play.

Reserve: Cards that may be used in certain maneuvers but not as contact cards.

Reverse: To transfer a descending sequence, one card at a time, onto an ascending sequence, or vice versa. In two-deck games, this maneuver is often subject to strict rules of play.

Round: Consists in turning up the entire talon, one card – or a group of cards – at a time, according to the rules of play. Some games allow more than one round per game.

Row: The horizontal alignment of cards.

Royal Quint: Five same-suit cards in sequence from 10 (jack, queen, king) to ace.

Run: Cards of the same or alternating colors that follow in correct order of rank. A run may be ascending or descending.

Sequence: Cards following one another in correct order of rank, regardless of suit or color. A sequence may be ascending or descending.

Glossary

Shadow card: In two-deck solitaire games, a card of the same rank and suit, such as any of the two 4s of hearts or the two jacks of spades. Also called **double card**.

Shuffle: To mix the order of cards before dealing so that they are randomly arranged.

Slide: To place a card, face up or face down, underneath another card or an entire packet or pile.

Space: The spot occupied by a card in a tableau, at the junction between a row and a column. For example, the following space in row 2 and column 4 is indicated by the letter O:

X   X   X   X   X   X   X   X

X   X   X   O   X   X   X   X

Square: Any group of four same-rank cards. Also called **four-of-a-kind**.

Suit: A succession of 13 cards bearing the same symbol. In playing cards, the four suits are spades, hearts, diamonds and clubs.

Suit sequence: Same-suit cards following one another in correct order of rank. A suit sequence may be ascending or descending.

Suit sequence on the ace: Suit sequence starting from the ace. A suit sequence on the 2 has a 2-card as foundation; a suit sequence on the king has a king-card as foundation; and so on.

Talon: A pile of face-down cards that are left over after the opening tableau has been laid out and that are reserved for subsequent use.

Tierce: A sequence of three cards of the same suit. For example, a sequence of 4, 5 and 6 of spades or of jack, queen and king of hearts.

Trio: Three cards whose respective ranks add up to a predetermined value. For example, a 7, a 3 and an ace form a trio with a total of 10; a 7, a 5 and a 3 form a trio with a total of 15.

Vacancy: A space or column that contains no card.

Value: A conventional ranking system for playing cards. It is both numerical – from two to 10, and figure-based – from jack to ace. Some games assign the ace the numerical value of one, the jack as 11 points, the queen as 12, and the king as 13.

Waiting space: A temporary destination for a card during a series of maneuvers.

Waste card: A card that is laid aside as unwanted or unplayable for the duration of a game.

Waste pile: A pile of cards that are laid aside as unwanted or unplayable.

PART I

Elimination and Amalgamation

CHAPTER 1

Elimination by Pairs

I. Nestor

This classic game of solitaire, named after the wise hero of the Trojan War, will hardly strain your intellectual capacities. It's primarily a game of chance, requiring a great deal of manipulation but little strategy. My grandmother said it was a favorite of the Empress Josephine but that Napoléon scorned the game.

Material
One deck of 52 cards.

Opening Tableau
Deal 48 cards face up in six overlapping rows of eight columns. A column cannot contain two cards of the same rank. If this happens, skip the second same-rank card by sliding it to the bottom of the talon and continue dealing. Keep the four remaining cards face down, to make the reserve.

Object
To eliminate all the cards in pairs of the same rank, regardless of suits.

Play
Only the available cards at the bottom of the columns can be matched and eliminated, regardless of their color. When play is blocked, use a card from the reserve pile. If none of the reserve cards can unblock play, the game fails. It is won when all the cards have been eliminated from the tableau.

Strategy
When faced with a choice between two pairs – say, when there are three same-rank cards at the bottom of the columns – opt for the pair that would either prevent an imminent impasse or generate the longest series of maneuvers.

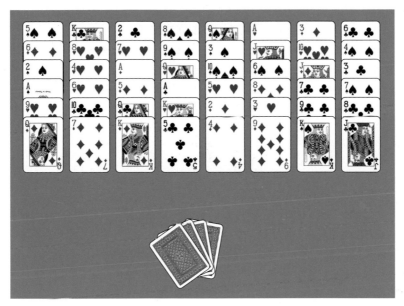

Tableau 1

Variant

Deal all four reserve cards, face up, and opt for the one you want.

2. Matchmaker

Grandmother wasn't terribly fond of this game, calling it strictly manual. Indeed, the game involves a lot of manipulation and little reflection – a solitaire game for long arms and small brains. Besides, the success rate is relatively high.

Material
One deck of 52 cards.

Opening Tableau
Deal the cards one row at a time into 13 piles of four cards each, arranged in two rows of five columns and one row of three columns. Only the top card of each pile is face up.

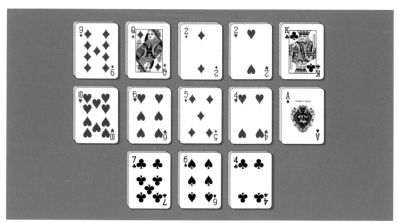

Tableau 2

Object
To eliminate all the cards from the tableau by removing same-color pairs, for example, two red 5s, or two black jacks.

Play

In Tableau 2, eliminate the pair of 2s (hearts and diamonds) in the first row. Turn over the two cards under them. Should new same-color pairs form, keep removing them. Otherwise, play is blocked.

To unblock play, eliminate any two same-rank cards of alternate colors and put them to the bottom of their respective piles, such as, say, the 6 of hearts in the second row and the 6 of spades in the third. Only one such maneuver is allowed per pile, so make sure you place the card perpendicular to the pile to remind yourself that you've already played that maneuver. If there is just one card left in one of the two piles involved, leave that pile alone and unblock the other. The game is won when all the cards have been eliminated from the tableau.

Variants

1. Deal 16 cards face down in four piles of four cards each. The top card of each pile is face up. Discard 20 cards and proceed to play with the remaining cards according to the same rules as those of the original version. The success rate of this abridged, 32-card version is much lower.
2. Deal 32 cards in eight piles of four cards each. The top card of each pile is face up. Proceed to play according to the same rules as those of the original version.

3. Monte Carlo

My grandmother dubbed this one Chain Weddings *because it consists in forming pairs and removing them. This reminded her of the hundreds of marriages that were hastily arranged in Montréal during the Second World War so that young men could escape conscription. The game is of French origin.*

Material
One deck of 52 cards.

Opening Tableau
Deal out 25 cards face up, forming five rows of five columns. Keep the talon face down.

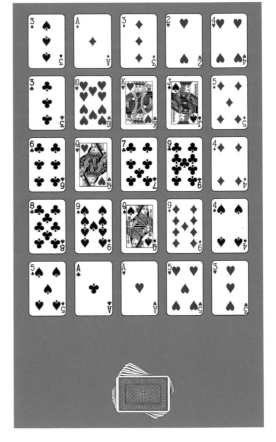

Tableau 3

Object

To eliminate all the cards from the tableau by pairs – or groups of two same-rank cards, regardless of color.

Play

Eliminate any two same-rank cards that are adjacent to each other either horizontally, vertically or diagonally. From the opening tableau as shown, eliminate the pair of 3s from the first column, the two 9s in the fourth column, the two 4s

Tableau 4

Elimination by Pairs

in the fifth column, the two aces in the fifth row and the two queens, which are diagonally placed in the second and third columns. Tableau 4 shows the vacant spaces left by the removal of those pairs.

Fill the spaces by sliding the cards to the left, or up from below – always starting from the left, and so on, as shown in Tableau 5. Cards are then dealt from the talon to complete the new tableau. Each time the tableau is reconstituted, the configuration changes and new pairs are formed. In Tableau 5, for example, there are three combinations of 5s – vertically in the third column, horizontally in the third row and diagonally in the third and fourth columns.

Tableau 5

Select the combination that will generate the greatest number of new pairs.

Continue to reconstitute the tableau and discard the pairs until there is nothing left to discard. The game is won only if both the tableau and the talon are empty.

Variants
1. Eliminate cards by pairs or by same-suit groups.
2. As soon as a pair is eliminated, fill the vacant spaces by moving cards leftward and/or up from below.
3. Put the talon in the waste pile and play only with the tableau.

4. Wish

This game requires more manipulation than calculation. According to Grandmother, who found it boring, the game was so named because some people believed that if you won it on your very first try, any wish you made before starting the game – however far-fetched – would come true. I remember that on my first try, I wished for a large castle in a deep forest atop a high mountain. I must have lost the game because I have never lived in a castle, large or small, let alone one secluded in a deep forest and atop a high mountain!

Material
One deck of 32 major cards – from 7 to ace.

Opening Tableau
Deal the cards face down in eight piles of four cards each, arranging the piles into two rows of four columns. Turn over the top card of each pile.

Object
To eliminate all the cards from the tableau by pairs.

Play
Eliminate all pairs from the tableau, regardless of their color. Turn up the cards that become exposed following each removal and continue removing the pairs. The game is won when all the cards have been eliminated from the tableau.

Variant
To make this game more difficult, Grandmother suggested eliminating the cards by same-color pairs, for example, a pair of black 8s, or red queens, and so on.

5. Furtive Pairs

Grandmother detested this particular solitaire game. Yet it was one of the first games she taught me.

Material
One deck of 52 cards.

Object
To eliminate all the cards by pairs or groups of two same-rank cards.

Play
There is no opening tableau. Turn over the cards one by one and deal them in two piles. Eliminate each pair as it is formed, regardless of color. Keep in mind that a pair can be formed only if the two cards in question are dealt out together. Let's suppose a 5 of hearts and 7 of spades are on the table, and the next deal produces a 7 of diamonds. The latter cannot be paired with the 7 of spades of the previous deal.

Once the deck is all dealt out, stack the pile on the left-hand side onto the other. Turn over the deck and, without shuffling the cards, start the process anew. Upon each new turn, the order of cards changes and new pairs are formed. The player is allowed as many deals as necessary to eliminate all the cards from play. However, if no pairs appear after two consecutive deals, the game is lost.

Variant
Eliminate each pair as it appears, whether it is formed with cards from the same deal or in tandem in the same column, or otherwise. The player is thus assured that the game will always be won.

6. Perpetual Motion

Grandmother taught me this game, although she dreaded it. As its name suggests, it consists in moving the cards about continually, though to no great purpose more often than not. Intelligence has nothing to do with this game, since it demands little attention. It's purely a game of chance.

Material

One deck of 52 cards.

Opening Tableau

Deal four cards face up in a row. Keep the talon face down.

Object

To eliminate all the cards from the tableau, by fours-of-a-kind, i.e., by groups of four same-rank cards.

Play

If the tableau contains two or three same-rank cards, stack them together atop the one farthest to the left. For example, if the tableau shows a 4 of spades, a 3 of hearts, a 3 of clubs and a 7 of hearts, pack the 3 of clubs atop the 3 of hearts.

Draw four more cards from the talon and lay them out face up atop the four columns. Let's suppose the new tableau shows a 5 of spades, a king of diamonds, a 5 of hearts and a king of clubs. Pack the 5 of hearts atop the 5 of spades, and the king of clubs atop the king of diamonds.

Move only one card at a time. If by removing a card, you release a card with the same rank as another, stack the card on the right atop that on the left. Continue the game in this manner until you have used up the talon.

The tableau now consists of four piles of cards. Stack them, face up, together – fourth onto third, and so on. Turn the entire deck over, and, without shuffling the cards, deal them out anew, four at a time. If a four-of-a-kind comes out in one deal, withdraw it from the deck.

Sometimes a four-of-a-kind may form in the talon that cannot come out entirely. In the meantime, another pair may be formed and break the square. Many more deals may be required before such a square can be whole again. Fours-of-a-kind thus form and unform, and the player goes on dealing the cards in a perpetual motion. The game is won if all the fours-of-a-kind have been eliminated. It fails if play is blocked; that is, when the order of the cards remains unchanged after, say, two consecutive deals. Usually, though, the player gives up before eliminating five or six fours-of-a-kind.

7. Clean Sweep

Despite its apparent simplicity, this game of solitaire has a low success rate.

Material
One deck of 52 cards.

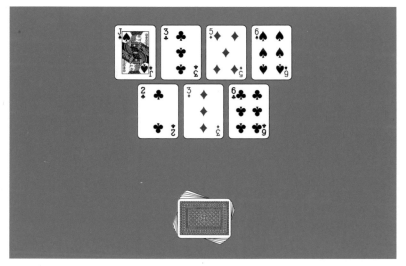

Tableau 6

Opening Tableau
Deal the cards face up, four in the first row and three in the second. Keep the talon face down.

Object
To eliminate all the cards in the first row.

Play

If a card in the second row is of the same rank as one or more cards in the first, it can "sweep" them off the tableau. In Tableau 6, for example, the 3 of diamonds can sweep the 3 of clubs, and the 6 of clubs can sweep the 6 of spades. The result is shown in Tableau 7.

Fill the vacant spaces in the first row with cards from the talon, and cover the second row with three new cards (see Tableau 8). Now, the 4 of clubs can sweep the 4 of hearts. Reconstitute the tableau until you can eliminate all four cards in the first row – in which case the game is won –

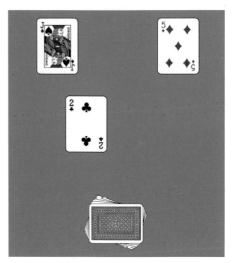

Tableau 7

or until the talon is exhausted. By then, if the first row is not entirely eliminated, the game is lost.

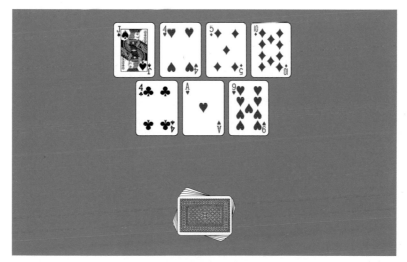

Tableau 8

8. Baker's Dozen

This is an easy game with a high success rate – a good one for beginners.

Material
One deck of 52 cards.

Opening Tableau
Deal 48 cards in a row of 12 piles and turn over the top card of each pile. Keep the four remaining cards face down, to make the reserve.

Object
To eliminate all the cards by pairs or groups of two same-rank cards.

Play
Eliminate all pairs from the tableau, regardless of their color. Turn over the cards under the eliminated ones, and continue removing all new pairs that form in the process.

    Whenever play is blocked, draw one of the four cards in the reserve pile. If it matches in rank with one in the tableau, eliminate them both and continue on. If not, draw another card from the reserve pile to unblock. The game is won when all the cards in the tableau are eliminated. It is lost if play is blocked and there are no cards left in the reserve pile.

Strategy
When faced with a choice between three cards with which to form a pair, opt for the cards in piles with the most face-down cards. Resist as much as possible the temptation to empty a pile too quickly because it will reduce your chance of matching pairs later on.

Variants

1. To make this game more difficult, some players suggest removing same-color pairs. For example, two red 5s, or black jacks.

2. There is also the two-deck variant, whereby the opening tableau is formed with 12 piles of four cards each, and the reserve pile contains eight cards. The 12 piles are arranged in two rows. The play consists in removing pairs of doubles, say, two 7s of hearts or two queens of spades.

9. Salamander

This very simple game depends entirely on chance. Nevertheless, it has a low success rate. It can hardly be considered attractive, since it is mainly a matter of manipulation. Often, the game fails the minute the opening tableau is laid out, in which case you should just start from scratch.

Material
One deck of 52 cards.

Opening Tableau
Deal seven cards, face up, in a row. Keep the talon face down.

Object
To eliminate all the cards from the tableau by squares, i.e., groups of four same-rank cards.

Play
If the tableau contains two or three same-rank cards, stack them together atop the one farthest to the left. Fill the resulting vacant spaces with cards from the talon.

Once all the spaces in the tableau are filled, turn over the cards from the talon, one by one, and stack each of them atop those of the same rank in the tableau until a square, or group of four same-rank cards, is formed. The game comes out if the player succeeds in removing all the cards from the tableau by squares – no mean feat, Grandmother said.

CHAPTER 2

Elimination by Sums

10. Aunt Lucile

A beginner's game, this one is simple and easy to win.

Material

One deck of 52 cards.

Opening Tableau

Deal 13 cards face up in two rows of five cards each and one row of three. Keep the talon face down.

Tableau 9

Object
To eliminate all the cards from both the tableau and the talon.

Play
Match and eliminate from the tableau all couples totalling 10, regardless of their color. From Tableau 9, for example, eliminate the 4 of hearts and the 6 of diamonds; and the 7 of clubs and the 3 of hearts.

Court cards (kings, queens or jacks) or 10s can be eliminated only by squares, that is, by groups of four same-rank cards. The two queens of diamonds and hearts in the tableau, for example, can be eliminated only after the two queens of clubs and spades show up in the tableau.

Continue to fill the vacant spaces with cards drawn from the talon, one by one. Eliminate all new couples or squares thus formed until no cards are left either in the tableau or in the talon. The game is lost if some cards remain with which neither couples nor squares can be formed.

Variants
1. Couples must be adjoining, either in the same row or in the same column, just like those in Tableau 9: the 4 of hearts and the 6 of diamonds in the first row, or the 4 of hearts and the 6 of spades in the third column.
2. Instead of squares, 10s and court cards can be eliminated if they constitute a sequence from 10 to king.

11. Pyramid

This game of solitaire got its name from the shape of the opening tableau. I asked Grandmother what a pyramid was when she taught me this one and was treated to fascinating stories about pharaohs building their fabulous tombs and the millions of slaves who perished in the process. She never missed an opportunity for a history lesson during our card-table encounters.

Material
A deck of 52 cards.

Opening Tableau
Deal 28 cards face up in seven rows arranged like a quincunx, that is, in the shape of a pyramid: one card in the first row, two in the second, three in the third and so on until the seventh row, which contains seven cards. Overlap each row with the one above so that each card is partially covered by two cards in the row below – except for the two end cards of each row. Keep the talon face down.

Tableau 10

Object
To eliminate all the cards from both the tableau and the talon.

Play
Eliminate from the tableau any two available cards that total 13. Ace is counted as one, jack as 11, queen as 12 and king as 13. Kings can be eliminated singly. Once all possible couplings – totalling 13, that is – have been eliminated from the tableau, draw the cards, one at a time, from the talon and try to match them with the available cards in the tableau. Eliminate all couples thus formed. If two consecutive cards from the talon total 13, eliminate them too.

For example, in Tableau 10, eliminate the king of clubs, the jack of hearts and the 2 of spades, then the 9 and 4 of hearts. Draw new cards from the talon. Should an 8 appear, match it with the 5 of spades and eliminate both cards. The game is won when all cards are eliminated from both the tableau and the talon.

Strategy
It's important to eliminate the cards from the tableau before those from the talon. When faced with a choice between two cards, choose the one that will generate the most maneuvers.

Variant
Grandmother's rules allow one deal for an expert, two for an apprentice and three for a beginner.

12. Decimal

Grandmother wasn't fond of this game. She particularly disliked the second variant, which she claimed was not a genuine solitaire game since it came out at virtually every try.

Material
One deck of 52 cards.

Opening Tableau
Deal 13 cards face up in a row. Keep the talon face down.

Object
To eliminate all the cards from both the tableau and the talon.

Play
Eliminate all adjoining cards totalling 10 or a multiple of 10, regardless of their color or the number of cards. For example, you may eliminate two 7s, a 2 and a 4, because they total 20 – that is, two times 10 – or a 3, an 8 and a 9, which also totals 20. Ace is counted as one. Tens and court cards (kings, queens and jacks), counted as 10 each, can be eliminated singly.

Tighten the row by sliding the remaining cards closer together, always from right to left. When matching is no longer possible, draw 13 new cards from the talon and continue to eliminate new groupings of cards totalling 10 or a multiple of 10. Continue play to include two more deals, of 13 cards apiece, from the talon. Only one round is allowed per game. The game is won when all the cards have been eliminated from both the tableau and the talon.

Variants

1. As the cards are being laid out, face up, one by one, eliminate any adjoining cards totalling 10, 20 or 30. Tens, jacks, queens and kings can be eliminated only if they are accompanied by other cards, from 9 down.

2. Some players suggest laying all the cards on the table, then start adding them up. I am puzzled by this because the cards are sure to come out each time. Can you guess the trick? See CLUES on page 503 for details.

13. Baroness

This game is a cousin of Pyramid *(no. 11). Its success rate is fair-ly high.*

Material
One deck of 52 cards.

Opening Tableau
Deal 10 cards, face up, in two rows of five columns.

Object
To eliminate all the cards from both the tableau and the talon.

Play
Eliminate same-color couples that total 13, regardless of suit. For example, a couple can be a 10 of spades and a 3 of spades, or a 9 of diamonds and a 4 of hearts. Kings can be eliminated singly. Fill the vacant spaces with cards from the talon. The game is won when all the cards are eliminated from both the tableau and the talon.

Strategy
When faced with a choice between various couplings, choose the one that would generate the most maneuvers. At times, the game has some surprising twists.

Variant
Deal five cards in one row and eliminate any couple totalling 13, regardless of color. Continue dealing five cards at a time. Only the available cards atop the piles can be eliminated.

14. Duke

This one has a low success rate, but if you play the second variant – that is, without taking the colors of the cards into consideration – it will almost always come out.

Material
One deck of 52 cards.

Tableau 11

Opening Tableau
Deal 12 cards, face up, in three rows of four columns.

Object
To eliminate all the cards from both the tableau and the talon.

Elimination by Sums

Play

Eliminate from the tableau all same-suit couples that total 11. Using Tableau 11, eliminate the 7 and 4 of diamonds, and the 5 and 6 of clubs. Court cards can be eliminated only if they can form a tierce – a sequence of three same-suit cards, such as the jack, queen and king of spades. Fill the vacant spaces with cards from the talon. Repeat these maneuvers until the talon is used up. If cards remain in the talon and the tableau no longer contains couples totalling 11, the game fails. It is successful when all the cards from the tableau and the talon have been eliminated.

Variants

1. Eliminate same-color couples or three-card sequences, regardless of suit. From Tableau 11, for example, eliminate the 6 of hearts and the 5 of spades.
2. A three-card sequence containing, say, a jack of diamonds, a queen of clubs and a king of hearts would also be eligible for removal.

15. Grand Departures

This seemingly simple game contains a few difficulties and requires a good sense of anticipation. Nevertheless, its success rate is relatively high.

Material
One deck of 52 cards.

Opening Tableau
Deal all the cards face up in four overlapping rows of 12 columns. The last four cards are added onto the first four columns.

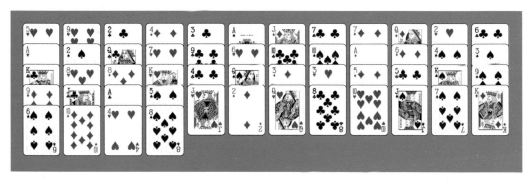

Tableau 12

Object
To eliminate all the cards from play.

Play
Ace is counted as one, king as 13, queen as 12 and jack as 11. Eliminate all couples that total 14. Only the available cards at the bottom of each column can be eliminated.

Elimination by Sums

Strategy

If two cards totalling 14 are placed in the same column, it is important to eliminate the first one as soon as possible. Before the game starts, try to locate any such couples, as well as any couple-chiasms, and anticipate a way to break them. For example, if you spot a 6 and a 4 in one column, a 10 and an 8 in another, make sure you don't eliminate the other three 4s or 8s beforehand, because it will be impossible later on to break that particular chiasm. A 4 or an 8 would be needed to detach these two groups.

16. Calculation

When I was a small boy, Grandmother often played this game while I looked on so that she could teach me how to count.

Material
One deck of 52 cards.

Opening Tableau
Deal all the cards, one by one, in two rows of five columns each and one row of three columns. Only the top card of each pile is face up.

Tableau 13

Object
To eliminate the cards from the tableau, by groups of 13 cards totalling 91.

Elimination by Sums

Play

Ace is counted as one, king, 13, queen, 12, and jack, 11. Add the 13 face-up cards. If they total 91, eliminate them from the tableau and turn over the 13 cards underneath. If the total is higher or lower than 91, pick one card and put it at the bottom of its pile, then turn over the next card of that same pile. Add the cards up again. If the new total is 91, eliminate these cards and continue. If not, put another card at the bottom of its pile and turn over the next card.

In Tableau 13, the total of the 13 face-up cards is 95. Suppose you choose to put the jack of hearts at the bottom of its pile and the next card you turn over is a 7. The total is now 91, and you can eliminate all the face-up cards from the tableau. Continue play in this manner.

You can put a card at the bottom of its pile only once per pile. Make sure you place it in a perpendicular position to remind yourself that you've already resorted to that maneuver for that particular pile. The game is won when you have eliminated all the cards from the tableau, by groups of 13 cards totalling 91.

Strategy

When the total is higher than 91, select and put a major card at the bottom of its pile. You'll have a better chance to find a lesser card that will help reduce the total. If, on the contrary, you need to increase the total, choose a minor card.

17. Good Omen

Grandmother attributed divine powers to this game. "If it comes out the first time you play it," she said, "you'll enjoy great happiness." Its high success rate will no doubt guarantee many a rosy future.

Material
One deck of 52 cards, with the four 10 cards removed.

Opening Tableau
Deal 16 cards in four rows of four columns. Keep the talon face down.

Object
To eliminate all the cards from play.

Play
Eliminate all same-suit cards that total 15 and all tierces containing kings, queens and jacks. Ace is counted as one. Fill the vacant spaces with cards from the talon and continue play. The game is successful only if no cards are left in the talon or in the tableau.

Strategy
When matching cards totalling 15, it's important to choose minor cards in order to free up as many spaces as possible. Choose a 2 and a 5 instead of a 7, for instance, or a 4, a 3 and a 2 instead of a 9. When faced with a choice between several solutions, try to remember the cards that have already been eliminated so as to leave in the tableau the ones you might need later on to match with – and eliminate – the cards still in the talon.

Elimination by Sums

Variants

1. Use the entire deck of 52 cards. Eliminate quarts, that is, four-card suit sequences containing kings, queens, jacks and 10s, rather than only court-card tierces. Thus, to eliminate say, a jack, queen and king of hearts in a given tableau, you'd have to wait for a 10 of hearts to show up.

2. Some players suggest eliminating major cards by squares, such as four kings, four queens, four jacks or four 10s.

18. Total Pair

This simple but cumbersome solitaire game has a rather high success rate.

Material
One deck of 52 cards, stripped of all the court cards (kings, queens and jacks).

Opening Tableau
Deal 40 cards in a long row, snaking or zigzagging it if the table is too short.

Object
To eliminate all the cards from play.

Play
Starting from the left, eliminate each couple of adjoined cards whose sum is an even number. For example, an 8 and a 4, or a 9 and a 5. Obviously, if two consecutive cards have either even or odd numbers, their sum is always even. And by extension, if an even card sits next to an odd card, their sum is always odd. Each time you eliminate a couple, push the cards closer together and eliminate any new couples that might form in the process. The game is successful when all the cards have been eliminated from the tableau.

Elimination by Sums

19. Combinations

A unique elimination game requiring two decks of cards. Combinations is only fairly interesting, but Grandmother was quite a devotee.

Material
Two decks of 52 cards.

Opening Tableau
Deal 12 cards face up in three rows of four columns. Keep the talon face down.

Object
To eliminate all the cards from play.

Play
Aces are eliminated singly. In Tableau 14, eliminate the three aces of spades, diamonds and hearts. Next, eliminate a set of four cards at a time – one court card with three others of different ranks and that total 18. Eliminate the jack, the 9, the 5 and the 4 in the first row; as well as the king, the 8, the

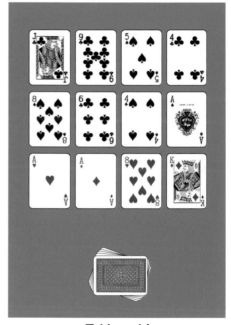

Tableau 14

6 and the 4 in the second row. Fill the spaces as they appear with cards from the talon. Success is achieved when all the cards have been eliminated from play. The game usually fails for lack of a court card or because no further groups totalling 18 are available.

20. Gleaner

Also called Hit or Miss, *this game is one of a kind. The object is to eliminate cards in numerical order. A puerile game that requires no mental effort whatsoever, its purely mechanical, mind-numbing manipulation always left Grandmother exasperated.*

Material
One deck of 52 cards.

Object
To eliminate all the cards from play.

Play
Turn up one card at a time from the pack. At the same time, call out the ranks of the cards in ascending order from the ace to the king. Every time the card you turn over corresponds, by pure chance, to the rank that you are calling out, that card is eliminated.

After calling out the king, start over again from the ace, and continue turning up cards in the search for a match. When you get to the end of the pack, start over again without shuffling the cards or interrupting the count. The game is successful when all the cards are eliminated.

The only time you can get stuck is when you have a multiple of 13 cards left (13, 26, 39 or 52) and you can't eliminate any cards because no matches come up.

Elimination by Sums

CHAPTER 3

Elimination by Proximity

21. Frog

This game is somewhat like Accordion *(no. 42), and its chances for success are just as slim. According to Grandmother, it got its name because the cards "behave" like a frog: they hop here, hop there, suddenly disappearing to the bottom of the pond.*

Material
One deck of 52 cards.

Opening Tableau
Deal four cards face up in a row. Keep the talon face down.

Object
To eliminate all the cards from the tableau and the talon.

Play
The only mobile card is the one at the right, dubbed "the frog" by my grandmother. The mobile card, or frog, can make only one move: it may skip over any card on the way to its exit except one of its own suit, in which case it must land on that particular card, called the "contact card." Thus, a spade may skip over any heart, diamond or club, but not over another spade.

Here are some examples:

1. If the three cards to the left of the mobile card are not of the same suit as its own, it can skip over all three cards and will thus be squarely eliminated from the tableau, like a frog diving into the pond. Let's suppose the tableau is made up of a 7 of diamonds, a 2 of hearts, an ace of spades and an 8 of clubs, in that order. The 8 of clubs, the mobile card, thus skips over all three adjoining cards and is eliminated from play. A new card is drawn from the talon, say, a jack of spades, to fill the space left by the 8 of clubs.

2. The tableau now has a 7 of diamonds, a 2 of hearts, an ace of spades and a jack of spades. The mobile card is now side by side with a same-suit card that is also of higher rank. It must then move onto this card, the contact card, which, in turn, can retain the mobile card because it is of a superior rank. The mobile card, packed onto the contact card, must now wait for yet another higher-ranked card, which could then drag the entire pile toward the exit. Figuratively speaking, the frog has hopped onto a water lily, where it sits, waiting. The next card drawn from the talon is, say, a 9 of diamonds.

3. The next tableau has a 7 of diamonds, a 2 of hearts, a jack of spades and a 9 of diamonds. The mobile card skips over the two intermediary cards and encounters a same-suit but lower-ranked card – the 7 of diamonds – which it can drag with it on its way out. If there were other cards under the 7 of diamonds, they, too, would have been eliminated in the process. The frog has jumped into the pond again. Let's suppose a 7 of spades and a 9 of spades are drawn from the talon to fill the first and fourth spaces.

4. The row now shows a 7 of spades, a 2 of hearts, a jack of spades and a 9 of spades. The mobile card must move onto its left-hand-side neighbor, the jack of spades, which is of higher rank. There the mobile card remains – since it can make only one move at a time – and must wait for a higher-ranked card to come along and drag the entire pile off the tableau. Suppose a king of spades is drawn from the talon to fill the vacant space left by the 9 of spades.

5. The new alignment has a 7 of spades, a 2 of hearts, a 9 of spades and a king of spades. The mobile card soon encounters a same-suit but lower-ranked card, which it can drag with it toward the exit. To its left, however, is another same-suit and lower-ranked card. Since the mobile card can only make one move, it must stop and land on this last card. The king of spades has succeeded in dragging the 9 of spades with it, but is now blocked by a 7 of spades.

Continue to draw cards until the talon is exhausted. At the end, when only three cards remain in the tableau, the third one will become the frog. Soon, the second card will get its turn.

The game is won when the talon is exhausted and all the cards have been eliminated from the tableau. To obtain this result, the last two cards must be of the same suit and the mobile card must be of higher rank.

Elimination by Proximity

Variants

1. The opening tableau is a row of 13 cards. When all the moves have been made, 13 new cards will be drawn, and so on. There are four deals in all.

2. Deal all the cards face up in one row, zigzagging it if the table is too short. In this way, the player starts out with all the information.

22. Might Is Right

This version of solitaire – though relatively simple – has a low success rate. It requires little attention and so little strategy that it can almost be considered a game of chance. It was one of Grandmother's favorites, especially when she had little time or space.

Material
One deck of 52 cards.

Opening Tableau
Deal four cards face up in a row. Keep the talon face down.

Object
To eliminate all cards, except the aces.

Play
The rule of the game is that a card may eliminate any other card of the same suit and lower rank. If the four cards that make up the tableau are of different suits, none can be eliminated. In this case, draw four new cards and lay them out on a second row, overlapping the first. Only the cards at the bottom of each column are available for play. Fill vacant spaces with any available card from the tableau, providing it contains more than three cards. If the tableau has only three cards, use cards from the talon.

Sometimes, one sole maneuver can generate a series of removals. Let's suppose the opening tableau shows a jack of spades, a 5 of spades, a 5 of hearts and a 2 of hearts, in that order. The jack of spades eliminates the 5 of spades and the 5 of hearts eliminates the 2 of hearts.

To fill the second and fourth columns, draw two new cards from the talon, for example, a 4 of spades and a king of spades. The latter, in turn, can eliminate both the jack and the 4 of spades. Suppose the next two cards drawn from the

Elimination by Proximity

talon are a 7 of clubs and a king of diamonds. In this new tableau, no card can be
eliminated.

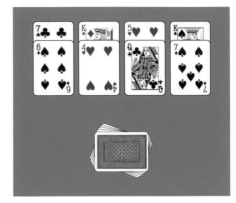

Next, draw four new cards and lay them
out on a second row, overlapping the first
(see Tableau 15). Now, the 6 of spades is
eliminated by the 7 of spades, and the 7 of
clubs by the queen of clubs. Fill the first column with the 7 of spades. This maneuver
releases the king of spades, which, in turn,
eliminates the 7 of spades.

Tableau 15

Fill the first column with the queen of
clubs; this maneuver releases the 5 of hearts, which, in turn, eliminates the 4 of
hearts. The new tableau now shows the queen of clubs, the king of diamonds, the
5 of hearts and the king of spades. Continue play in this manner until the talon is
exhausted. The game is won when the aces alone remain in the tableau.

Strategy

When filling a vacant space with a card from the tableau, choose a card that will
generate the longest chain of removals. Think also about unblocking eventual
impasses; for example, if a king overlaps a same-suit ace, use the king as soon as
possible to fill a vacant space. In this way you release the ace, which you will later
need to eliminate the king.

Variants

1. There's an abridged version of this game, requiring a deck of 32 major cards,
from 7 to ace.

2. A second variant allows the player to fill a vacant space with a card from
either the tableau or the talon. If you opt for a card from the talon, beware of
the risk involved, since you don't know what card will turn up.

3. Upon the appearance of the first ace, you can choose to assign it the highest
or lowest rank. In the latter case, the game is won when the four kings are the
last cards to be aligned.

23. Irish Solitaire

Grandmother called this game Irish Solitaire *because the focus is on clubs, which resemble the shamrock. This easy game of chance requires so much manipulation and so little concentration that it eventually becomes tedious.*

Material
One deck of 32 major cards, from 7 to ace.

Opening Tableau
Deal 15 cards face up in five rows of three columns.

Object
To eliminate all club cards from play.

Play
Eliminate all club cards from the tableau. Add the remaining tableau cards to the talon, reshuffle, then deal 15 new cards face up in five rows of three columns. Again, eliminate all club cards. Start the process again for the third and final time. If all 13 club cards are eliminated, the game is won. If not, have patience and start again!

Elimination by Proximity

24. Royal Nuptials

This resembles Leapfrog *(no. 43) but it is more difficult.*

Material
One deck of 52 cards.

Opening Tableau
Place the queen of hearts on the table, and put the king of hearts to the bottom of the talon.

Object
To eliminate all the cards save the royal couple – queen and king of hearts, side by side.

Play
Draw the cards from the talon one by one and place them to the right of the queen of hearts. Whenever a card is flanked by two cards of the same suit or rank, for example, two spades or two 5s, it is discarded and the card on its right is moved to the left to fill the vacant space. Continue the play until the talon is exhausted. The game is won when the royal couple is united. It is lost if cards remain between them.

25. Forty Thieves

While this one involves a modest degree of manipulation, it also demands considerable attention, a good memory and sober calculation as well as a keen sense of anticipation and deduction. My grandmother, who adored the game, told me many detective stories as she manipulated the cards; even Sherlock Holmes would have lost his Latin. Grandmother never could solve the enigma of the name, however. "Why is it called 'Forty Thieves,'" she often wondered, "when there are only 35 criminals?"

Material
One deck of 52 cards.

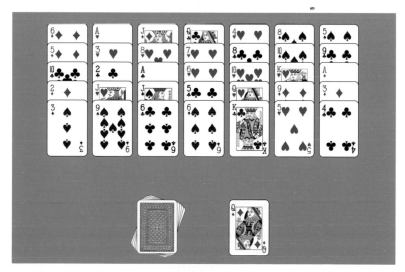

Tableau 16

Elimination by Proximity

Opening Tableau

Deal 35 cards face up in five overlapping rows and seven columns. Keep the talon face down. Turn over the top card of the talon and place it, face up, to the side to start the discard pile.

Object

To eliminate all 35 cards from the tableau.

Play

Eliminate from the tableau any available card that ranks immediately higher or lower than the one atop the discard pile, regardless of suit or color. On a 7 atop a discard pile, for example, you can place either a 6 or an 8, and on a 10, a jack or a 9. The exception is the king, which, though it can be placed upon a queen, cannot be covered by any other card. When a king appears, it blocks play and you have to resort to the talon in order to continue.

It is not necessary to move a card onto the discard pile. If you prefer to keep a particular card in the tableau for later use, you may do so. But you cannot transfer back to the tableau any card that has already been moved to the discard pile. If no available card in the tableau can be moved onto the discard pile, draw one from the talon, place it upon the discard pile and continue the play.

From Tableau 16, eliminate the king of clubs and place it upon the queen of spades. Eliminate also the 4 of clubs, then the 3 of diamonds, but the game will stop there. Alternately, eliminate in order the 4 of clubs, the 5 of hearts, the 6 of spades, the 7 of diamonds, the 6 of clubs, the 5 of clubs, the 6 of hearts and the 7 of hearts. When all possible maneuvers have been executed, draw a new card from the talon.

If the talon is exhausted and there are still cards in the tableau, the game is lost.

Strategy

Since aces can only cover 2s, and kings can only cover queens, it's important to eliminate aces and kings from the tableau as soon as possible. The chances of finding a contact card for aces and kings are far lower – about half – than they are for other cards.

When you have a choice, eliminate cards from columns with the most cards. Sometimes, though, it's better to opt for a lesser column, especially if such a maneuver will generate a greater series of withdrawals. It helps to remember what cards have been eliminated.

It's possible to keep a card in the tableau, instead of transferring it to the discard pile at the first opportunity, if you think that this card will be needed to eliminate another card later on. This strategy applies particularly to queens – the only cards that can eliminate kings from the tableau. For example, you may decide to keep a queen instead of placing it upon a jack, in order to eliminate a king that is placed higher in the tableau and not available for play in the meantime. There are no hard-and-fast tactical rules, however. Tactics result from experience and sometimes they are simply a matter of flair.

Variant

The opening tableau can be arranged in the shape of a pyramid – a layout of 28 cards over seven rows, the lower ones overlapping those immediately above them. Thus the talon will contain 24 cards, instead of 17. The game is played according to the same rules governing the original version.

26. Storming of the Bastille

Despite its apparent simplicity, this game requires anticipation, cunning and flair. Chance plays a secondary role, but the game's success rate is low, nevertheless.

Material
One deck of 52 cards.

Opening Tableau
Deal 48 cards face up in six rows of eight columns. Keep the remaining four cards face up. They will serve as reserve cards to unblock play.

Object
To eliminate all the cards from the tableau.

Play
The rule of the game is to eliminate two adjoining cards at a time, provided they are of the same rank or suit, without forming a crenel – that is, a confined gap created by the withdrawal of cards. Thus, from Tableau 17, you can eliminate the 6 and 4 of spades, the jack and 6 of diamonds, the 9 and 5 of hearts. You can't, however, eliminate the 5 and 2 of hearts, nor the kings of clubs and spades, nor the 2s of clubs and spades, for such removals would result in crenels being formed.

After each removal of any two cards, you may wish to move a card by two spaces, or two cards by one space. For example, after eliminating the jack and 6 of diamonds, and then the 4 and 7 of clubs, you may want to move the 4 of diamonds by one space to the left, and then upward, again by one space. This maneuver will enable you to eliminate the 2s of clubs and spades.

After all possible maneuvers have been executed, use one of the four reserve cards to match with, and eliminate, a card of the same suit or rank. The tableau will thus be reactivated. For example, use either the 2 or 10 of diamonds to eliminate the 4 of diamonds in the tableau, a maneuver that will enable you to eliminate the 10 and ace of spades.

The game is won only when all the cards in the tableau have been eliminated.

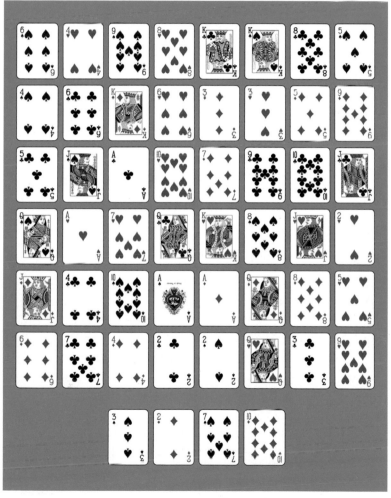

Tableau 17

27. Romanian Solitaire

This version of solitaire is essentially a game of chance. Its success rate is very low — only one in 50, according to my grandmother.

Material

One deck of 52 cards.

Opening Tableau

Deal 21 cards face up in three rows of seven columns. Keep the talon face down.

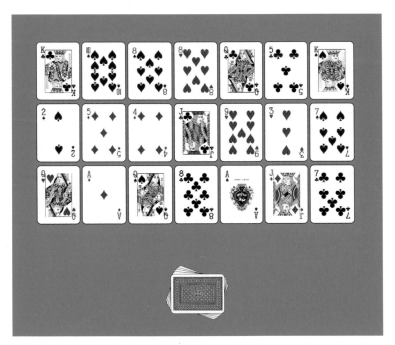

Tableau 18

Object

To eliminate all cards from both the tableau and the talon.

Play

Match and eliminate any card from the second row with one in the first or third row, provided they are in the same column and of the same suit or rank. For example, from Tableau 18, eliminate the 5 and ace of diamonds, the jack and 8 of clubs, as well as the 7s of spades and clubs. In columns that thus far have been untouched, shift the cards in the first and second rows. Then fill the vacant spaces with cards from the talon.

Continue the play by shifting cards in the second and third rows. These shifts cease after the third deal. If the talon still holds cards and no more couples can be formed and eliminated, the game is lost. If the talon is empty but the tableau still holds cards, eliminate any two adjoining cards in the same row as long as they are of the same suit or rank. The game is won when both the tableau and the talon are empty.

CHAPTER 4

Amalgamation by Suit

28. Osmosis

This game relies entirely on chance. Nonetheless, if enough atten-tion is paid to all the maneuvers, success will not be very far off.

Material
One deck of 52 cards.

Tableau 19

Opening Tableau

Deal the cards into four piles of four cards each, and arrange the piles in a column. Only the top card of each pile is face up. These are the reserve piles. Deal the next card, face up, to the right of the first reserve pile. This card is the first foundation card. In this game, the foundation zone and the maneuver zone are one. Keep the talon face down.

Object

To gather all the cards by suit, regardless of rank.

Play

If the reserve column contains a card of the same rank as the first foundation card, immediately place it below the first foundation card. For example, in Tableau 19, place the queen of spades below the queen of diamonds. The other foundation cards will eventually turn up and take their places in the right-hand-side column, one below another.

Furthermore, if the reserve column contains one or more cards of the same suit as that of the first foundation card, lay them out to its right, regardless of rank – in overlapping fashion so that all cards are visible. Thus, in Tableau 19, overlap the queen of diamonds with the 5 of diamonds. Turn up the cards in the reserve column as soon as they become available for play.

Two conditions must be fulfilled before you can shift a card from the reserve column to the foundation zone: first, the foundation card must be in place beforehand; second, a card of the same rank as the one you wish to shift must be among the cards in the row immediately above it. The order of appearance of the cards is not crucial. For example, if the cards in the upper row are 5, 8, 2 and 7, and the card you have just drawn is a 7, you can move that 7 onto the lower row, even if the row hasn't as yet received the 5, 8 and 2.

When all possible maneuvers have been executed with cards from the reserve column, deal the cards from the talon in groups of three, the top card of which is available for play. If the latter can be played, then the one under it becomes available, and so on.

Move unplayable cards to a discard pile. When the talon is exhausted, turn to the discard pile and, without changing the order of the cards, start dealing the pile in groups of three. Tableau 20 shows the hypothetical evolution of Tableau 19 following several maneuvers.

The game is successful only if all four suits have been completed.

Variant

You may lay out all the reserve cards face up, in an overlapping fashion, and use the cards as they become available. This initial layout allows the player to spot any potential impasse early on and to anticipate ways to avoid it. The player may then opt for one foundation over another in order to, say, release a blocked card later on. My grandmother liked this variant because she saw it as a way to free herself from the tyranny of chance and inject some measure of strategy into the play.

Tableau 20

29. Cascades

This game of solitaire is interesting because it contains many surprising twists. It requires a great deal of concentration, since the player must be prepared to control different aspects of the game at any given time. Its success rate is moderately high, and the suspense it sustains until the bitter end makes this game a favourite.

Material
One deck of 52 cards.

Opening Tableau
Deal four cards face up in one reserve column. Keep the talon face down.

Object
To gather all the cards according to suit.

Play
Move the lowest-ranked card from the reserve column to its right, in the first row. This is the first foundation card. Below this card place the lowest-ranked card of another suit. Continue until the foundation column has four cards representing the four suits, on which ascending sequences are built.

In Tableau 21, move the 3 of hearts to the right of the 8 of hearts (the latter stays in the reserve column) then the 6 of spades below the 3 of hearts, and the 7 of clubs below the 6 of spades, as shown in Tableau 22.

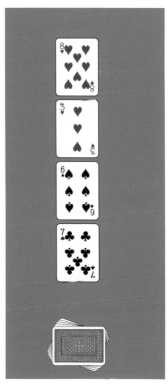

Tableau 21

Since no further maneuvers are possible, draw four cards from the talon one by one, placing them face up in the reserve column, top to bottom, as shown in Tableau 23. First, move the 7 of spades onto the 6 of spades, then the 9 of diamonds below the 7 of clubs. The foundation column is now complete. When shifting cards, if you have a choice between several cards of the same suit, always

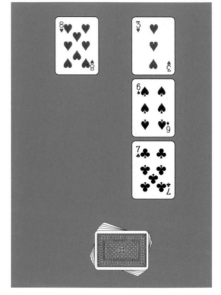

Tableau 22

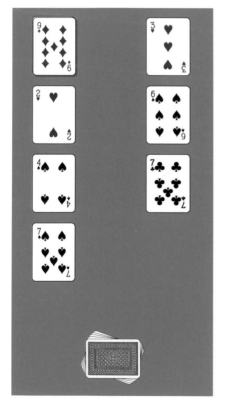

Tableau 23

opt for the lowest-ranked card, since the object is to build ascending sequences. Ace counts as one.

Now that the first foundation column is complete, and no other cards from the reserve column can be played onto any of its rows, start a new foundation column, always top to bottom. Here, move the 2 of hearts next to the 3 of hearts, then the 4 of spades next to the 7 of spades.

Draw four cards from the talon and place them, face up, in the reserve column. Incidentally, any vacant space in the reserve can only be filled with a card from the talon following a new redeal. Suppose Tableau 24 is the result of the latest redeal. Cards to the right of the reserve column constitute the foundations on which segments of ascending sequences are built. Here, move the 4 of hearts onto the 3 of hearts – a maneuver that releases the 8 of hearts in the reserve column. Next, move the 3 of clubs next to the 7 of clubs. As for the 8 of hearts, it cannot be moved next to the 2 of hearts, because the second foundation column is not yet complete.

Place four new cards in the reserve, as shown in Tableau 25. Move the 10 of diamonds onto the 9 of diamonds, the 5 of diamonds next to the 10 of diamonds,

Tableau 24

then the 6 of diamonds onto the 5 of diamonds. Now that the second foundation column is complete, move the 8 of hearts next to the 2 of hearts, then the ace of spades next to the 4 of spades. And so cascades are built until the talon is exhausted.

The number of foundation piles depends entirely on chance. The more foundation piles there are, the better the chance that the game will be won. It is successful only when all the cards have been aligned in four rows according to their suits.

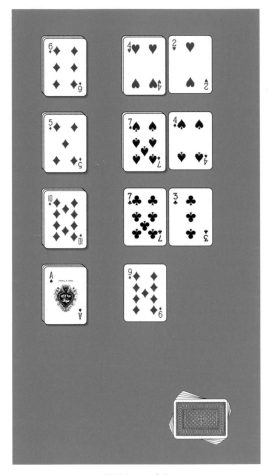

Tableau 25

30. Partners

Partners *was not one of my grandmother's favorites. It is essentially a game of chance and requires a great deal of manipulation and no strategic judgment. Just a little attention is enough to bring this game to its end; nevertheless, its success rate is relatively low.*

Material
One deck of 52 cards.

Opening Tableau
Remove the four queens from the deck and lay them out in a row. Then, deal 16 cards face up in four rows of four columns below the four queens. Keep the talon face down.

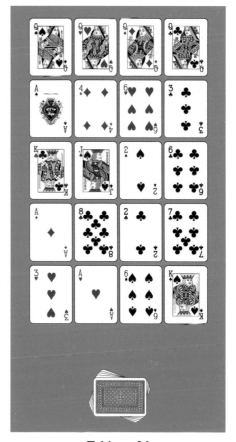

Tableau 26

Object

To bring each of the four kings to the same column as their same-suit queen.

Play

If, in the opening tableau, a king is in the same column as its same-suit queen, there's no point moving the king anywhere else, since the couple has already been formed. To introduce a king in the same column as its same-suit queen, you must free up certain spaces by removing all same-color pairs.

From Tableau 26, eliminate the 2s of spades and clubs, the 6s of spades and clubs, and the aces of diamonds and hearts. Move the king of spades to the space created by the removal of the ace of diamonds, then the king of clubs in the space left by the 6 of clubs. Two queens have thus found their partners. Fill other vacant spaces with cards from the talon, starting from left to right, top to bottom, as illustrated in Tableau 27.

The new tableau shows that a third queen has found her partner: following the latest redeal, the king of diamonds has appeared in the column of its same-suit queen. The king of hearts has yet to show up. But there are no more same-color pairs to discard and so the play is blocked. The queen of hearts will not find its partner. The game is lost. It is won only if each queen has found its king within its column, regardless of what row the king is in.

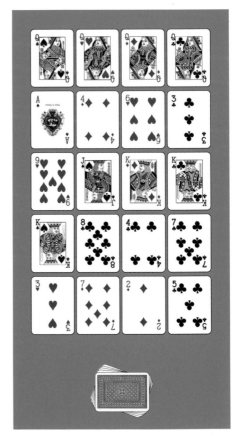

Tableau 27

31. Royal Couple

This is one of the first games of solitaire I learned from my grand-mother – I was five or six years old at the time. It is very simple, but its success rate is so low – some would say one in 100 – that even the most persevering players can fail. Whenever I lost patience try-ing to work it out, Grandmother would invent variants to make it easier for me. One day, following a series of illegal moves, I pre-tended that I'd won. Grandmother went along with the charade and promised me a brilliant career as a matchmaker.

Material
The four kings and four queens from a deck of cards.

Object
To match each king with its queen.

Play
There is no opening tableau. Shuffle the eight cards thoroughly and keep the pile face down. Draw the first card and place it face up on the table. Draw a second card and slide it face down under the pile. Then, draw the third card and place it to the right of the first card. If the first card is a king and the second is a queen of the same suit, continue. If not, the game has already been lost. It is won when the four pairs of same-suit king-queen are formed, regardless of the order of appearance. Tableau 28 shows a successful game.

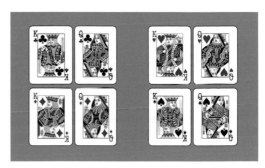

Tableau 28

Variants

1. Ignore the order of appearance of the partners. The queen may appear before the king of the same suit.

2. It is not necessary that the king and queen be of the same suit or color. You can thus pair off a king of hearts with a queen of clubs.

32. Royal Alignment

This game doesn't demand much concentration, but its success rate is still extremely low. Even though it wasn't one of Grandmother's favorites, she'd gladly spend an evening or two playing it.

Material
One deck of 52 cards.

Opening Tableau
Place the king and queen of hearts side by side, then the queen and king of spades. Below them, deal 16 cards in three rows of four columns. Keep the talon face down.

Object
To bring the king and queen of diamonds below the king and queen of hearts, and the queen and king of clubs below the queen and king of spades.

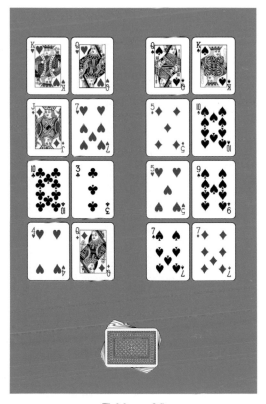

Tableau 29

Play

In the left-hand section, below the king or queen of hearts, if you find a card of the same color and rank as one in the right-hand section, below the king or queen of spades, transfer both cards to a waste pile. From Tableau 29, for example, eliminate the 7s of hearts and diamonds, and the 10s of clubs and spades. Incidentally, you can't eliminate the two red 5s since they are both in the same section, under the queen of spades.

Fill the spaces with cards from the talon, left to right, top to bottom. Eliminate all same-color and same-rank pairs, provided they come from different sections, with the exception of, of course, the kings and queens.

Play is blocked when no more pairs can be formed and discarded. To unblock, gather all the cards, except those in the first row, and shuffle them with the remaining cards in the talon. Reconstitute the tableau as before and start the maneuvers anew. Repeat the cycle until the talon holds no more cards.

Tableau 30

If cards other than kings and queens remain in the tableau, the game is lost, as shown in Tableau 30. The game is won if the king of diamonds is aligned vertically with the king of hearts, the queen of diamonds with the queen of hearts, the queen of clubs with the queen of spades, and the king of clubs with the king of spades, regardless of what row they are in. Tableau 31 shows a successful game.

Tableau 31

33. Hidden Royal Quint

My grandmother hated this game and made no attempt to hide it.

Material
One deck of 52 cards.

Opening Tableau
Deal all the cards face down in a row of five piles, placing the last two cards on the first two piles.

Object
To eliminate all the cards save for the royal quint.

Play
Turn over the first pile and draw cards individually until one appears that can be part of a royal quint, such as the 10 of hearts, the queen of spades or the ace of clubs. This card will determine the suit of the sought-after royal quint. If the first pile did not contain any card between 10 and ace, discard the entire pile.

Let's suppose the first pile contains the 10 of hearts; hearts will then be the suit of the royal quint. Turn over the second pile and start drawing cards until the second eligible card appears. If the pile contains no card higher than the 10 of hearts, discard the entire pile. Move to the third pile, then the fourth and fifth.

Once all the cards have been dealt, gather the piles – first onto second, and so on – and, without shuffling the cards, redeal them into four piles. For the next round, redeal the cards into three piles, then, for the final round, two piles. The game is won if the last two piles hold only the royal quint.

34. Court of the Great Kings

This game is charming and colorful. It takes only a short time to play and leaves a lot of room for strategy. Nevertheless, its relative simplicity is misleading. It actually demands complete concentration and a good memory at all times. There's also an element of chance. Grandmother estimated that the success rate was about one in 100.

Material

One deck of 52 cards.

Opening Tableau

The opening tableau is composed of 16 cards laid out in four rows of four columns. There are two distinct zones: a core of four spaces – the maneuver zone; and the perimeter area, comprising 12 spaces, one for each court card – the foundation zone.

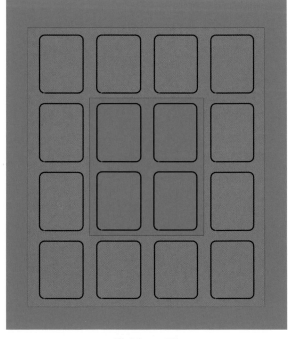

Tableau 32

Object

To place all the court cards on the perimeter, as follows: the four kings in the four corner spaces (the king of hearts in the top left; the king of spades, top right; the king of diamonds, bottom left; and the king of clubs, bottom right); two queens in the top row and two queens in the bottom row; and two jacks on each side. Each king must be flanked by his same-suit queen and jack.

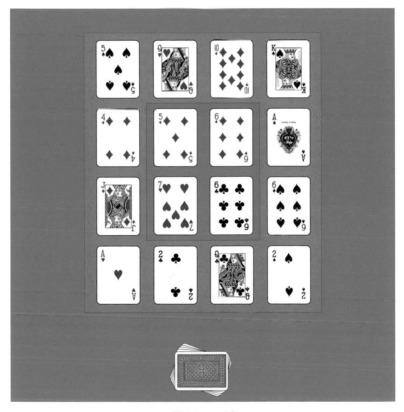

Tableau 33

Amalgamation by Suit

Play

Deal out 16 cards one by one, face up, in random order, taking care to place any court cards that turn up in their designated spaces. When the tableau is filled, discard all the pairs, regardless of their suit or color, such as the aces, the 2s, the 5s and the 6s, as illustrated in Tableau 33.

Note that the queen of hearts, the king of spades, the jack of diamonds and the queen of clubs have been placed in their designated spaces. Fill the vacancies with cards from the talon, taking care to place the cards as strategically as possible to ensure success. Never place a court card in the four spaces that form the core of the tableau, for instance, or in any space on the perimeter that's not designated for it. Continue to eliminate pairs and fill the vacant spaces.

The game is successful when all the court cards are in their places. It fails if the tableau is full but contains no removable pairs, or else if you draw a court card from the talon and its space in the tableau is not available. This would be the case if, considering the above example, the queen of spades or the jack of hearts had been drawn during the second redeal.

Variants

Generally speaking, all variants aim at making this game of solitaire easier to solve.

1. Instead of assigning spaces in advance for the kings, place them in any space as they turn up during the deal.
2. Match the court cards by color rather than by suit.
3. Match the court cards regardless of color or suit.
4. Instead of discarding pairs, try couples that total 10, say, 2 and 8, 6 and 4, and so on. Ace counts as one and 10s can be eliminated singly.
5. Switch the places of the queens and the jacks: queens on the side and jacks in the top and bottom rows.

6. Place a court card temporarily in any core space or any space on the perimeter if its own designated place is not available. When it's freed up by the removal of a pair, move the court card to its destination.

Let your imagination take flight using the above variants as guides.

CHAPTER 5

Amalgamation by Rank

35. Tournament

Grandmother taught me this game as if it were a tournament involving four horsemen. As a small boy I loved the game, and I loved to win! A simple solitaire, to be sure, but one with a rather low success rate.

Material
One deck of 52 cards.

Opening Tableau
Remove the four jacks from the deck and place them in a row. Under the jacks, deal four cards face up. Keep the talon face down.

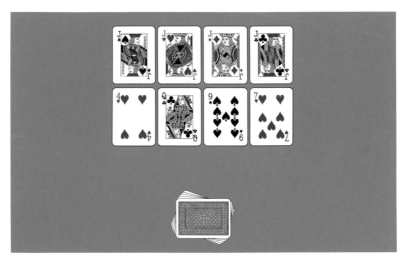

Tableau 34

Object
The jack of hearts must have the greatest number of cards beneath it.

Play

Ace counts as one, queen as 12 and king as 13. If a card with an even value rests in the same column as a red jack, it is placed beneath that jack; and if a card with an odd value rests in the same column as a black jack, it is placed beneath that jack. Remove cards that do not satisfy these conditions. In Tableau 34, place the queen of clubs under the jack of hearts and the 7 of hearts under the jack of clubs. Draw two more cards. Deal another round of four cards and start the same maneuvers. Repeat until the talon is exhausted. Count the number of cards under each jack. If the jack of hearts has more cards than any of the other three jacks, the game is successful. If not, good luck on your next try!

36. League of Twelve

This one is easy to play, and its success rate is high. "A good game for beginners," said Grandmother.

Material
One deck of 52 cards.

Opening Tableau
Deal 12 cards face up in three rows of four columns. Keep the talon face down.

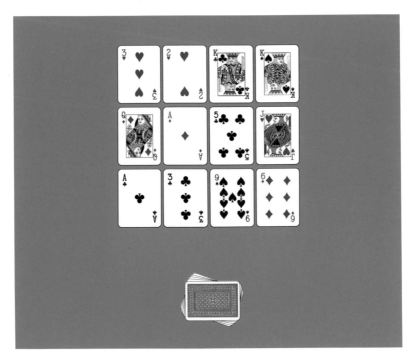

Tableau 35

Object

To eliminate all the cards from ace to 10, keeping only the 12 court cards in the tableau.

Play

Eliminate the court cards from the tableau and place them under the talon. Fill the vacant spaces with other cards from the talon. If more court cards show up, eliminate and place them under the talon. Continue until the tableau no longer contains court cards. For example, in Tableau 35, eliminate the kings of clubs and spades, the queen of diamonds and the jack of hearts and place them under the talon. Let's suppose that the next four cards drawn from the talon are the 8 of hearts, the 8 of diamonds, the 5 of diamonds and the jack of clubs. Eliminate the latter and replace it with another card from the talon, say, a 2 of spades. See the results in Tableau 36.

Once the tableau no longer contains a court card, take the cards from the talon and turn them over one by one, packing them onto any two cards totalling 11. For example, the 9 of spades and the 2 of spades or hearts, the 6 of diamonds and the 5 of clubs or diamonds, the 8 and 3 of hearts, the 8 of diamonds and the 3 of clubs. If a court card is turned up, the space on which it is placed is off-limits. If the tableau has no more couples totalling 11 and the talon still holds cards, the game is lost. It is successful when the tableau is covered with the 12 court cards.

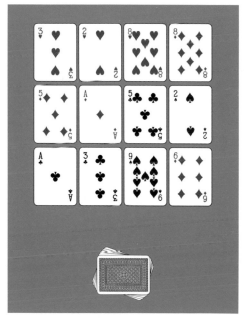

Tableau 36

37. Chiasms

Grandmother always maintained that she invented this game. It is extremely difficult and requires a precise memory and exceptional tenacity. It takes up little space, so it is great for traveling.

Material
One deck of 32 major cards, from 7 to ace.

Opening Tableau
Deal eight cards face up in two rows of four columns. Keep the talon face down.

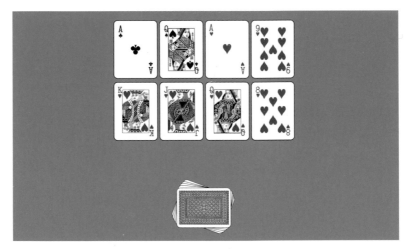

Tableau 37

Object
To find four pairs forming three chiasms as per the following formula:

$$X \quad Y \quad X \quad Y$$
$$Y \quad X \quad Y \quad X$$

Play

With two ready-made chiasms in Tableau 37, the game is off to a good start: the first is the pair of queens, which are placed diagonally in different rows and columns; the second is the pair of aces, which, although placed in the same row, are separated by another card. Leave both pairs in the tableau but discard the other cards and fill the vacant spaces with cards from the talon. The results are shown in Tableau 38.

From the new tableau, eliminate the 8 of clubs, since its counterpart – the 8 of hearts – was discarded in the earlier round, and the pair of jacks, which sit side by side in the same row and thus do not constitute a pair chiasm. Fill the vacant spaces with cards from the talon.

Tableau 38

Tableau 39 shows three queens forming two pairs: vertically in the second column and horizontally in the second row. The earlier chiasm is gone. Eliminate the three queens and the king of spades, given that its counterpart – the king of hearts – was discarded in the earlier round. Keep the 7 of spades, since no 7 has been discarded up till now. Continue the play until the talon is exhausted.

If the tableau ends with four chiasms, the game is successful. If not, have patience and start again. In other words, to succeed, you must achieve two fours-of-a-kind or squares, that is, two sets of four cards each of the same rank, as shown in Tableau 40.

Tableau 39

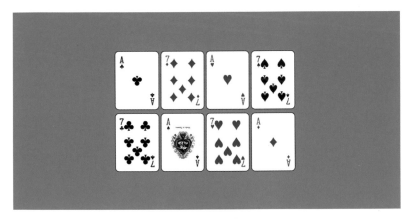

Tableau 40

38. Major Squares

This version of solitaire requires little time or space and will provide many a lonely player with delightful moments. It's essentially a game of chance and has a high success rate, making it popular with young beginners. Grandmother much enjoyed winning at this one.

Material
One deck of 16 major cards, from jack to ace.

Opening Tableau
Deal the 16 cards in four rows of four columns. Only one card is face up – fourth row, fourth column.

Object
To form four squares, i.e., four groups of four same-rank cards, arranged in four columns: jacks in the first column, queens in the second column, kings in the third column and aces in the fourth column.

Play
Since the object of play is to form fours-of-a-kind, suit or color is not relevant. Cards are moved by row, starting from the top. Thus, the first ace that comes along will be placed in the first row of column 4, the second ace in the second row, and so on.

Start by moving the face-up card onto the first row of its respective column. If, for example, the face-up card is the queen of clubs, place it in the first row of the second column. Turn up the card that was in that space and move it to its appropriate spot. If it's a king, move it to the third column; if it's a jack, it goes to the first column. The game is over the moment the fourth ace comes out. It is successful if, by then, all the cards have been turned up and thus placed in their appropriate spots or if the as-yet-unturned cards turn out to be in their appro-

Amalgamation by Rank

priate spaces. In Tableau 41, for example, the fourth ace comes out before three other cards – in the first three columns – have a chance to come out. For the game to be successful, the hidden cards must be the jack of spades in the first column, the queen of diamonds in the second column and the king of diamonds in the third.

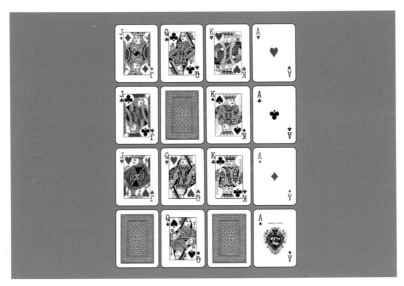

Tableau 41

Variant

Arrange the squares in four rows instead of four columns: aces in the first row, kings in the second row, queens in the third row and jacks in the fourth row. In this case, move the cards by column – the first card of the square goes to the first column, the second to the second column and so on.

39. Clock

Visually attractive, Clock requires only a brief attention span. The rules are simple, and each and every maneuver depends strictly on chance. Furthermore, the success rate is relatively high. It's a perfect game for young children.

Material
One deck of 52 cards.

Opening Tableau
Deal the cards in 13 piles of four cards each, face down. Arrange 12 piles in a circle to represent the hours of a clock, with the 13th pile, called the cuckoo, in the center. Each card indicates a precise hour: ace is one o'clock; 2, two o'clock; 3, three o'clock and so on. Jack is 11 o'clock; queen, 12 o'clock; and the king is the cuckoo in the center.

Object
To get all 13 fours-of-a-kind together, each at its designated hour, and the four kings in the center.

Play
Turn up the first card of the pile in the center. Place this card face up underneath the pile of its number. For example, if the card is a 2, put it under the pile at "two o'clock." Now, turn up the top card of the pile at "two o'clock" and continue in the same way. When a king turns up, put it underneath the cuckoo pile and turn up its top card.

Amalgamation by Rank

If the last face-down card of a pile, say, at "three o'clock," happens to be a 3, leave it face up on its pile and turn up the top card of the "four o'clock" pile. The game is lost if the fourth king joins the cuckoo in the center before all the other cards are turned up and placed in their appropriate spots.

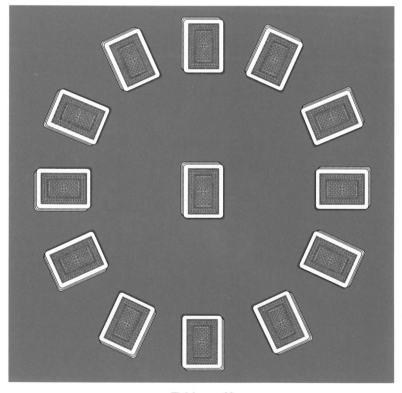

Tableau 42

40. Right Time

Grandmother didn't like this game of solitaire; she found it too mechanical. Indeed, it requires a great deal of manipulation and almost no reflection.

Material
One deck of 52 cards.

Opening Tableau
Deal the cards face up and one by one, in 13 piles of four cards each. Arrange 12 piles in a circle to represent the hours of a clock, with the 13th pile, called the cuckoo, in the center.

Object
To retain 12 cards – each at the hour corresponding to its number – plus one king in the center.

Play
Turn up the top card of the cuckoo pile and put it underneath the pile of its number. In Tableau 43, put the 3 of diamonds underneath the "three o'clock" pile. Turn up the top card of the latter pile, say, the king of spades, and put it underneath the "four o'clock" pile. Then turn up the top card of the "four o'clock pile" and put it underneath the "five o'clock" pile. Continue in the same way until "noon." Then, turn up the top card of the "12 o'clock" pile and put it underneath the cuckoo pile, and turn up the top card of the cuckoo pile and put it underneath the "one o'clock" pile and so on. Note that ace counts as one, jack as 11, queen as 12 and king as 13.

When the top card of a pile chances to be at the "right time," skip this pile and go to one whose top card is still at the "wrong" time. As the game progresses, more cards will appear at the right time, reducing the number of cards to be put underneath the piles.

Amalgamation by Rank

Tableau 43

When the 12 top cards are at their right time and the cuckoo pile is topped by a king, eliminate all 13 cards and start a second round with the remaining cards. If all goes well, proceed to the third round, then the fourth and final round. The game is only successful if the last 13 cards are placed at their appropriate spots.

41. Double Clock

This game is a two-deck variant of Clock *(no. 39). Also visually attractive, it demands more dexterity than application, since the opening tableau takes up a lot of space and the play is essentially mechanical. The success rate, however, is on the low side.*

Material
Two decks of 52 cards.

Opening Tableau
Deal the cards face down in the same fashion as that for *Clock*, only in two dials, one inside the other. Each hour thus has two piles of four cards each, and the cuckoo pile in the center has eight cards.

Object
To get all the cards at their designated hour – the red cards in the outer dial, the black ones inside, and the eight kings in the center.

Play
Like *Clock*, turn up the top card of the cuckoo pile and put it underneath the pile of its number – in the inner dial if the card is black and in the outer dial if it is red. The game is successful if all the cards are in their prefixed positions before the eighth kings joins the cuckoo.

Tableau 44

CHAPTER 6

Piling Up

42. Accordion

This game is very difficult to play. Grandmother won it just once in her long career as the "queen of solitaire." Even though the object is to end the game with a single pile of cards, Grandmother said anything less than four piles would be victory enough. One evening I balked at playing the game, whereupon my sententious grandmother waxed eloquent about the intense happiness her only victory had brought her. "After such a long wait," she said, quivering with emotion, "success is simply exquisite." Once, I asked her, "Why is it called Accordion? *"Just take a good look at the movement of the cards," she said. "Sometimes the row is shortened, sometimes it's lengthened. Doesn't it remind you of Uncle Arsène playing the accordion?" "If you say so," I replied, without much conviction.*

Material
One deck of 52 cards.

Opening Tableau
Deal four cards face up in a row. Keep the talon face down.

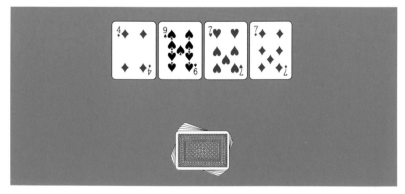

Tableau 45

Object

To bring all the cards back into a single pile.

Play

Whenever a card matches either its left-hand neighbor or the third card to its left in either suit or rank, move it onto its match and close the gap by pushing the row leftward and filling it with new cards from the talon. If piles are created, the top card designates the suit or rank of the pile, which can be moved according to the rules of the game. After all the possible maneuvers have been executed, continue dealing from the talon until a "matchable" card turns up. If you have a choice between the left-hand neighbor or the third card to the left, choose wisely because your decision may determine the outcome of the game. For Grandmother, however, it was simply a question of flair. Since the object of play is to gather all the cards back into one pile, the top cards of the last two piles must match either in suit or rank. If they don't, the game fails.

Tableau 45 offers the choice of placing the 7 of diamonds upon either the 7 of hearts (same rank) or the 4 of diamonds (same suit) two cards away (third to its left). "Play your hunches," Grandmother would say. The first scenario would result in the tableau showing the 4 of diamonds, the 9 of spades and the 7 of hearts; the second scenario would yield the 7 of diamonds, the 9 of spades and the 7 of hearts.

Suppose you opt for the first possibility and draw the queen of spades from the talon. Since the latter matches no card in the tableau in either suit or rank, you must draw another card, say, the 8 of hearts. Again, there's no match. Suppose the next card from the talon is the 10 of diamonds, which matches the 7 of diamonds, the third card to its left. This brings us to Tableau 46.

Continue dealing from the talon and moving cards and/or piles to the left until the talon is exhausted. The game is successful if only two piles are left in the tableau, whose top cards match either in suit or rank. Alas, this has never happened to me.

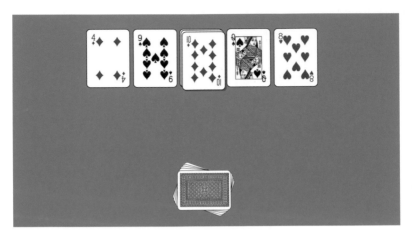

Tableau 46

Strategy
When there is a choice between two or more maneuvers, it is preferable to choose the card farthest to the left.

Variants
1. Deal 13 cards at a time – instead of four – from the talon.
2. Instead of four cards, deal the entire deck face up in a row, zigzagging it if the table is too short. Match cards of the same suit and rank, regardless of their position in the tableau. Opt for maneuvers that will yield the most matches in the long run.
3. If you're faced with a choice between two or more maneuvers, draw four cards from the talon in order to assess the situation more clearly.

43. Leapfrog

This deceptively simple game is actually one of the most difficult. It requires concentrated attention just to keep track of all the possibilities. Grandmother spent many a long evening playing it, without much success.

Material
One deck of 52 cards.

Opening Tableau
Deal four cards face up in a row. Keep the talon face down.

Object
To gather all the cards in three piles.

Play
If the first and fourth cards match in either suit or rank, place the first card upon the fourth and close the gap by pushing the row leftward. As piles are created, the top card designates the suit and rank of the pile, which can be moved as a unit. Continue turning up cards from the talon from left to right, packing the first and fourth cards according to the rules of the game, until the talon is exhausted. The game is successful if, in the end, all the cards are gathered in three piles.

Strategy
Pay close attention to the order of cards, which changes constantly. Moving a single card may generate a whole series of maneuvers. Generally speaking, it is preferable to move the card farthest to the left before any other. Consider Tableau 47: move the 6 of diamonds onto the 6 of hearts first, then the 3 of spades onto the jack of spades.

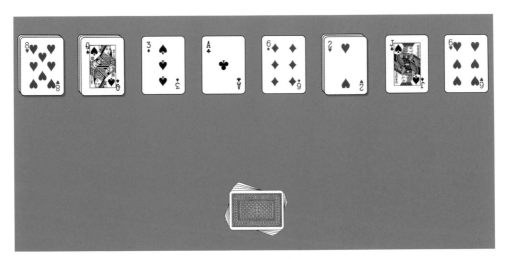

Tableau 47

Before moving the queen of spades onto the 3 of spades in Tableau 48, consider moving the 8 of hearts onto the 2 of hearts. The latter maneuver would

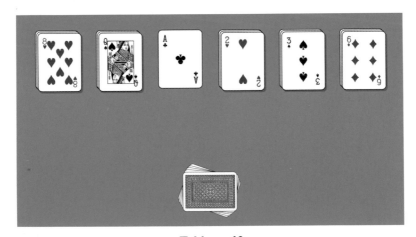

Tableau 48

have been impossible once the queen of spades was removed, for there would have remained only one card between the 8 and 2 of hearts.

Since Tableau 49 offers no possible maneuvers, continue turning up cards from the talon until it is exhausted.

Tableau 49

44. Germaine

Grandmother seemed very mysterious one particular day, lost in an endless reverie punctuated with enigmatic smiles and deep concentration. Then, all of a sudden, she grew agitated. Taking me by the arm, she dragged me into her room, where a huge solid oak table sat imposingly – the scene of many of her games of solitaire. She handed me a deck of cards and said, "Shuffle them well and deal them face up in four rows of 13 columns." After I laid out the tableau, she said: "Now tell me, is it a masterpiece or what! That's what I dreamed about the other night. I spent three days working on this tableau. My boy, never has anyone invented anything so beautiful!" Then, with tears in her eyes, Grandmother set about teaching me this striking game, which one can't possibly win without an extraordinary sense of anticipation, a prodigious memory, a rare gift of total concentration and a watchfulness worthy of a Sioux warrior. Busting with pride, Grandmother named the game after herself.

Material
One deck of 52 cards.

Opening Tableau
Deal all the cards face up in four rows of 13 columns.

Object
To gather all the cards back in one pile.

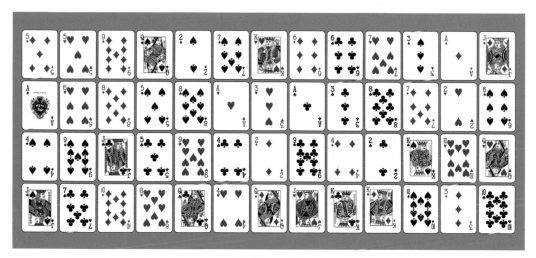

Tableau 50

Play

Select a card and place it upon any of its four neighbors – north or south, east or west – provided its rank is immediately lower or higher. Color is irrelevant. As the game progresses, piles will form whose sequences may be ascending, descending or circular. A king may rest upon a queen or an ace; an ace, upon a king or a 2; and a 2, upon an ace or a 3 and so on. As piles are created, the top card designates the suit and rank of the pile, which can be moved as a unit.

What follows is a hypothetical sequence of play as per Tableau 50. This is by no means the best strategy – others may well be more fruitful. Start by packing the 3 of hearts upon the 2 of diamonds in the seventh column, then push the king of hearts down by one space. This move helps bring the king out of isolation and closer to other court cards in the fourth row.

Push the first row of cards to the right to close the crenel that has just been created. This move also leaves the trio of cards in the 11th and 12th columns intact (3 of spades – ace of diamonds – 2 of hearts) and brings the 2 of spades into the same column as the ace of hearts.

We have now arrived at Tableau 51. Continue to bring the king of hearts closer to the queen of diamonds by moving the 3 of hearts onto the 4 of clubs. Close the gap in the seventh column and fill the crenel by moving the right-hand portion of the first row to the left, temporarily forsaking the previously trio.

Tableau 52: Pack the 4 of hearts upon the 3 of hearts and fill the crenel by moving the left-hand portion of the fourth row to the right. Pack the king of hearts upon the queen of diamonds and move the right-hand portion of the third row to the left. Close the crenel in the 13th column by pushing the 10 of clubs up by one space.

Tableau 51

Tableau 53: Pack the 9 of hearts upon the 8 of hearts and close the gap in the third row by pushing the cards to the right. Pack the 10 of diamonds upon the 9 of hearts and close the gap in the first row by pushing the cards to the right. Pack the 8 of spades upon the 9 of spades and close the gap in the fifth column by pushing the cards downward and the first row to the right. Pack the 7 of clubs upon the 8 of spades and push the jack of spades to the right; pack the queen of

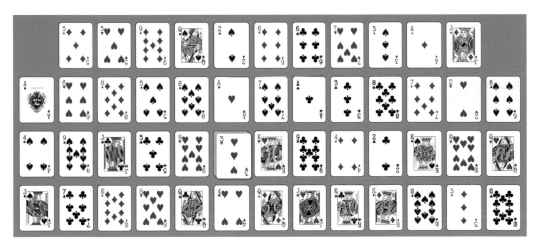

Tableau 52

spades upon the jack of clubs in the row below, tighten the fifth column by pushing it downward and move the 5 of diamonds to the right.

Tableau 54: Pack the jack of spades upon the queen of spades, then the queen of clubs upon the jack of spades and push this pile to the right. Move the queen of clubs onto the king of hearts, then onto the jack of hearts, the king of clubs,

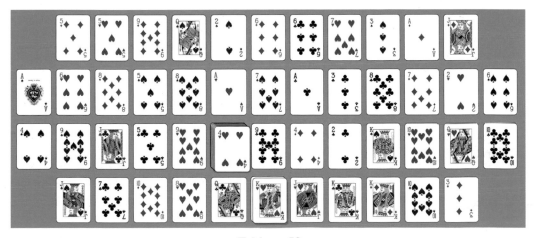

Tableau 53

the king of diamonds and finally onto the king of spades in the row immediately above it. The fourth row is now left with the 10 of spades and the 3 of diamonds.

Continue the play until all the cards are gathered in one pile.

Strategy

Since the configuration of the tableau changes constantly, it's important to memorize the entire tableau after each maneuver. A move may be useful in one area while creating an impasse in others. Wise is the player who tries early in the game to locate the various positions of "matchable" cards and plot a tactic to bring them closer together.

Tableau 54

Avoid piling up all same-rank cards too hastily, lest you risk blocking play later on. For example, if you have covered all the 7s early in the game, you reduce by half your chances of finding a match for the 6s and the 8s. And if both 7s and 5s are buried under other cards, it will be impossible to pack a 6 upon a pile – a sure recipe for failure. It is thus essential always to remember which cards are buried in what pile in order to make judicious choices concerning isolated cards. For example, if you can choose between one 7 and three 9s on which to pack an 8, opt for one of the 9s and save the 7 for a subsequent maneuver.

45. Revolt of the Tens

Beginners are generally turned off by this game. Its success rate is very low and, despite its apparent simplicity, play is usually blocked after a couple of maneuvers – pretty discouraging for most beginners.

Material
One deck of 52 cards.

Opening Tableau
Deal nine cards face up in three rows of three columns. Keep the talon face down.

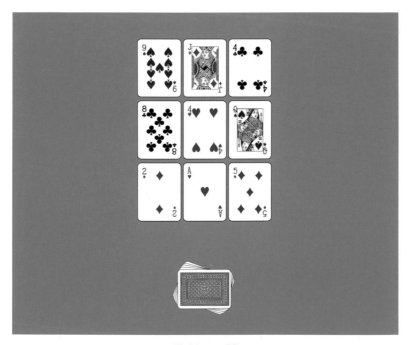

Tableau 55

Object

To empty the talon by laying out all the cards atop the nine cards in the tableau.

Play

Cover – with cards from the talon – any pairs of jacks, queens and kings in the tableau – as well as any two cards totalling 10, regardless of color. Tens are the exceptions – they're the rebels that "refuse" to be covered – and thus tend to block play whenever they appear. In Tableau 55, draw from the talon to cover the 8 of clubs and the 2 of diamonds, as well as the 9 of spades and the ace of hearts. If by chance you draw a 3, a king, a 2 and a 10, play will be blocked and the game fails. On the contrary, if you draw a queen instead of a king, cover the pair of queens and continue the play. The game is won when all the cards from the talon are dealt out in the tableau.

46. Evangeline

This undemanding solitaire game requires little manipulation, attention or memory, except perhaps in the variant, which requires a bit of strategy. It's essentially a game of chance. Grandmother played it from time to time, especially when she wanted to think about other things. She named it for a distant cousin from whom she inherited the game.

Material
One deck of 52 cards.

Opening Tableau
Deal nine cards face up in three rows of three columns. Keep the talon face down.

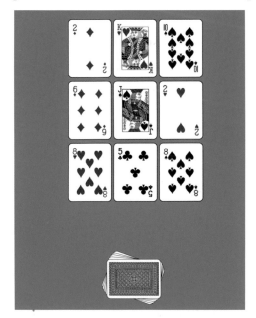

Tableau 56

Object
To lay out all the cards over the nine cards in the opening tableau.

Play
Cover – with cards from the talon – any two cards in the tableau that total 10, regardless of colour, as well as any pairs of 10s, jacks, queens and kings. In Tableau 56, cover the 8 of spades and the 2 of hearts, and the 8 of hearts and the 2 of diamonds. If you draw a 3 and a 10, then a 9 and an ace, cover the latter couple. If by chance you subsequently draw a 10 and a 5, cover the two 10s.

   If the next draw produces a queen and a 9, there will be no more pairs or couples totalling 10 in the tableau. Play is thus blocked – in other words, the game fails. It is successful when all the cards from the talon have been dealt out.

Variant
Cover as many cards as it takes, so long as they total 10. With regard to the above game, you could have continued by covering the 5 of clubs, the 3 of hearts and the 2 of spades. As you may suspect, the success rate of the variant is much higher than the original version's. Nevertheless, the variant does call for some degree of memory and strategy.

47. Dragnet

This solitaire version depends entirely on chance, but it produces enough twists and turns during play to keep things interesting. Just when you think play is blocked, the right card will come along and keep your hope of success alive.

Material
One deck of 52 cards.

Opening Tableau
Deal four cards face up in a row. Keep the talon face down.

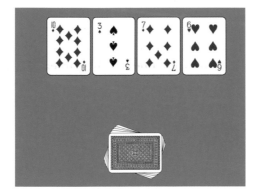

Tableau 57

Object
To lay out all the cards from the talon atop the four cards in the opening tableau.

Play

Cards from the talon are turned up one by one. If none matches rank with any of the four cards in the tableau, place them in the discard pile. If a card does match, place it upon its same-rank "twin" and cover the pair with the top card of the discard pile. Should a freshly released card from the discard pile match a card in the tableau, place it upon the latter and cover the pair with the next card, and so on. Note that a pair can only be matched with one card each from the talon or the discard pile and the tableau.

Suppose the next cards drawn from the talon are the ace of clubs, the 8 of diamonds, the king of diamonds, the king of spades and the 10 of clubs, in that order. Pack the 10 of clubs upon the 10 of diamonds (see Tableau 57), and cover the pair with the top card of the discard pile – the king of spades. Pack the king of diamonds, which becomes available following the removal of the king of spades, upon the latter, and cover the pair of kings with the 8 of diamonds. The discard pile is now left with just one card – the ace of clubs.

Continue the play in this manner until the talon is exhausted. Only one redeal is allowed. The game is successful if all the cards from the talon and the discard pile have been moved onto the four piles in the tableau. It fails if there are still cards in the discard pile.

48. Millefeuille

This speedy game of solitaire takes up little space, and the success rate is low enough to be challenging. Ideal for travel.

Material
One deck of 52 cards.

Opening Tableau
Deal out four cards face up in a row. Keep the talon face down.

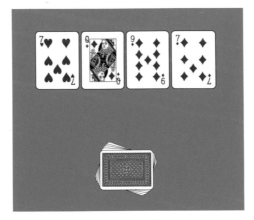

Tableau 58

Object
To place all the cards in the talon onto the tableau.

Play
If the tableau contains two or more same-suit or same-rank cards, cover them with cards from the talon. In Tableau 58, for example, cover the pair of 7s or the three diamond cards. Continue the play as long as two or more same-suit or same-rank cards turn up. The game is successful if and when the talon is exhausted.

49. Carousel

Although this highly colorful game is purely a matter of luck, it demands the player's full concentration.

Material

One deck of 52 cards.

Object

To place all the cards in the talon onto the carousel.

Opening Tableau

Remove the four queens and the four kings from the deck and arrange them alternating from king to queen, in a circle. These cards represent horses on a carousel (see Tableau 59). Keep the talon face down.

Tableau 59

Tableau 60

Play

Consider the circle as a compass. Starting from top center and going clockwise, turn up and place each card from the talon above each of the "horses" on the carousel. Any card matching its horse in suit or rank can mount it. Cards that cannot mount their own horse advance clockwise to adjoin the next horse. Fill the vacant spaces with cards from the talon. Suppose that after two rounds of the carousel, we arrive at Tableau 60.

Place the 3 of hearts upon the 3 of spades; the jack of spades upon the jack of hearts; then the 2 of clubs upon the king of clubs. Since no other cards can now mount their horses, move the 7 of hearts above the 3 of hearts, the 5 of hearts above the king of hearts, the 6 of diamonds above the queen of spades and the 10 of diamonds above the 2 of clubs. Fill the vacant spaces with cards from the talon and continue the play in this manner until all the cards are mounted on the carousel.

50. Recruiters

This simple game nonetheless demands complete attention and a good memory of past maneuvers in order to guide your choice between various options.

Material
One deck of 52 cards.

Opening Tableau
Deal out eight cards face up in a row. Keep the talon face down.

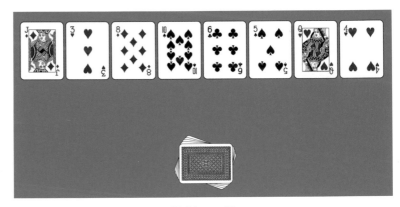

Object
To deal out the entire talon onto the tableau.

Tableau 61

Play
Cover – with cards from the talon – any two-card sequences in the tableau, whether they're ascending or descending, regardless of suit, color, rank or position. In Tableau 61, for example, cover any of the following couples: queen and jack; jack and 10; 6 and 5; 5 and 4; or 4 and 3. With new cards from the talon being injected into the tableau, other sequences will form that prompt yet more cards to be drawn from the talon. The game is successful when all the cards from the talon are placed in the tableau.

51. Patio

This version, though easy to play, has an extremely low success rate. It was one of the first "real" solitaire games that Grandmother taught me.

Material
One deck of 52 cards.

Opening Tableau
Deal out eight cards face up: three each in the first and third rows, and two in the second row – one at each end. The object is to form a closed court as shown in Tableau 62.

Tableau 62

Object

To place all the cards from the talon onto the tableau.

Play

Turn up cards from the talon one by one. Move any card in the tableau – whether it be single or carrying a pile underneath it – onto another card of immediately lower rank, regardless of color. In Tableau 62, for example, move the 8 onto the 7, the jack onto the 10, the queen onto the jack and the king onto the queen. An ace can have a 2 placed upon it but cannot be moved onto a king. A king may be placed upon a queen but cannot host any cards – neither ace nor queen. A vacant space must be filled as soon as it appears with a card from the talon.

Whenever play is blocked, draw a card from the talon and place it on another card in the tableau according to the game's rule. Continue in this manner until the talon is exhausted. The game is successful if all the cards from the talon can be placed in the tableau.

Strategy

If two or three same-rank cards and one of immediately higher rank appear in the tableau, say, three 4s and a 5, it's preferable to move the 5 upon one of the 4s before any other maneuver. A card from the talon may eventually turn up to unblock other cards. In the absence of pairs, move the lowest-ranked cards first. For example, if the tableau includes a three-card sequence – 5, 6, 7 – place the 6 upon the 5 first, then the 7 upon the 6. You will thus obtain two maneuvers instead of one had you chosen to move the 7 onto the 6 first.

52. Mixed Pairs

This particular game is not really solitaire, Grandmother always claimed, because a quick glance at the opening tableau usually indicates whether or not it will be successful. "But how?" I asked. "It's like Christopher Columbus' egg," scoffed Grandmother. "Use your head, my boy." Go figure!

Tableau 63

Material
One deck of 52 cards.

Opening Tableau
Remove the ace of spades, and the king and queen of hearts from the deck and place them in a column. These three cards represent the "mayor" and two "witnesses." Deal out 15 cards face up in three rows of five columns, as in Tableau 63. Keep the talon face down.

Object
To form 15 mixed pairs.

Play
Turn up cards from the talon one by one, pausing to make possible plays. As soon as a card finds its mixed-pair match (same rank, different color) in the tableau, place it atop the latter. Eliminate cards that find no match in the tableau. Only one deal is allowed per game. The game is successful if all the cards in the tableau are covered.

Clue
A quick glance at the opening tableau will tell whether or not the game will come out. Five combinations, each considered separately, mean failure. Can you figure it out? If not, see CLUES on page 503.

53. Mixed Pairs II

Grandmother wasn't terribly keen on this game, which requires more manipulation than attention or reflection.

Material
One deck of 52 cards.

Opening Tableau
Deal six cards face down directly into the waste pile. Then deal out 18 cards face up in three rows of six columns. Keep the talon face down.

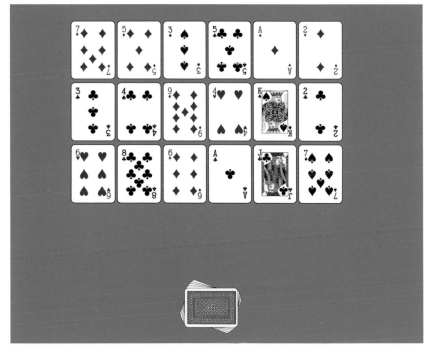

Tableau 64

Object

To cover the 18 cards in the tableau with face-down cards from the talon.

Play

Turn up cards from the talon one by one, pausing to make possible plays. As soon as a card finds its match (same rank, different color) in the tableau, place it face down upon the latter. Consider Tableau 64: Suppose you draw the 7 of clubs from the talon, place it face down upon the 7 of diamonds. If you draw the jack of hearts, place it face down upon the jack of clubs. And so on. The game is successful when all the cards in the tableau are covered.

The six cards that were removed beforehand ensure the random nature of the game. If it weren't for them, this game would come out at every try, with the exception of the following two cases: a) if the opening tableau contains a four-of-a-kind or a pairs-royal (or proil), you might as well start over because the game will certainly fail. The four-of-a-kind is doomed to stay uncovered since there will be no same-rank card in the talon with which to cover it; b) in the case of the pairs-royal, there's only one card left in the talon with which to cover all three cards – an impossible task.

Variant

To make this game more difficult, some players suggest removing eight, 10 or even 12 cards beforehand.

54. Lovers' Lane

This game is less than exciting, based as it is on luck rather than skill. But Grandmother was fond of it because it gave her the opportunity to recount some of the world's most enduring love stories, such as Romeo and Juliet, Tristan and Isolde, Caesar and Cleopatra, and many others.

Material
One deck of 52 cards.

Opening Tableau
Remove the king and queen of hearts from the deck. Deal out 21 cards face up in three rows of seven columns. Place the queen of hearts above the first card at the left of the top row and the king of hearts below the last card at the right of the last row (see Tableau 65).

Tableau 65

Object

To cover one of the two following routes whereby the two lovers – the king and queen of hearts – can reunite.

Queen of hearts   Queen of hearts

```
X                                    X  X  X  X  X  X  X
X                                                      X
X  X  X  X  X  X  X                                    X
         King of hearts                        King of hearts
```

       Route A   Route B

Play

Turn up cards from the talon one by one. As soon as a card finds its match (same rank, alternate color) in the tableau, place it face down upon the latter. Put unmatchable cards into the waste pile. To win, however, it is not necessary to cover all the cards in the tableau, which comprises two distinct sections: a core of five cards and a perimeter made of 16 cards, as shown in Tableau 65. You need only cover half the perimeter in a continuous manner – as shown in Tableau 66.

Tableau 66

Strategy

If faced with a choice over which card to cover – in the core or on the perimeter – opt for a card on the perimeter, since the core is irrelevant as far as the "lovers' lane" is concerned. Consider Tableau 65: If you draw a red 9 from the talon, place it upon the 9 of spades rather than the 9 of clubs; if it's the queen of diamonds, place it upon the queen of spades rather than the queen of clubs; if a black 3 turns up, place it upon the 3 of diamonds rather than the 3 of hearts.

However, the game will automatically fail if the opening tableau shows a four-of-a-kind – say, four 7s, of which each route contains at least one card, regardless of color. Both routes are thus blocked since there are no 7s left in the talon with which to cover them.

CHAPTER 7

Potpourri

55. Good Old King Dagobert

This game amused Grandmother. "We all assume that when good King Dagobert died, he went straight to heaven. But that wasn't the case," Grandmother said. "Even though he was a king, he still had to stand before Saint Peter. And I tell you, Saint Peter didn't have an easy job letting him through. Maybe Dagobert wasn't as good as he was reputed to be. For example, if he could be so distracted as to put his pants on back to front, he might also have forgotten to confess a couple of little sins, in which case the impartial Saint Peter would have felt obliged to put his foot down." This version of solitaire requires total concentration and a good dose of mental calculation. The success rate is low.

Material
One deck of 52 cards.

Opening Tableau
In the foundation zone, deal all 13 diamond cards in ascending order, in the shape of a staircase – from 2 at the bottom to ace at the top. Place the king of hearts – representing King Dagobert – at the foot of the stairs. In the maneuver zone, deal the 38 remaining cards face up in seven rows – six rows of six columns, and one row of two columns.

Object
To lead Dagobert up the stairs on his way to heaven.

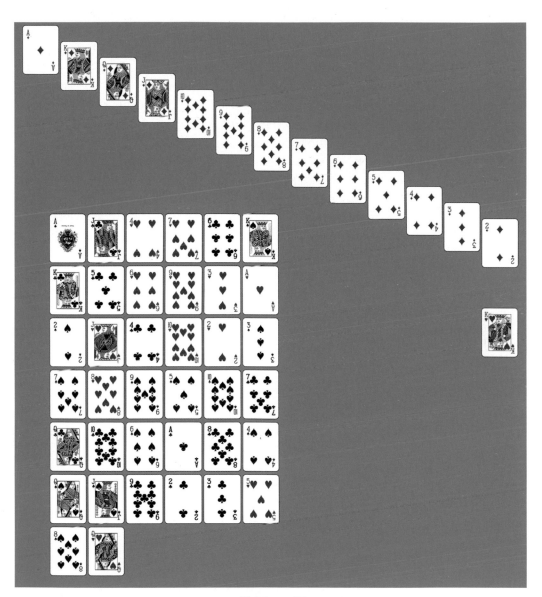

Tableau 67

Play

Ace counts as one, king as 13, queen as 12 and jack as 11. Select two cards in the first row and deduct the lowest-ranked card from the highest; the result or difference indicates the number of steps King Dagobert is allowed to climb. For example, if you deduct the 4 of hearts from the jack of clubs, the king is allowed to climb seven steps. Choose two other cards in the first row and repeat this operation. Suppose they are the king of spades and the 7 of hearts, the difference of which is six – exactly the number of steps Dagobert would need to climb before Saint Peter opens the door to heaven to him. The game is successful.

But things are rarely that simple. To be admitted to heaven, King Dagobert must arrive exactly at the last step. If he should go past it, he will bang his nose against the closed door and must go down again. For example, if Dagobert is given six steps, but needs only two to reach the top, he will have to climb two steps up and come down four steps. What's more, once the king has started to descend, he must go all the way down to the foot of the stairs before he can ascend again. Use as many cards – row by row – in the maneuver zone as it takes to get the king through the pearly gates.

Variant

To get the number of steps for King Dagobert, use one card at a time, instead of choosing two cards and substracting one from the other. This variant obviously offers a higher success rate.

56. Free the Princess!

This simple game will please children. Its success rate is high.

Material

One deck of 52 cards.

Opening Tableau

Deal 10 cards face down in a row. Place the queen of hearts – the imprisoned princess herself – below the fourth card.

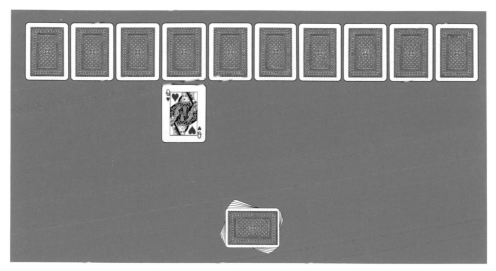

Tableau 68

Object

To get the princess out of prison.

Play

Turn up the card directly above the princess. If it's red, move the princess one step to the left. If it's black, move her one step to the right. Repeat the maneuver with the third or fifth card, as the case may be, and continue in this manner until the princess reaches either end of the row. In her back-and-forth movements, if the princess finds herself below an already-turned-up card, cover same with another card, face up, drawn from the talon.

If the princess finds herself at the left end and the card above her is red, she may make her exit there. If she's at the right end, the card above her must be black before she can exit. Whichever the case, the princess is freed and the game is successful. On the contrary, if the talon is exhausted and the princess is nowhere near the exit, it fails.

57. Thermometer

This yoyo-style game closely resembles Free the Princess *(no. 56), except that play proceeds vertically. Grandmother considered these kinds of games puerile. She taught them to me when I was small but later encouraged me to cultivate more sophisticated games.*

Material
One deck of 52 cards.

Opening Tableau
Deal seven cards face down in one column, representing a thermometer. To the right of the fourth card, place a card face up. Like mercury, this card will move up and down, recording the temperature's fluctuations.

Object
Forcing the thermometer to burst by elevating the "witness card" past the top of the column.

Play
Turn up the fourth card, which sits to the left of the witness card. If both are of the same color, the witness card moves up a degree; if not, it goes down by one degree. Repeat the maneuver with the third or fifth card, as the case may be, and continue the play in this manner. In its up-and-down movements, if the witness card finds itself next to an already-turned-up card, cover same with another card, face up, from the talon. If the witness card goes below the lowest card in the column, the game is lost. However, if it towers above the top card, the thermometer bursts and the game is successful.

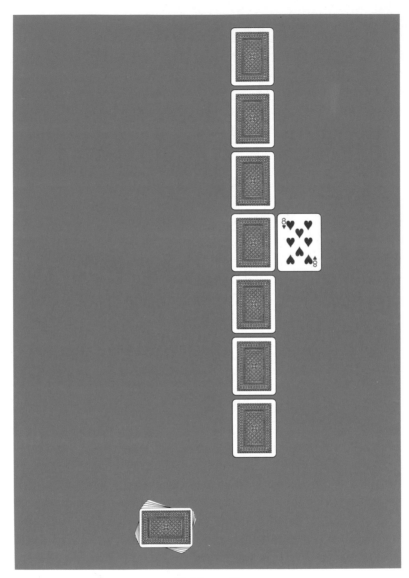

Tableau 69

58. Globe-Trotters

Another yo-yo game that has a round tableau, representing the globe. The two red jacks represent the globe-trotters.

Material
One deck of 52 cards.

Opening Tableau
Remove from the deck all the aces, kings and queens as well as the two red jacks. Create a circle large enough to hold 39 cards by placing the four aces at the top (north), the king and queen of diamonds to the northeast, the king and queen of clubs to the southeast, the king and queen of spades to the southwest, and the king and queen of hearts to the northwest (Tableau 70). These five groups represent, in this order, five continents: North America, Europe, Asia, Africa and Oceania. The continents are separated by groups of five face-down cards. The red jacks represent the globe-trotters, the jack of hearts is in Oceania and the jack of diamonds is in Europe. Keep the remaining 13 cards – the talon – face down.

Object
To guide the globe-trotters through all five continents.

Play
Turn up the first card from the talon. If it's black, put it aside. If it's a heart card, the jack of hearts will advance the number of spaces indicated by the rank of the card. If it's a diamond card, the jack of diamonds will travel. Once both jacks are en route, if you draw a spade card, the jack of hearts will retreat the number of spaces indicated by the rank of the spade card; if it's a club card, the jack of diamonds will retreat. Three redeals are allowed to guide the red jacks around the world…and to win the game.

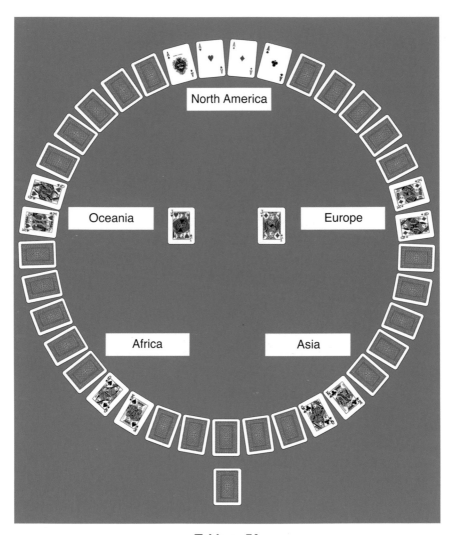

Tableau 70

59. Knight

This one gets its name from the way the knight moves in a chess game. Each move represents a jump by the knight. It's a difficult solitaire game, requiring an acute sense of anticipation and a good memory to compute complex combinations. Grandmother claimed she had found four different itineraries for the knight that were surefire winners. No doubt the great chess master Anatoly Karpov would discover others.

Material
A deck of 32 major cards, from 7 to ace; one knight.

Opening Tableau
Deal the cards face down in four rows of eight columns.

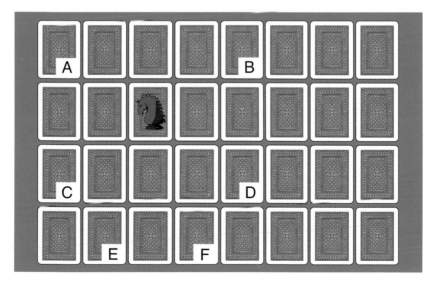

Tableau 71

Object

To turn up all the cards in the tableau in 32 jumps by the knight.

Play

Select a card at random and place the knight on it. Move the knight as you would in a chess game. In Tableau 71, for example, the knight is located in the second row, third column. His first move may be in any of the six directions indicated by the letters A, B, C, D, E and F. As the knight jumps, turn up the card upon which he rests. He may jump in any direction except back onto a turned-up card. Continue until all 32 cards are turned up, in which case the game is successful. It fails if the knight is left with no possible direction other than onto an already turned-up card.

Strategy

To succeed, you must discover four different itineraries. See CLUES on page 503.

Variants

1. To simplify things, two rounds are allowed on turned-up cards.
2. The knight can go back over its initial position only once.
3. The knight can go back as many times as you wish over turned-up cards, but to win the game you must turn up all the cards in 40 jumps or less.

60. Clairvoyance

This is the first game that Grandmother taught me. Its success rate is low at best. As soon as she noticed my unswerving determination to beat the odds, Grandmother knew at once that I was a worthy partner and took me on as such – an odd decision by Grandmother in the eyes of the rest of our family.

Material
One deck of 52 cards.

Object
To predict the color of cards.

Play
There is no opening tableau. Hold the deck face down and, as you deal, announce the color of the card as it's turned up: red or black. If you're wrong, put the card aside. When the talon is exhausted, take the discard pile and redeal. After two redeals, if you manage to call the right color for all the cards, the game is won. Some players claim you need a genuine gift of clairvoyance to win this game.

61. Announcement

This is the second game Grandmother taught me. It wasn't among her favorites by a long shot, even though its success rate is very low – less than one percent, she said.

Material
One deck of 52 cards.

Object
To turn up the entire deck without once announcing the right rank of a single card.

Play
There's no opening tableau. Hold the deck and turn up the cards one by one while calling out the ranks from ace to king: ace, 2, 3...jack, queen, king. Repeat four times. If the turned-up card corresponds to the rank called out, the game fails. If you manage to turn up the entire deck without announcing the right rank of a single card, you've succeeded beyond any player's wildest dreams.

62. Poker Solitaire

This is a case where the disciple supplanted his master. Grandmother knew nothing about Poker Solitaire *until I taught her. It's not solitaire in the strict sense of the term because it doesn't necessarily end in terms of success or failure; when you play poker, you always win something.* Poker Solitaire *is nonetheless a highly entertaining game. A poker lover will enjoy it because it has all the characteristics of a poker game, whereas a novice will have a chance to learn something about poker while appreciating the value of its various hands. Grandmother was all the more interested in the game because it calls for absolute concentration, a reliable memory, tenacity, a rare sense of direction and a gift for mental calculation.*

Material
One deck of 52 cards.

Opening Tableau
Deal 25 cards face up in five rows of five columns. The rest of the deck goes to the waste pile.

Object
To form the best possible total score in poker hands.

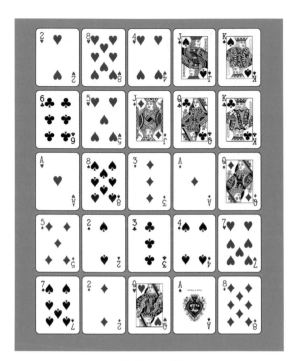

Tableau 72

Value of Poker Hands

Bear in mind that the ace can be used either as the highest- or lowest-scoring card.

1. **Royal flush:** A hand of five same-suit cards in sequence from ten (jack, queen, king) to ace. 100 points.
2. **Straight flush:** A hand of five same-suit cards in sequence, such as 3, 4, 5, 6, 7. 75 points.
3. **Four-of-a-kind, or square:** A hand of four same-rank cards with one odd card. For example, four 7s and a king. 50 points.
4. **Flush:** A hand of five same-suit cards, regardless of rank. For example, 3, 4, 8, jack and king of clubs. 40 points.
5. **Full house:** A hand containing a three of a kind, or pairs-royal, and a pair. For example, three jacks and two 7s. 30 points.

6. **Straight:** A hand of five cards in sequence, regardless of color or rank. For example, a 5 of clubs, 6 of hearts, 7 of hearts, 8 of spades and 9 of diamonds. 20 points.
7. **Three of a kind, or pairs-royal:** A hand of three same-rank cards with two odd cards. For example, three 6s, a 9 and an ace. 10 points.
8. **Two pairs:** A hand of two pairs with one odd card. For example, two 8s, two queens and a jack. 5 points.
9. **Pair:** A hand containing two same rank cards and three odd cards. For example, two 3s, a 10, a 6 and a 4. 2 points.

Play

A poker hand has five cards. The opening tableau comprises five horizontal poker hands and five vertical poker hands, to which real professionals may add two diagonal poker hands. Study the tableau carefully and modify the position of cards to form the best scoring hands possible. You can move a card only once.

Tableau 72 offers no possibilities for royal flush, straight flush or four-of-a-kind. But it's certainly possible to form a few poker hands with the four existing pairs-royal (aces, queens, 8s and 2s) and the six pairs (kings, jacks, 7s, 5s, 4s and 3s). Furthermore, you may form a pairs-royal with the three 7s (spades, hearts and diamonds), as well as two straights thanks to the two pairs-royal (aces and 2s) and the three pairs of 3s, 4 and 5s.

Make sure you didn't miss any maneuver so as to obtain the best possible score. Count the hands you've formed and add up the total value.

Variant

There's no opening tableau. Turn up 25 cards one by one and place them face up on the table. The second card must be placed next to the first card, either right or left, above or below, or diagonally. Continue in this manner with the remaining 23 cards until the tableau includes five rows of five columns. Once laid out, a card may not be moved. Count the hands thus formed – horizontally, vertically and diagonally.

PART II

Ascending Suit
Sequences on the Ace

CHAPTER 8

Ascending Suit Sequences on the Ace – One-Deck Games

63. Gold Rush

This game is also commonly called Klondike. *According to Grandmother, this classic was invented in the Klondike itself, during the gold rush at the end of the 19th century. Its high success rate and easy manipulation make it an all-time favorite.*

Material
One deck of 52 cards.

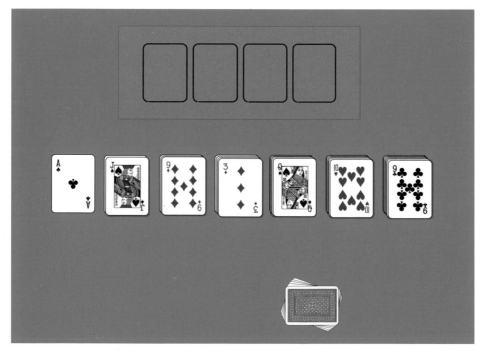

Tableau 73

Opening Tableau

To form the maneuver zone, deal a row of seven columns from left to right. Place one card in the first column, two in the second, three in the third, and so on, until you place seven cards in the seventh column. Only the top card of each pile is face up.

Reserve spaces above the row for the four aces. They are the foundations upon which to build the four suit sequences. Keep the talon face down.

Object

To complete four ascending suit sequences from ace to king.

Play

Move the aces as they appear over to the foundation zone and build on them in suit and ascending sequence with available cards from the maneuver zone. Once a card is moved to its foundation, it cannot be moved back.

In the maneuver zone, move available cards onto those next higher in rank and of alternating colors, so as to build down in sequence. Once a face-down card is bared, turn it face up for a subsequent maneuver.

When all possible maneuvers have been executed, turn up cards from the talon in packets of three. If the first card can be placed upon a suit sequence or a run, the one under it becomes available for play. You can move a sequence as a unit onto an available card if the contact cards are in correct sequence and color. A vacant column may be filled only by an available king, alone or with its pile. Once a move is made, it cannot be undone.

Three redeals are allowed. After each redeal, gather the remaining cards and, without shuffling, deal them again in packets of three. After three redeals, if there are still face-down cards in the tableau and in the talon, play is blocked and the game fails.

Here is a hypothetical play as per Tableau 73. Move the ace of clubs to the foundation row. In the maneuver zone, move the 9 of clubs onto the 10 of hearts, then the 10 of hearts onto the jack of spades. Suppose you find the 2 of hearts beneath the 10 of hearts, and the king of clubs beneath the 9 of clubs.

Fill the first column (left vacant by the removal of the ace of clubs) with the king of clubs – a move that bares the 7 of spades. We now arrive at Tableau 74.

Since no further maneuvers are possible, turn up cards from the talon in packets of three. Suppose the first packet yields the 5 of diamonds, which has no place to go. The second packet yields, say, the 8 of spades, which can be placed upon the 9 of diamonds, baring the next available card: the 3 of clubs.

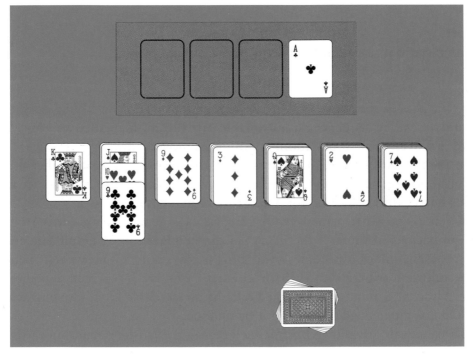

Tableau 74

The third packet yields the ace of diamonds, which goes immediately onto the foundation row and, in the process, releases the 7 of diamonds for play. The latter goes upon the 8 of spades and releases, say, the 2 of clubs, which, in turn, can be placed upon the ace of clubs in the foundation row. We're left once again with the 3 of clubs from the previous packet. This time around, however, it can join the 2 of clubs in the foundation row. Let's suppose the next available card is the 9 of hearts, which has no place to go. We now arrive at Tableau 75.

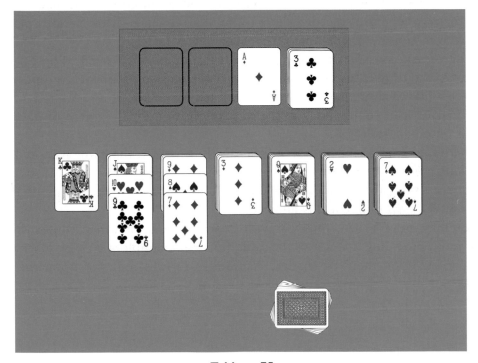

Tableau 75

Turn up the fourth packet of three cards, and continue play in this manner.

Strategy
When faced with a choice between two maneuvers, for example, which of two red sixes to place upon a black seven, opt for the one with the most cards

underneath. Also, when a king blocks a column, try to vacate another column as soon as possible and move the king there, in order to unblock play.

Variants

1. Keep any card that may prove crucial for play in the maneuver zone, instead of moving it immediately to the foundation zone.
2. One variant allows moving a card from the foundation zone back to the maneuver zone if it's needed there to build a sequence. Most serious players, however, consider this maneuver a cheat.
3. If necessary, consider breaking a run, for example, if you need to bare a face-down card or release a particular card to develop a suit sequence. Suppose you have a five-card run made of a black 7, a red 6, a black 5, a red 4 and a black 3. If you wish, you may break the run and move only a segment of it, say, 5-4-3 onto another red 6.
4. There's no limit to the number of redeals. In this way, the game is more likely to come out.
5. Turn up the cards in the talon one by one, instead of in groups of three. However, only one redeal is allowed.
6. You may move a card, singly or with its sequence, upon any card next higher in rank, providing it is not of the same suit. For example, you may place the 6 of hearts upon the 7 of spades, diamonds or clubs, but not upon the 7 of hearts.

64. Alaska

Grandmother assumed this game was so named because of its resemblance to Gold Rush *(no. 63). In fact, both have almost the same rules.*

Material
One deck of 52 cards.

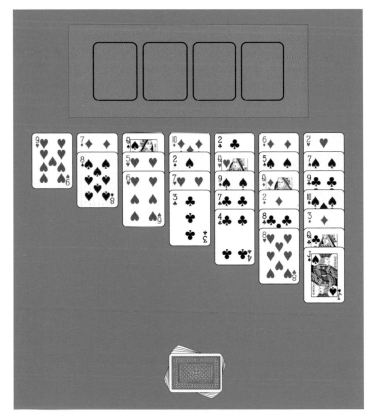

Tableau 76

Opening Tableau

Reserve a foundation zone above the tableau for the four aces, on which to build the four suit sequences. The maneuver zone consists of 28 face-up cards arranged in seven overlapping rows of seven columns – one card in the first row, two in the second, three in the third, and so on. Keep the talon face down.

Object

To complete four ascending suit sequences from ace to king.

Play

Place the aces, as they appear, in the foundation zone. In the maneuver zone, move available cards upon one another, provided they are of the same color, although not necessarily of the same suit, so as to build down in same-color sequence. You may fill any vacant column with any card, whether it be alone or with its run. As well, you may break any column and move only a part of it upon another. When all the possible maneuvers have been executed, turn up cards from the talon in groups of three and proceed in the same manner as in *Gold Rush* (no. 63). Three redeals are allowed. The game is successful when the four suit sequences are complete.

65. Russian Solitaire

Some maintain that this is the most difficult game of solitaire in the world. But Grandmother, who knew the game well, didn't agree. For her, nothing beat L'Impériale (no. 112) in terms of difficulty. It is true, however, that the success rate of Russian Solitaire is extremely low. What's more, it requires a good deal of manipulation, which makes it unattractive. Sometimes failure looms after a mere couple of moves or even as the tableau is being laid out; in these cases, the best thing to do is start over.

Material
One deck of 52 cards.

Opening Tableau
As in *Gold Rush* (no. 63), lay out 28 cards in a row of seven columns – one card in the first column, two in the second, three in the third, and so on, until you place seven cards in the seventh column. Only the top card of each pile is face up. Then, starting from the second column, lay out the 24 remaining cards, face up, in four overlapping rows of six columns (see Tableau 77).

Reserve spaces for the four aces above the maneuver zone. They are the foundations on which to build the four ascending suit sequences.

Object
To complete four ascending suit sequences from ace to king.

Play
Place the aces, as they become available, into the foundation zone. All other available cards must be moved immediately to their appropriate rank in the foundation zone and, once there, cannot be returned to the maneuver zone. In Tableau

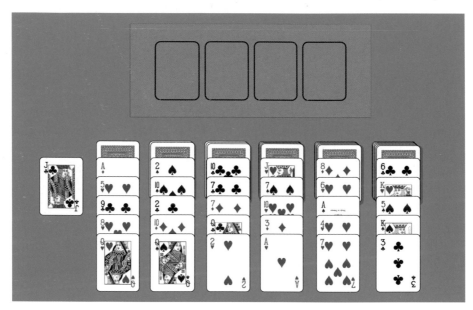

Tableau 77

77, for example, move the ace of hearts to the foundation zone, followed by the 2 of hearts. If a card finds its place in the foundation, there's no point in retaining it for a descending sequence in the maneuver zone.

In the maneuver zone, move one available card at a time – singly or with its pile, as the case may be – onto one another, providing the latter is of the same suit and next higher in rank, so as to build descending suit sequences. Face-down cards that become available for play are turned up. A vacant column can be filled only by a king, singly or with its sequence. The game is successful when all four ascending suit sequences are complete.

The following is a hypothetical play as per Tableau 77. Move the ace of hearts to the foundation zone, followed by the 2 of hearts. In the maneuver zone, move the jack of clubs onto the queen of clubs. Fill the vacant first column with either the king of spades or the king of hearts. If you opt for the latter, move its entire pile as a unit. Next, move the pile topped by the jack of hearts upon the queen of hearts and turn up the newly bared card in the fifth column, say, the 6 of diamonds. Move the pile topped by the 2 of clubs onto the 3 of clubs. We now arrive at Tableau 78.

By now, though, no further maneuvers seem possible. Play is blocked, and the game is lost.

Strategy

When faced with a choice between two maneuvers, opt for the one that will generate the most subsequent maneuvers. It's also important to bare the face-down cards as soon as possible, for they can unblock play and help advance the game.

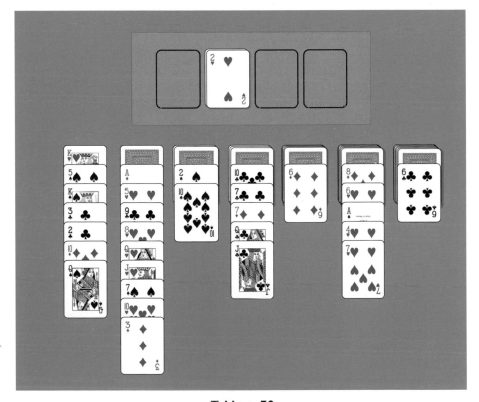

Tableau 78

Ascending Suit Sequences on the Ace – One-Deck Games

Variants

1. Build runs instead of suit sequences in the maneuver zone. For example, move a card onto another next in rank and alternate color, rather than same suit. In this way, the game is easier to play, since you'll get twice as many possible combinations.

2. Delay moving cards to the foundation zone if you think they'll come in handy for subsequent play in the maneuver zone.

66. Old-fashioned Solitaire

This is an all-time classic. Relatively simple, but with a low success rate, it was one of Grandmother's favorites. She claimed she won this one more often than anyone else. It was also one of the first varieties she taught me.

Material
One deck of 52 cards.

Opening Tableau
Reserve a foundation zone to host the four aces as they appear, and four discard columns in the maneuver zone. Keep the talon face down.

Object
To complete four ascending suit sequences from ace to king.

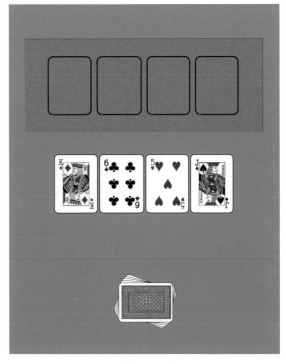

Tableau 79

Play

Place the aces, as they appear, in the foundation zone. Turn up cards in the talon one by one. Cards that do not fit in the foundation zone are placed in each of the four columns in the maneuver zone – the lower rows overlapping the upper ones – until they can be moved onto suit sequences. Only available cards at the bottom of the columns can be moved onto the suit sequences. Cards in the maneuver zone cannot be moved from one column to another. Only one redeal is allowed. The game is successful when the four suit sequences are complete.

Strategy

Think ahead when placing cards in the discard columns so as not to block play unwittingly. It's important to reserve a column for high-ranking cards and avoid blocking lower-ranked cards with higher ones, especially if they are of the same suit. For example, it's impossible to move a 9 of hearts onto its rank in an ascending suit sequence if the 7 of hearts is already buried under it. Bear in mind, though, that you can't always avoid a bad turn of events. Otherwise, solitaire wouldn't be solitaire, would it?

Variants

1. Some variants suggest increasing the number of discard columns to five or even six. But then the game will become too easy. "Must have been the work of a coward," Grandmother sneered.
2. In the foundation zone, build ascending runs of alternating colors, instead of suit sequences.
3. Reverse the order and build down suit sequences or runs, from king to ace. As you lay out the opening tableau, take out the aces beforehand and place them directly in the foundation zone.

67. Egyptian Solitaire

Egyptian Solitaire is the oldest version of solitaire. I learned it from my grandmother, who, in turn, inherited it from her grandmother, and so on, all the way back to the pharaohs, said Grandmother, smiling mischievously. Come to think of it, she wasn't entirely wrong, considering the Egyptian origins of the tarot pack from which modern card games derive. Egyptian Solitaire is a simple game that requires little space or manipulation. In the original version, the rules were so strict that the game depended solely on luck. However, a couple of variants have been invented along the way that call for some reflection and strategy.

Material
One deck of 52 cards.

Opening Tableau
In the foundation zone, reserve space for the four aces, on which to build suit sequences. The maneuver zone consists of four face-up cards in a row. If an ace turns up, place it immediately in the foundation zone and fill the space with another card from the talon. Keep the talon face down.

Object
To complete four ascending suit sequences from ace to king.

Ascending Suit Sequences on the Ace – One-Deck Games

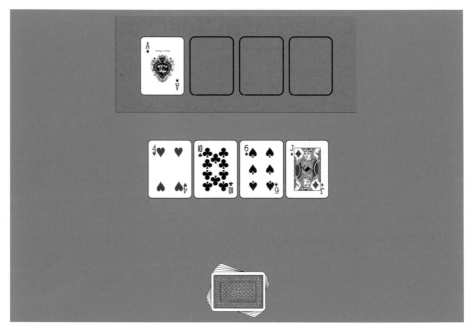

Tableau 80

Play

Place the aces, as they appear, in the foundation zone, followed immediately by all available cards that fit in the suit sequences. Once there, the cards cannot be moved back to the maneuver zone.

In the maneuver zone, build down runs of alternating colors by moving an available card onto another of opposite color and next in rank. When all the possible maneuvers have been executed, turn up cards from the talon in groups of three. If the top card can be played, it releases the next one under it for play. For example, if the first card is a 2 of spades, place it upon the ace of spades. If the next card is a 9 of diamonds, place it upon the 10 of clubs. Cards that cannot be played either in the foundation or maneuver zones are placed in a discard pile, the top card of which may be reintroduced into the game at the first opportunity.

You can move an already formed run only as a unit. For example, if you have a run made of a 7 of hearts, a 6 of clubs, a 5 of diamonds, a 4 of spades and a 3 of hearts, you must move the entire run, from 7 to 3, not just a segment of it. Fill a vacant column with an available card from the discard pile or from the talon if there's no discard pile.

When the entire talon has been dealt, turn it over and, without shuffling, redeal it in groups of three. Continue until play is blocked, that is, until the time when no cards fit in the suit sequences or runs. The game is successful only when the four suit sequences are complete.

Variants

1. Remove the four aces and place them directly in the foundation zone when laying out the opening tableau.

2. Use only the 32 major cards and form suit sequences from seven to ace.

3. Use the first card drawn from the talon as the foundation on which to build a sequence. For example, if the first card is a seven, build a circular sequence from seven to six, as follows: seven, eight, nine, ten, jack, queen, king, ace, two, three, four, five and six.

4. Build sequences regardless of suit in the foundation zone. For example, on an ace of spades you may place a 2 of hearts, or of clubs or diamonds. Grandmother did not approve of this variant, however, considering it cheating.

5. Keep any card that may prove crucial for play in the maneuver zone instead of moving it immediately to its foundation.

6. You may break a sequence and move only a segment of it onto another run, if such a maneuver helps advance play. This variant, needless to say, makes play infinitely easier.

7. To unblock play, you may move a card from its foundation back to the maneuver zone. Grandmother did not approve of this variant.

68. Good Fortune

This game's high success rate makes it a beginner's favorite.

Material

One deck of 52 cards.

Opening Tableau

Lay out the four aces in a row as foundations on which to build ascending suit sequences. In the maneuver zone, lay out 12 cards face up in a row. Keep the talon face down.

Object

To complete four ascending suit sequences from ace to king.

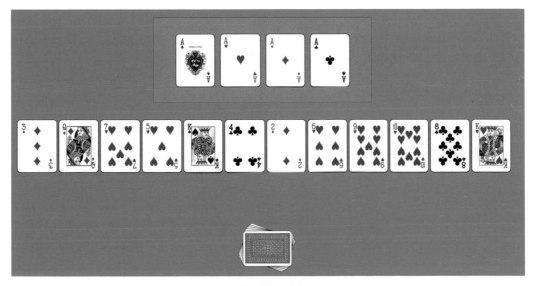

Tableau 81

Ascending Suit Sequences on the Ace – One-Deck Games

Play

In the maneuver zone, move an available card onto another, provided that the latter is of the same suit and immediately higher rank, so as to build descending suit sequences. In Tableau 81, for example, move the 6 of hearts onto the 7 of hearts; the 5 of hearts onto the 6 of hearts; the 2 of diamonds onto the 3 of diamonds; then the 9 of hearts onto the 10 of hearts. You can move only one card at a time. Fill any vacant column with an available card drawn from the discard pile, or from the talon if there is no discard pile.

Turn up cards from the talon one by one and place them wherever they fit – either in the ascending sequences being built in the foundation zone or in the descending sequences being built in the maneuver zone. Cards that do not fit in either zone are placed in the discard pile, the top card of which is always available for play and can be reintroduced into the game at the first opportunity. Only one redeal is allowed. If the entire talon has been dealt and play is blocked, the game fails. It is successful when all four ascending suit sequences have been completed.

69. Quartet

This game requires scant attention and depends entirely on luck. Its success rate is very low, however, and that was enough to attract Grandmother, bless her card-playing heart.

Material
One deck of 52 cards.

Opening Tableau
Place the four aces in a row in the foundation zone, on which you will build the four ascending suit sequences. Below the aces, lay out four cards face up. Keep the talon face down.

Object
To complete four ascending suit sequences from ace to king.

Play
Deal four cards at a time and place them so that they slightly overlap the four cards in the maneuver zone. At the first opportunity, transfer available cards from the maneuver zone to their appropriate rank in the foundation zone. In the maneuver zone, however, cards cannot be moved from one column to another. Turn up cards from the talon, four at a time, pausing to make what plays are possible, until the talon is exhausted. The game is successful if and when all four suit sequences are complete. Alas, this has never happened to me.

Variants
Given this game's low success rate, it's hardly surprising that many variants have been invented to make it easier to play.

1. Instead of four suit sequences, build four runs of alternating colors in the foundation zone.

Ascending Suit Sequences on the Ace – One-Deck Games

2. Build sequences, regardless of color.

3. Up to three redeals are allowed.

4. Some players even combine the second and third variants into one game. "That's pure cowardice!" Grandmother exclaimed.

70. Seven in a Row

If well executed, this apparently simple game can bring about surprising twists and turns. Its high success rate – 90 percent, according to Grandmother – makes it another favorite for beginners.

Material
One deck of 52 cards.

Opening Tableau
Reserve space for the four aces in the foundation zone, upon which to build suit sequences from ace to king. In the maneuver zone, lay out seven cards face up in a row. Transfer aces as they appear immediately to the foundation zone and fill the vacant spaces with cards from the talon. Keep the talon face down.

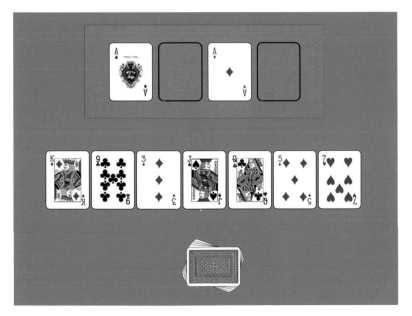

Tableau 82

Ascending Suit Sequences on the Ace – One-Deck Games

Object

To complete four ascending suit sequences from ace to king.

Play

In the maneuver zone, build descending runs of alternating colors by overlapping one card upon another, provided the latter is immediately higher in rank and of opposite color – black upon red, red upon black. For example, in Tableau 82, move the queen of clubs onto the king of diamonds.

When all the possible maneuvers have been executed, turn up cards from the talon in groups of three. If the top card can be placed upon a suit sequence in the

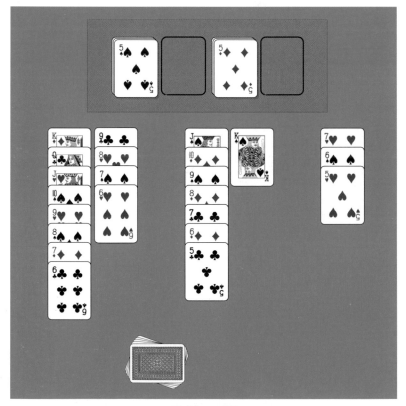

Tableau 83

The Complete Book of Solitaire

foundation zone or a run in the maneuver zone, the one under it becomes available for play.

A vacant column can be filled only by a king, either single or with its run. Suppose the top card is the king of clubs with which you use to fill the vacant column, and suppose the second card is the 2 of clubs, which you can place upon the 3 of hearts. Continue in this manner until the talon is exhausted. Once the first redeal is done, turn over the talon and, without shuffling, deal again in groups of three. There's no limit to the number of redeals, as long as new available cards keep turning up for play. The game is successful if and when all four ascending suit sequences are complete.

Up until now, things seem simple enough. However, certain maneuvers may produce spectacular developments. Suppose that following a series of maneuvers, we arrive at Tableau 83, according to which the following moves are possible:

- 5 of hearts onto 6 of clubs;
- 6 of spades onto its suit sequence;
- 5 of clubs onto 6 of hearts;
- 6 of diamonds onto its suit sequence;
- 6 of hearts and 5 of clubs onto 7 of clubs;
- 7 of spades onto its suit sequence;
- 6 of clubs and 5 of hearts onto 7 of hearts;
- 7 of diamonds onto its suit sequence;
- 8 of spades onto its suit sequence;
- 7 of clubs, 6 of hearts and 5 of clubs onto eight of hearts;
- 8 of diamonds onto its suit sequence;
- 9 of spades onto its suit sequence;
- 9 of clubs, 8 of hearts, 7 of clubs, 6 of hearts and 5 of clubs onto
- 10 of diamonds.

As you can see, the above series of maneuvers contributes considerably to the building of both the spade and diamond sequences. We now arrive at Tableau 84.

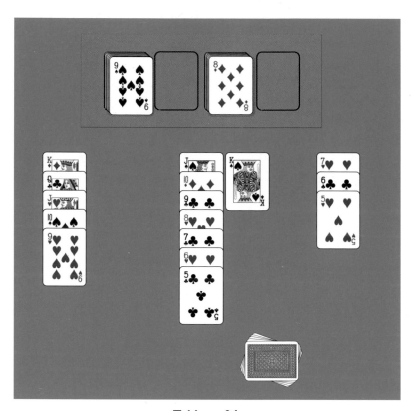

Tableau 84

Let's consider a scenario in which you must temporarily undo a suit sequence in the foundation zone in order to unblock play in the maneuver zone. For this purpose, let's suppose the foundation zone includes a third suit sequence running from ace to 4 of hearts.

Instead of placing the 5 of hearts upon its suit sequence in the foundation zone, move the 4 of hearts from its foundation onto the 5 of clubs in the maneuver zone. Suppose this maneuver releases the 3 of spades for play. As a result, the order of appearance of the cards in the talon will be modified, and this will probably lead to further possible maneuvers. As you might have already noticed, it's even permissible to move several cards – albeit one by one – from their suit sequence back to the maneuver zone.

What's unusual about this game is that the flexible nature of its rules actually favors strategic moves. For example, instead of transferring a suitable card at once to its foundation, you may keep it in the maneuver zone for as long as you deem necessary. You can even transfer one or more cards already in the foundation zone back to the maneuver zone and use them to build runs. What's more, you may even split a run at will and place part of it at a strategic point so as to obtain new maneuvers; or you may delay placing a suitable card upon another run, say, a red 6 upon a black 7, in the hope of drawing the other red 6 from the talon.

This game clearly flaunts all usual game rules in favor of fairly liberal combinations of cards. No wonder its success rate is high. To quote Grandmother, "This is a 'patience' for people who haven't any."

71. Roaming Proils

As this game progresses, threes-of-a-kind, or proils, form and unform, only to form again, though differently – hence its name. It requires absolute concentration and an acute sense of anticipation. Luck, too, plays a key role. Its success rate is very low – one out of 50, according to Grandmother.

Material
One deck of 52 cards.

Opening Tableau
Reserve space for a foundation zone to host the aces, on which you will build suit sequences. In the maneuver zone, deal 17 piles of three cards each – the top card face up, the other two face down. The remaining card, called the "Solitaire," is placed face up at the bottom right of the tableau.

Object
To complete four ascending suit sequences from ace to king.

Play
Place the aces, as they appear, in the foundation zone. Consider Tableau 85: Start the game by moving the ace of spades to the foundation zone, a maneuver that will release, say, the 10 of clubs. Move any available card upon another of the same rank, regardless of color, provided the receiving pile doesn't yet contain a proil. Thus, in Tableau 85, move the queen of clubs onto the queen of spades or vice versa, then the 5 of hearts onto the 5 of clubs or vice versa, and so on. You may also move the queen of diamonds onto the queen of spades and form a proil of queens in the process. Note, however, that this maneuver will block the seventh pile as well as the two face-down cards at the bottom of it.

Tableau 85

Turn up any freshly bared card for play. You can only move one available card at a time. For example, if you decide to move the two queens of clubs and spades onto the queen of diamonds, move the club queen first, then the spade queen – a maneuver that reverses the position of the two cards. In this way, proils form and unform according to various maneuvers. A pile may never contain more than three face-up cards. What's more, piles may completely disappear.

If an available card fits in a suit sequence, you may move it immediately to the foundation zone or keep it for a time in the maneuver zone to help develop play. You may also place a card upon the Solitaire and even form a proil there. The Solitaire, too, can be moved onto a pile, providing the contact card is of the same rank, regardless of color. However, only a king can fill the space left vacant by the Solitaire. In Tableau 85, for example, move the 9 of diamonds onto the 9 of clubs and move the kings of hearts and spades into the vacant space left by the Solitaire. Suppose a series of maneuvers ensues and we now arrive at Tableau 86.

Since no further maneuver seems possible, the game fails. It is successful if and when the four ascending suit sequences are complete.

Strategy

Generally speaking, it's important to bare as many face-down cards as possible. It also helps to release minor cards first in order to build sequences as fast as possible. At some point, though, it may be advantageous to keep a card in the maneuver zone instead of transferring it to the foundation, especially if it helps turn up one or more face-down cards.

Let's suppose the following scenario: the foundation zone shows the heart sequence built up to five, and the maneuver zone shows the 6 of hearts as the last card in a pile, and that the 6 of spades is atop another pile. In this case, moving the 6 of hearts upon its suit sequence wouldn't serve any purpose except to empty a pile. But if you transfer the 6 of spades onto the 6 of hearts, you will release a face-down card and thus advance play. Remember that it's advantageous to retain as many piles as possible in play. To this end, do not be in a rush to empty piles, nor to form proils only to eliminate them later. Instead, build proils in columns that contain only face-up cards.

Tableau 86

72. Flamboyant Solitaire

This highly colorful game proceeds at a fast clip. It requires some attention but little reflection. Grandmother found it both flamboyant and cumbersome. With a high success rate, it can hardly be considered a major challenge.

Material

One deck of 52 cards.

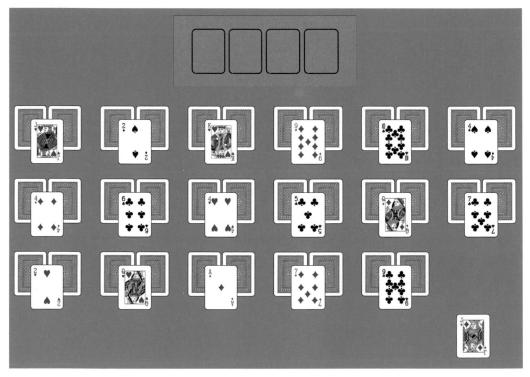

Tableau 87

Opening Tableau

Reserve space for the aces in the foundation zone, upon which you will build suit sequences. In the maneuver zone, deal 17 groups of three cards – each with two face-down cards placed side by side and the third one, face up, overlapping both, as shown in Tableau 87. The last card, called the "Solitaire," is placed face up at the bottom right of the tableau and will play a special role in the game.

Object

To complete four ascending suit sequences from ace to king.

Play

Remove any aces among the face-up cards and place them in the foundation zone. In the maneuver zone, build descending runs by packing an available card upon another, provided the latter is of opposite color and immediately higher rank. For example, in Tableau 87, move the 10 of clubs onto the jack of hearts, the 9 of diamonds onto the 10 of clubs, the 4 of diamonds or hearts onto the 5 of clubs, and so on. You may also build a descending run upon the Solitaire card. Any card that fits in its suit sequence must be moved immediately to the foundation zone and cannot be transferred back to the maneuver zone.

Turn up freshly bared cards for play. If removing the ace of diamonds releases the ace and jack of clubs, transfer the ace of clubs to the foundation and the jack of clubs onto one of the two red queens. Any released card must be turned up either for play or to host another card or a sequence.

When all the possible maneuvers have been executed, place the Solitaire upon an available card in the tableau, provided the latter is of opposite color and next rank. For example, you may move the jack of diamonds, singly or with its run, as the case may be, onto the queen of clubs or spades. The space left vacant by the jack of diamonds may be filled by any king in the tableau, single or with its run. This maneuver, however, is allowed only once. By now, if play is blocked, the game fails. It is successful if and when all the four ascending suit sequences are complete.

Variants

1. Deal all the cards in the tableau face up. This approach will make things much easier; it will be more a game of strategy than of chance.

2. Instead of descending runs, build ascending runs in the maneuver zone.

73. Alsatian Solitaire

Grandmother appreciated this version of solitaire. All the cards in the tableau are face up, thus you can organize play right from the outset. This is one for the experts, complete with a low success rate.

Material

One deck of 52 cards.

Opening Tableau

Reserve space for the aces in the foundation zone. In the maneuver zone, deal the cards face up in four overlapping rows of 13 columns, as shown in Tableau 88.

Object

To complete four ascending suit sequences from ace to king.

Tableau 88

Play

Place the aces, as they become available, in the foundation zone. In the maneuver zone, build descending sequences, regardless of color, by moving one card at a time onto another of immediately higher rank. Already formed sequences cannot be moved. A vacant column can be filled only by a king. Any card that has been placed onto its suit sequence in the foundation zone cannot be transferred back to the maneuver zone. The game is successful if and when all four ascending suit sequences are complete.

Strategy

Before starting the game, look in each column to see if any card is blocked by another of the same suit and higher rank; if this is the case, try to unblock it as soon as possible. Build suit sequences in the foundation zone at the same pace as you would descending sequences in the maneuver zone. The important thing is that you should keep cards in the maneuver zone for as long as necessary, rather than rushing them immediately into the foundation zone.

Variant

Remove the first two aces as they appear and place them in the foundation zone. Spread the rest of the cards face up in five overlapping rows of 10 columns, instead of four rows of 13 columns. Play proceeds as in the original version.

74. Comforter

This game is so easy that it would take a genuine effort to lose.

Material

One deck of 52 cards.

Opening Tableau

Remove the four aces from the deck. Deal 20 cards face up in four rows of five columns. This forms the "comforter" that will serve as reserve in the maneuver zone. Place an ace in each corner of the tableau as the foundations upon which to build ascending suit sequences. The four corners thus form the foundation zone. Keep the talon face down.

Object

To complete four ascending suit sequences from ace to king.

Play

Turn up cards from the talon one by one, pausing to place suitable ones onto their suit sequence and others in the discard pile. At first opportunity, move "reserve" cards, that is, those in the maneuver zone, upon their suit sequence. These cards, once moved, cannot be transferred back into the maneuver zone. Vacant spaces are immediately filled by cards from the discard pile or – in the absence of a discard pile – the talon. In Tableau 89, for example, move the 2 of diamonds immediately onto the ace of diamonds and replace it with a card from the talon. The game is successful when the four suit sequences are complete.

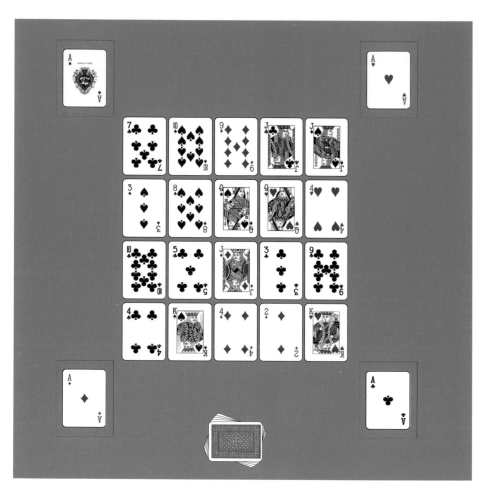

Tableau 89

75. The Gate

This game takes its name from the shape of the opening tableau. Its high success rate attracts many a beginner, though Grandmother – ever fussy – found the game insipid.

Material
One deck of 52 cards.

Opening Tableau
Deal five cards each, face up, into two columns set a distance apart. These are the two posts that form the gate and constitute the reserve cards. Between the posts, deal a row of four cards, face up, upon which to build runs. This is the maneuver zone. Above this row, form a foundation row for the aces upon which to build suit sequences. Keep the talon face down.

Object
To complete four ascending suit sequences from ace to king.

Play
As aces appear, place them in the foudation zone. Move suitable cards in the maneuver zone onto their suit sequence in the foundations. Once moved, however, these cards cannot be transferred back. In the maneuver zone, build descending runs of alternating colors. A pile may be moved as a unit from one column to another.

Try to empty the reserve – that is, the two posts – as soon as possible, starting with the bottom card, which may be moved to one of the following destinations: a) onto its suit sequence in the foundation zone; b) upon a suitable card in the maneuver zone, provided it is of opposite color and immediately higher rank; or c) to fill a vacant spot in the maneuver zone. Once the reserve is exhausted,

Ascending Suit Sequences on the Ace – One-Deck Games

fill vacant spots in the maneuver zone with cards from the discard pile, or, in the absence of a discard pile, the talon.

When all the possible maneuvers have been executed, draw cards from the talon one by one and place them either upon their suit sequence in the foundation zone or upon their respective descending run in the maneuver zone. Unsuitable cards are placed in the discard pile, the top card of which is reintroduced in the game at the first opportunity. The game is successful when all four suit sequences are complete.

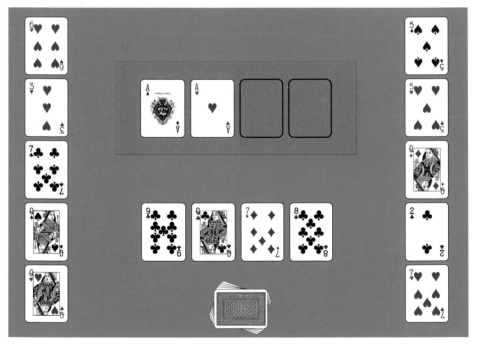

Tableau 90

76. Beleaguered Castle

Grandmother was very fond of this one. It requires absolute concentration and a dash of clairvoyance so as to anticipate long strings of maneuvers.

Material

One deck of 52 cards.

Opening Tableau

Lay out the four aces face up in a column. This is the foundation zone. The maneuver zone is divided into two wings, one on each side of the foundation column. As shown in Tableau 91, each wing has four rows of six face-up and

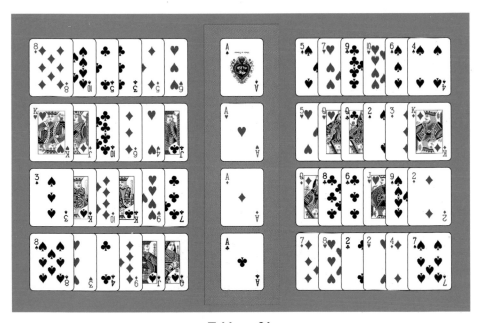

Tableau 91

overlapping cards, so as only the outermost cards in each row are available for play.

Object
To complete four ascending suit sequences from ace to king.

Play
Move available cards from the maneuver zone onto their proper suit sequence in the foundation zone. Once there, though, these cards cannot be transferred back to the maneuver zone. Within the maneuver zone, build descending sequences by moving available cards upon one another, provided the latter is of immediately higher rank, regardless of color. Move only one card at a time. Sequences cannot be moved. Any vacant row, be it to the right or left of the foundation column, can be filled by any available card in the maneuver zone – a rule that makes the game easier to win. If no more plays are possible, the game fails. It is successful if and when the four ascending suit sequences in the foundation column are complete.

Strategy
The sooner you vacate a row, the more flexible the maneuvers. Don't be in a hurry to build an ascending suit sequence in case you use a card that you may need to unblock play later. Try to build suit sequences at an equal pace. If you have a choice, it is more advantageous to build suit sequences than descending sequences in the maneuver zone, since cards in suit sequences are generally easier to transfer to the foundation zone.

Variants
1. Do not remove the aces. Deal all the cards face up – seven cards in the first four rows and six cards in the last four rows. Reserve an empty space in the center for the aces when they turn up in the process. The rest of the game proceeds as in the original version.

2. Place the aces in the foundation zone as they appear during distribution. If a card turns up that fits into the foundation zone, transfer it at once. However, you cannot transfer a card that's already in the tableau until after distribution. For example, suppose the ace of hearts is already in its spot in the foundation zone when the 2 of hearts turns up. Place the latter at once upon the ace. At this point, if the 3 of hearts is already in the tableau and available for play, you must wait until after distribution to transfer it onto the 2 of hearts, assuming it's still available for play. Spaces made by clearing away cards are not filled, which results in rows appearing uneven.

77. La Belle Lucie

This is a very "French" game – highly colorful and particularly difficult. Grandmother absolutely adored it. Needless to say, it demands total concentration, a keen sense of anticipation and a good memory so that you can plan a lengthy series of maneuvers.

Material
One deck of 52 cards.

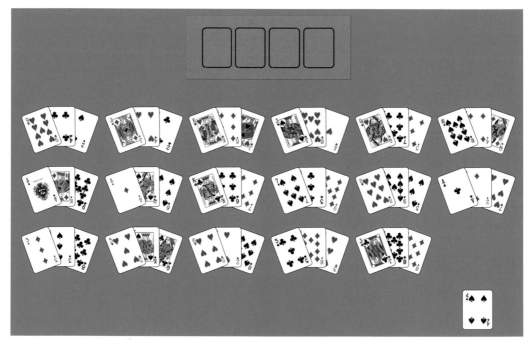

Tableau 92

Opening Tableau

To form the maneuver zone, deal the whole deck in 17 fans of three cards each, face up.

Within each fan, the left card overlaps the one in the center, which, in turn, overlaps the right card. The leftover card, called the "Solitaire," is placed at the bottom right of the tableau. Above the maneuver zone is the foundation zone, which hosts the aces upon which you will build ascending suit sequences. The cards available for play are the top cards in the fans and the solitaire which can be played at any time.

Object

To complete four ascending suit sequences from ace to king.

Play

Move each ace, as it becomes available, to the foundation zone. If no aces are free, check to see if any available card in the tableau is of the same rank as the Solitaire. If not, the game fails. The game consists of moving an available card from one fan to any incomplete fan – that is, one with less than three cards – whose contact card is of the same rank, regardless of color. Move only one card at a time.

Fans will form and unform following various maneuvers, and once eliminated they are not replaced. A fan can never contain more than three cards. A card may be transferred upon its suit sequence as soon as it becomes available, or it may be kept in the maneuver zone for as long as it's deemed useful. Once a card is moved to its foundation, it cannot be transferred back.

Consider Tableau 92: start by moving the aces of spades, diamonds and clubs to the foundation zone. You now have three incomplete fans and three newly available cards. Move the 2 and 3 of diamonds onto the diamond sequence in the foundation zone; the queen of hearts onto the queen of spades, the seven of clubs onto the 7 of hearts, and the 7 of spades onto the 7 of clubs. Next, move the king of hearts onto the king of diamonds, the 3 of clubs onto the 3 of spades, and so on. The game is successful if and when the four ascending suit sequences are complete.

Ascending Suit Sequences on the Ace – One-Deck Games

Strategy

It's advantageous to keep as many fans in play as possible. Avoid moving the last card in a fan onto its suit sequence or onto another fan unless this maneuver is necessary to maintain play. Also, avoid having three same-rank cards in a fan, for as such they are much less flexible. Build suit sequences at an even pace.

Variants

1. Remove the four aces and place them in the foundation zone beforehand. Spread the 48 remaining cards in 16 fans of three cards each. There is no Solitaire. Proceed as in the original version.
2. Instead of packing same-rank cards in each fan, build down partial suit sequences whereby a card is moved onto another of the same suit and next in rank. If a king finds itself upon a card of the same suit in the opening tableau, reverse the order. Otherwise, the game is doomed before it even starts since there's no possible way to release the card underneath.
3. In the maneuver zone, build either ascending or descending sequences, regardless of color.
4. Whenever play is blocked, gather all the cards in the maneuver zone, shuffle them anew and lay them out in fans of three cards each, starting over according to the same rules. Some players even allow a second redeal. "Pathetic!" Grandmother used to say, gnashing her teeth.

78. Strategy

This game stands out in that the actual play kicks in straight away. In fact, the outcome of the game depends first and foremost on how you choose to shape the opening tableau.

Material

One deck of 52 cards.

Opening Tableau

Remove the four aces and place them in the foundation zone, on which you will build suit sequences. In the maneuver zone, deal the remaining 48 cards – one by one and face up – into two rows of four columns. Choose a space for each card, bearing in mind that this will have an impact on whether or not the game will be won.

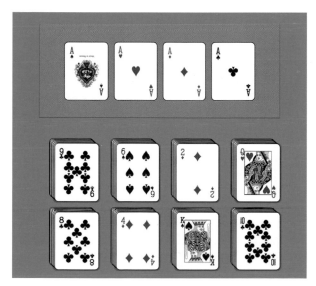

Tableau 93

Object

To complete four ascending suit sequences from ace to king.

Play

Once distribution is over, move one card at a time to its suit sequence in the foundation zone. The game fails if and when such a move is no longer possible. It is successful when all four ascending suit sequences are complete.

Strategy

Reserve at least two spaces for kings and queens. Place a queen upon a king, provided they are not of the same suit. Always fill a vacant space with a major card first. Keep minor cards together in two or three columns in such a way as not to block suit sequences. Anticipate upcoming major cards and reserve spots for them so as to avoid placing them upon minor cards.

Build as many descending sequences as possible. At times it is advantageous to place a card upon another of different suit and next lower in rank. In this way, you can easily remove this card to place it upon its suit sequence when the time comes. Sometimes, though, luck can play mischief, dealing you several minor cards in a row followed by major cards.

It's important that you memorize cards as they are being stacked in a pile. Placing a card upon another of the same suit and lower rank, for instance, is a no-no since it will automatically block play. Also, avoid building long suit sequences; instead, scatter same-suit cards in different piles and build descending sequences of alternating suit or color.

79. Tandems

This attractive game takes practically no time to play. Nevertheless, it requires great attention since it is deployed on two fronts: suit sequences and pairs. Because its success rate is very low, many variants have been invented to make it easier. Grandmother hesitated a long time before teaching it to me.

Material
One deck of 52 cards.

Opening Tableau
Reserve space for a foundation zone to host the four aces and plan a reserve area to hold pairs. In the maneuver zone, deal two cards face up side by side. These are the two base cards on which columns will be built, with the lower card overlapping its upper neighbor. Keep the talon face down.

Object
To complete four ascending suit sequences from ace to king.

Play
If the two face-up cards form a pair, move them to the reserve area and draw two new cards from the talon. If an ace appears, place it immediately in the foundation zone. If the face-up cards do not form a pair nor contain an ace, deal two new cards from the talon, overlapping the first cards so that all cards are visible. Continue to build overlapping columns in this manner. If the cards atop the two columns form a pair, remove the pair and place it in the reserve area. If two consecutive cards at the bottom of a same column form a pair, remove it as well.

The right column cannot contain more cards than the left column. If such a situation arises, say, following the removal of a pair, transfer an available card from the right column to the left column. Transfer any pairs that may result from this maneuver to the reserve area. You can move any available card at will from one column to the other so as to form pairs, except when both columns contain exactly the same number of cards.

Move any available card in the maneuver zone to its appropriate suit sequence in the foundation zone. However, pairs in the reserve area can only be transferred to their suit sequence in tandem, that is, simultaneously. For example, if you wish to transfer, say, a pair of 4s, of hearts and clubs, to their respective suit sequences, you must first make sure that the foundation zone contains both the 3 of hearts and the 3 of clubs upon which to place the pair of fours.

Before moving on to the next deal, make sure that all possible maneuvers have been executed. Consider Tableau 94: Move the ace of diamonds to the foundation zone, then the pair of 5s (spades and clubs) to the reserve area. Since the right column now has more cards than the left column, move the 10 of clubs from the right to the left. Suppose on the next deal you draw the jack of clubs and the ace of hearts. Move the latter to the foundation zone and, since no other maneuver is possible, draw two new cards, say, the 8 of hearts and the ace of spades. Transfer the latter to the foundation zone at once. Suppose the next deal yields the 8 of spades and the jack of hearts. We now arrive at Tableau 95.

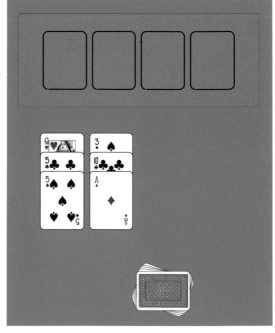

Tableau 94

Move the pair of 8s (hearts and spades) and the two jacks (clubs and hearts) to the reserve area. Continue in this manner until the talon is exhausted. The game is successful when all four ascending suit sequences are complete.

Variants
1. When play is blocked, gather the remaining cards in the two columns, shuffle them thoroughly and proceed anew.
2. Some players allow pairing off an available card with another one in the other column. Suppose the bottom card of the left column is an 8, and that

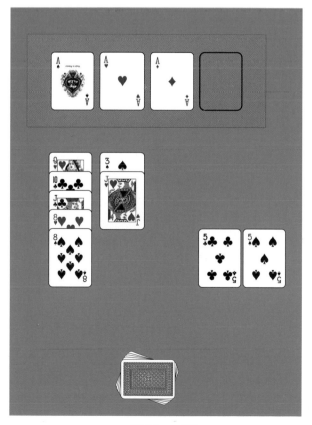

Tableau 95

the middle card in the right column is also an eight. Move the latter, together, with the cards that overlap it, onto the left column. A pair of eights is thus formed. To release the pair to the reserve area, transfer the overlapping cards back to the right column. This variant, if judiciously executed, will guarantee success at every try, especially if there's no limit to the number of cards a column can hold.

3. Play the game with a deck of 32 major cards, from 7 to ace.

80. Masked Ball

*This attractive game calls for manual dexterity simply to manip-
ulate an unusually dense tableau, but Grandmother found it
pleasant, nonetheless. It's essentially a game of chance in which
cards are turned up gradually, creating possibilities – just like the
hidden identity of partners at a masked ball. A good strategy
involves flair, clairvoyance and flexibility.*

Material
One deck of 52 cards.

Tableau 96

Opening Tableau

Remove the four aces from the deck and place them face up in a row in the foundation zone. Deal out the other cards in four rows of 12 columns. Cards are face down in the first, third, fifth, seventh, ninth and eleventh columns. They are face up in the other columns.

Object

To complete four ascending suit sequences from ace to king.

Play

In the maneuver zone, move any available card upon another of opposite color and immediately higher rank so as to build descending sequences and to release suitable cards for the suit sequences in the foundation zone. Only the card at the far end of a row can be transferred to its suit sequence. Once moved to its foundation, a card cannot be transferred back to the maneuver zone. However, you may delay transferring a card to its suit sequence if this strategy helps advance play. You may also move an entire sequence, but only as a unit. A face-down card can be turned up only if the space immediately to its right is vacant. A vacant row can be filled only by a king, singly or with its sequence. The game is successful when all four suit sequences are complete.

The layout as shown in Tableau 96 was successful for me at first try – in 87 maneuvers, although I have no doubt it can be won faster. My first 10 moves were as follows:

1. Move the 3 of hearts onto 4 of clubs and turn up the 9 of diamonds.
2. Move the 2 of spades onto the 3 of hearts and turn up the 5 of diamonds.
3. Move the 2 of spades onto its suit sequence since there's no card to its right.
4. Move the 3 of spades onto its suit sequence because it is at the far right of the row, and turn up the 7 of diamonds.
5. Move the sequence 4 of clubs and 3 of hearts onto the 5 of diamonds and turn up the 8 of clubs.

6. Move the 5 of clubs onto the 6 of diamonds and turn up the 6 of hearts.

7. Move the 7 of diamonds onto the 8 of clubs and turn up the 10 of hearts.

8. Move the 9 of hearts onto the 10 of clubs and turn up the jack of hearts.

9. Move the 9 of diamonds onto the 10 of spades.

10. Move the sequence 10 of clubs and 9 of hearts onto the jack of hearts and turn up the jack of clubs.

Strategy

It's important to turn up cards as soon as possible. Build descending sequences in the maneuver zone rather than suit sequences in the foundation zone. If and when all four sequences are placed in the first column, the game is successful, since by then nothing can prevent the cards from being transferred to their appropriate suit sequence in the foundation zone. Try to clear a row or two as soon as possible so as to fill them with any kings that might be blocking a row.

81. Flower Garden

This game is more difficult than it appears. Since all the cards are face up, you might imagine that its success rate is high, but nothing is further from the truth. What's difficult is that you can move only one card at a time. Grandmother spent hours in her "flower garden."

Material
One deck of 52 cards.

Opening Tableau
In the maneuver zone, spread 36 cards face up in six overlapping rows of six columns. That's the garden. The 16 remaining cards are the "bouquet," that is, the reserve whose face-up cards are available for play at the first opportunity. Above the maneuver zone, reserve space for a foundation zone in which to build suit sequences.

Object
To complete four ascending suit sequences from ace to king.

Play
Place the aces, as they become available, in the foundation zone. Any available card from the garden or the reserve may be moved onto its appropriate suit sequence and may not be transferred back. In the maneuver zone, build descending sequences by moving any available card (either in the garden or the reserve) onto another, next in rank, regardless of color. You can move only one card at a time. When a column in the garden becomes vacant, fill it with any available card. All the cards in the reserve are available and may be moved at will either to the foundation zone or the garden. The game is successful if and when all four suit sequences are complete.

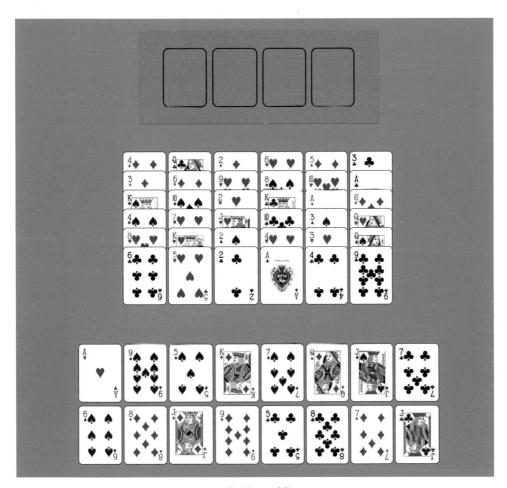

Tableau 97

Strategy

Try to bare minor cards as soon as possible, as they are the first to follow the aces to the foundation zone. Use cards from the reserve only when necessary because each use diminishes the number of available cards you might need to unblock play. Avoid overstacking a column, especially if it contains minor cards.

82. Scorpion

Grandmother didn't like this one at all. She thought it was too easy and that the card manipulation was unnatural. Yet, Scorpion requires great concentration in order to anticipate and select the most advantageous maneuvers. Strategy and luck play equal parts in this game. Grandmother claimed that it was one of the favorites of Belgium's Queen Fabiola.

Material
One deck of 52 cards.

Opening Tableau
Reserve space for a foundation zone for the aces above the tableau, on which you will build suit sequences. In the maneuver zone, spread all the remaining cards over seven overlapping rows of eight columns. The upper four cards in each of the last four columns are face down; all other cards are face up. The seventh row contains only four cards spread over the first four columns (see Tableau 98).

Object
To complete four ascending suit sequences from ace to king.

Play
Remove the aces as they become available and place them in the foundation zone. In the maneuver zone, move any card, along with those covering it, regardless of rank or color, onto any available card of the same suit and next in rank. Turn up face-down cards as they become available. At the first opportunity, move available cards to their appropriate suit sequence in the foundation zone. Only a king, alone or with cards covering it, can fill a vacant column. The game is successful if and when all four suit sequences are complete.

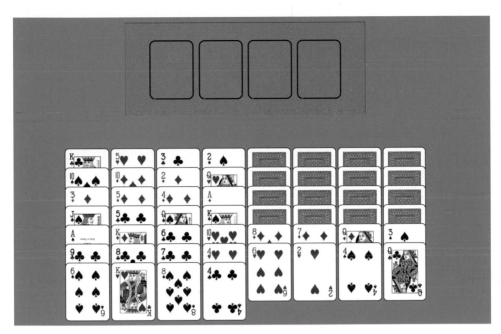

Tableau 98

Consider Tableau 98: Move the 3 of clubs and all the cards covering it – in other words, the entire third column – onto the 4 of clubs. You may fill the newly vacant third column with any one of the three kings: diamonds, hearts or spades. By opting for the king of spades, for example, you will release the ace of diamonds, which you must move immediately to the foundation zone. Next, move the 3 of spades onto the 4 of spades. This allows you to release and turn up a face-down card in the eighth column. Let's suppose this card is a five of spades, which you can move onto the 6 of spades, releasing yet another face-down card in the eighth column, say, the ace of clubs. Transfer the latter to the foundation zone.

Let's suppose the next available card in the eighth column is a jack of clubs. By moving it upon the queen of clubs, you will release, say, the 10 of clubs. Place the latter upon the jack of clubs. The eighth column is now empty and can be filled by the king of hearts. Now, move the 7 of clubs onto the 8 of clubs; the 5

Ascending Suit Sequences on the Ace – One-Deck Games

of clubs onto the 6 of clubs; the 4 of diamonds onto the 5 of diamonds; the 2 of diamonds onto the ace of diamonds in the foundation zone; and the 5 of hearts onto the 6 of hearts. Now that descending suit sequences have been established in the maneuver zone, move them to the foundation zone, card by card, as they become available.

Strategy

Remove aces as soon as possible to start suit sequences. Try to turn up face-down cards very early in the game, lest they block play. When faced with a choice between two maneuvers, opt for the one that will help advance play.

Variants

1. Build simple sequences rather than suit sequences in the maneuver zone. Instead of moving a card onto another of the same suit and next in rank, move it onto a card which is immediately higher in rank but of opposite color – red upon black or black upon red. This variant is easier to play since it provides twice as many possible combinations.

2. Keep available cards in the maneuver zone for as long as you deem necessary, rather than moving them immediately onto their appropriate suit sequence in the foundation zone.

3. Some players suggest placing the aces directly in the foundation zone as they appear during the initial deal.

83. King Albert

This game has a high success rate since all the cards are face-up in the opening tableau. The player can thus choose maneuvers that may contribute to its success. According to Grandmother, King Albert of Belgium played this one regularly.

Material
One deck of 52 cards.

Opening Tableau
In the maneuver zone, deal 45 cards face up over nine overlapping rows of nine columns – one card in the first column, two in the second, three in the third, and so on, until you have placed nine cards in the ninth column. Below this, lay out the remaining seven cards face up in a row; these will serve as reserve cards. Above the triangle, reserve space for a foundation zone to host the aces on which you will build suit sequences.

Object
To complete four ascending suit sequences from ace to king.

Ascending Suit Sequences on the Ace – One-Deck Games

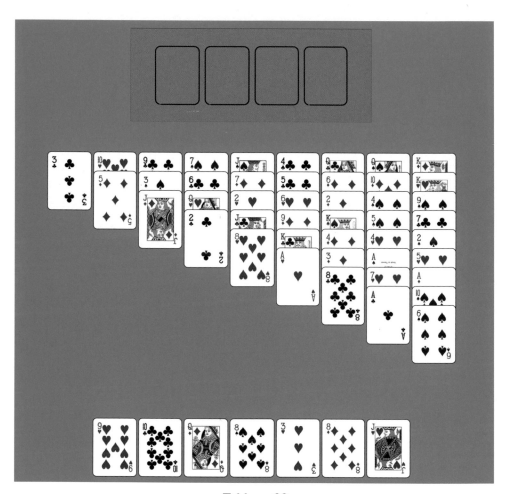

Tableau 99

Play

Transfer the aces to the foundation zone as soon as they become available, followed by other available cards. Once placed upon their appropriate suit sequences, these cards may not be returned to the maneuver zone. Within the maneuver zone, build descending sequences of alternating colors by moving one available card at a time upon a card of opposite color and that is next in rank.

Sequences cannot be moved as a unit. Empty columns can be filled with any available card. Reserve cards may be introduced into play at any time.

In Tableau 99, for example, move the aces of hearts and clubs to the foundation row, then the 2 and 3 of clubs onto the ace of clubs. The first column is now empty. Move the 7 of hearts onto the 8 of clubs, the 6 of spades onto the 7 of hearts, and the 10 of spades onto the jack of diamonds. Transfer the aces of diamonds and spades to the foundation zone, then move the 5 of hearts onto the 6 of spades and the 2 of spades onto its ace. Fill the empty column with the 7 of clubs, then move the 8 of hearts onto the 9 of spades and the 7 of clubs onto the 8 of hearts. Save the newly vacant column for other maneuvers. Continue in this manner until the game comes out or until play is blocked.

The game is successful if and when all four ascending suit sequences are complete. It fails when no further maneuvers are possible, even with the help of reserve cards. A secret: if you pursue the maneuvers as suggested for Tableau 99, success is guaranteed.

Strategy

Try to build the four suit sequences at a more or less equal pace. Do not rush to move a card to its appropriate suit sequence in the foundation zone, especially if its presence in the maneuver zone helps to move play along. Keep the cards in the reserve row for as long as possible, and use them only when play is blocked.

84. The General's Wife

This is the kind of game where astuteness can compensate and even overcome the luck of the draw. With all the cards face up, the player has the luxury of studying their positions and anticipating how each maneuver may affect play in the long run, then proceed accordingly. The success rate is relatively high. Grandmother maintained this one was a favorite of Madame Charles de Gaulle, hence its name. It's also known as Eight Off.

Material
One deck of 52 cards.

Opening Tableau
Set up a foundation zone above the tableau to house the aces on which to build suit sequences. In the maneuver zone, deal 48 cards face up over six overlapping rows of eight columns. Below this layout, spread the four remaining cards face up, to create the reserve.

Object
To complete four ascending suit sequences from ace to king.

Play
Transfer the aces to the foundation zone as they become available. You may move suitable cards onto their appropriate suit sequence in the foundation zone or keep them in the maneuver zone if they prove useful in developing play. Once moved to the foundation zone, however, cards cannot be transferred back to the maneuver zone. Within the maneuver zone, build descending suit sequences by moving one available card at a time upon another of the same suit and next in rank. Already formed sequences cannot be moved as a unit.

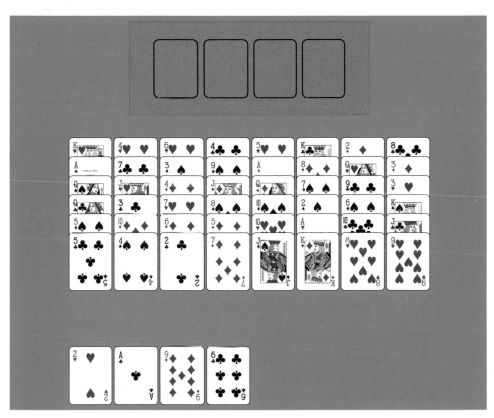

Tableau 100

You may also move any available card from the maneuver zone to the reserve row, which can contain up to eight cards. Reserve cards are available at all times and may be moved either to the foundation zone or the maneuver zone. In Tableau 100, for example, you may move the king of diamonds to the reserve row and release the ace of hearts for transfer to the foundation zone. Then, move the 2 of hearts onto the ace of hearts. A vacant column may be filled only by an available king. The game is successful when all four ascending suit sequences from ace to king are complete.

Strategy

A vacant space in the reserve row is much more useful than a vacant column. For example, if you wish to move a three-card run onto another card of the same suit, say, the 7, 8 and 9 of hearts upon the 10 of hearts, you may do so by first transferring the 7 and 8 of hearts to the reserve row, then placing the 9 upon the 10, followed by the 8 and then the 7 from the reserve row. By comparison, a vacant column can only host a king. Avoid building long suit sequences in a column that already contains a lower card of the same suit lest you cannot get at, let alone release, the lower card for play. If you manage to avoid this kind of pitfall, your chances of success are very good.

85. Napoléon on Horseback

"Now, I'm going to show you a Corsican on a white horse," said Grandmother as she set about teaching me this game. It has the same teaching goal as that of L'Impériale *(no. 112), although cards are moved differently – not unlike a knight's jumps in a chess game. The game is fairly difficult, requiring great anticipation and calculation. Its low success rate was what attracted Grandmother.*

Material
One deck of 52 cards.

Opening Tableau
Deal all the cards face up over four rows of 13 columns. The foundation and maneuver zones are one.

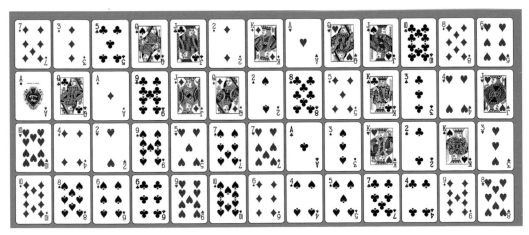

Tableau 101

Object

To complete four ascending suit sequences from ace to king, in the following order: spades in the first row, hearts in the second, diamonds in the third and clubs in the fourth.

Play

To start, guide the ace of spades to its destination – that is, row 1, column 1 – by moving it as a knight moves in a chess game, i.e., in a defined L-shape. The card that was previously in row 1, column 1 now becomes the "knight card" and moves in the same manner. The knight card can jump in any direction, as long as it arrives at its destination in six jumps or less.

Thus, in Tableau 101, the ace of spades can get to its spot in three jumps: row 4, column 2; row 2, column 3; and row 1, column 1. Next, the 7 of diamonds needs four jumps to arrive at its destination: row 2, column 3; row 4, column 4; row 2, column 5; and row 3, column 7. Then the 7 of hearts gets to mount its horse – to move to its spot in row 2, column 7, followed by the 2 of spades (row 1, column 2), and so on.

If the knight card should fall into an empty space, the game fails since no other maneuver is possible. It also fails if the knight card does not get to its destination in six jumps or less. The game is successful when all four suit sequences are complete.

Variant

The following rule will increase your chance of success. When the knight card lands in a vacant spot, leave it there and proceed with the ace of hearts, then the ace of diamonds and finally the ace of clubs. If the knight card lands again in a vacant spot, there's nothing else you can do, short of admitting defeat.

86. La Serenissima

Also called Bisley, *this game is a beginner's favorite. It boasts an original opening tableau, simple but strict rules and a high success rate. Grandmother named it* La Serenissima *because she said the game was popular in Venice during the city's heyday.*

Material
One deck of 52 cards.

Opening Tableau
Remove the four aces and the four kings from the deck. Set up a tableau of four rows and 13 columns. Place the four aces in the first four columns of the first row, on which you will build suit sequences. This is the foundation zone. Place the four kings in the last four columns of the fourth row, then deal out the rest of the deck into the remaining space in the tableau. Along with the kings, these cards constitute the maneuver zone.

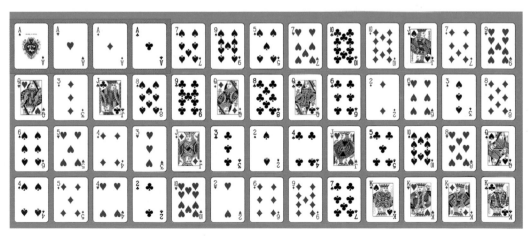

Tableau 102

Ascending Suit Sequences on the Ace – One-Deck Games

Object

To complete four ascending suit sequences from ace to king.

Play

The game consists of building ascending suit sequences on the aces and descending suit sequences on the kings, regardless of where the two kinds of sequences chance to meet. You can move only one card at a time. Any available card may be moved onto any suit sequence, be it ascending or descending, or upon another available card, provided the contact card is of the same suit and next-lower or next-higher in rank. A vacant column can be filled only by a single king. In other words, you cannot move a king and its suit sequence as a unit. To do so, you must first reverse the suit sequence upon another of the same suit – one card at a time. Aces are stationary because they constitute the foundation zone. There are no exceptions to these rules. The game is successful when all four ascending suit sequences from ace to king are complete.

With Tableau 102 as reference, here are the first 15 maneuvers to a successful game:

- 2 of clubs onto ace of clubs;
- 2 of hearts onto ace of hearts;
- 3 of hearts onto 2 of hearts;
- 4 of hearts onto 3 of hearts;
- 5 of diamonds onto 4 of diamonds;
- 5 of hearts onto 4 of hearts;
- 6 of diamonds onto 5 of diamonds;
- 2 of spades onto ace of spades;
- 3 of clubs onto 2 of clubs;
- 7 of clubs onto 8 of clubs;
- 10 of hearts onto jack of hearts;
- Queen of diamonds onto jack of diamonds;
- 9 of spades onto 8 of spades;
- King of hearts in the vacant sixth column.

Good luck!

Strategy

Move the kings as soon as possible in order to start play in the last four columns. You may move them onto their matching queens or onto a vacant column. To this end, it pays to clear any one of the five columns in the center quickly. Keep at least two suit sequences active – one descending, the other ascending – so as to enable necessary card transfers.

Avoid at all costs building a descending suit sequence in a column that already contains a lower card. For example, if you move the sequence 8-7-6 of spades to the bottom of a column that already contains a 5 of spades, play will be automatically blocked because it's virtually impossible to invert the suit sequence in question. By the same token, avoid building an ascending suit sequence in a column that already contains a higher card. What's important is that you recognize cards that need "rescuing" right at the start of play and plan maneuvers accordingly.

Generally speaking, it is more advantageous to move a king onto a queen than the other way around. This inversion will allow you to re-establish a suit sequence when a column becomes vacant.

87. Hide and Seek

This game is rather like L'Impériale *(no. 112), except that play depends uniquely on chance, as hinted by the face-down cards in the opening tableau. Grandmother much preferred this one to* L'Impériale. *The success rate is very low.*

Material
One deck of 52 cards.

Opening Tableau
Deal all the cards face down in four rows of 13 columns.

Object
To complete four ascending suit sequences from ace to king, left to right, with spades in the first row, hearts in the second, diamonds in the third and clubs in the fourth.

Play
To start, turn up the card furthest to the right in the last row – that is, the one occupying the 13th column of the fourth row, the final destination for the king of clubs – and place it in its appropriate spot in the tableau. For example, if the said card is the 4 of hearts, place it in row 2, column 4. Next, remove the card that was previously in row 2, column 4 – let's suppose it's the ace of spades – and place it in row 1, column 1. If the previous occupant of row 1, column 1, is the queen of clubs, move it to row 4, column 12. We now arrive at Tableau 103. Continue play until the king of clubs appears; if it is the last card to turn up, the game is successful.

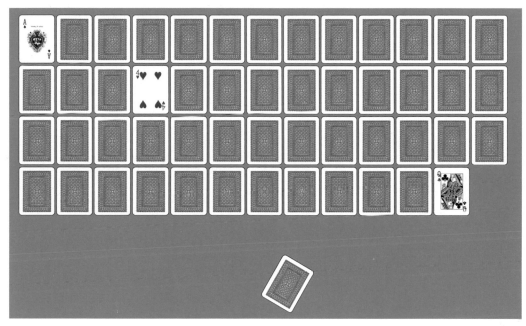

Tableau 103

Variants

1. If the king of clubs turns up mid-play, you may still continue the game by turning up the last card of the third row – the final destination for the king of diamonds. If the king of diamonds turns up, turn up the last card of the second row, which is reserved for the king of hearts. If the king of hearts turns up, turn up the last card of the first row, the spot assigned to the king of spades. And if the king of spades turns up, there's nothing else you can do, short of admitting defeat.

2. There's also an abridged version of the game, using only the 32 major cards, from 7 to ace. Spread the cards face down over four rows of eight columns. The tableau is identical with the original, and so is the order of rows: spades, hearts, diamonds and clubs. Ascending suit sequences run from 7 to ace. The ace of clubs is the last to be turned up.

88. Brainteaser

This game leaves little scope for chance and was one of Grandmother's favorites. It requires a keen sense of anticipation so as to set up an entire series of winnable maneuvers in advance. The same game may be played out according to various strategies, some leading to quick victory, others to sudden and unpredictable defeat. Grandmother used to spend weeks on just one game and even kept a notebook in which she meticulously recorded each of her maneuvers – down to numbering the columns from 1 to 8 and assigning the last four letters of the alphabet – w, x, y and z – to the four "waiting" spaces.

Material
One deck of 52 cards.

Opening Tableau
Deal all the cards face up into seven overlapping rows; the first six rows have eight columns and the seventh row has only four columns. Below the rows, set up a row of four "waiting" spaces to host transient cards. This is the maneuver zone. Above it is the foundation zone, reserved for the aces on which you will build suit sequences.

Object
To complete four ascending suit sequences from ace to king.

Play
The game involves building descending suit sequences in the maneuver zone, with a plan to release cards to their appropriate suit sequence in the foundation zone. You can move only one card at a time. If you wish to transfer an entire sequence, move the sequence, one card at a time, via the waiting spaces or vacant columns.

Ascending Suit Sequences on the Ace – One-Deck Games

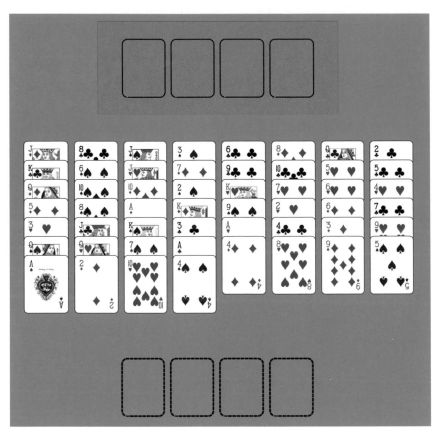

Tableau 104

You may transfer an available card to its appropriate suit sequence or keep it in the maneuver zone for as long as you deem it useful. Cards already in the foundation zone may not be transferred back to the maneuver zone. Within the maneuver zone, you may move an available card upon another of the same suit and next in rank, or to either a vacant column or an available waiting space. A vacant column can be filled by any available card. The game is successful when all four suit sequences on ace are complete.

I've won the game as shown in Tableau 104 in 88 maneuvers. Here are the first 11 moves:

- Ace of spades to its spot in the foundation zone;
- 4 of spades onto the 5 of spades;
- Ace of clubs to the foundation zone;
- 8 of hearts to a waiting space;
- 3 of clubs onto the 4 of clubs;
- King of diamonds to a waiting space;
- 2 of spades onto ace of spades;
- 7 of diamonds to a waiting space;
- 3 of spades onto the 2 of spades in the foundation zone;
- 4 of spades onto the 3 of spades;
- 5 of spades onto the 4 of spades.

Do continue on, and good luck! Obviously, things are not always this simple. There might very well be other routes to a quicker victory or a more sudden defeat.

Strategy

Contrary to popular belief, it doesn't pay to target aces and minor cards. Instead, aim at building down sequences in the maneuver zone. But watch out: if these sequences become too lengthy, they may be too cumbersome to move since you can move only one card at a time. Try to empty a column as soon as possible so as to use it as an extra waiting space when moving entire sequences.

Note, however, that there are no winning formulas. What's important is that you are alert to potential combinations and impasses, and maintain play accordingly. Sometimes it takes very little to win a game. First maneuvers are often the most important. Each game has its particular turning point: it will suffice to build a couple of short sequences, vacate a column and – voilà – victory! Still, you must decide which sequence to undertake and which column to vacate. Some games call for fairly complex moves and uncommon maneuvers. You can only prove that a game is winnable once you've won it. On the other hand, there's no proof that this game is unwinnable.

Ascending Suit Sequences on the Ace – One-Deck Games

Variant

In the maneuver zone, build descending sequences of alternating colors instead of simple descending sequences.

89. Feast

This game got its name from the opening tableau, which resembles guests seated around a luxuriously appointed dining table.

Material

One deck of 52 cards.

Tableau 105

Opening Tableau

Remove the four aces and the four kings from the deck. Place the aces in a row in the center of the table, to create the foundation zone, on which you will build suit sequences. The maneuver zone is comprised of 12 face-up cards, which are placed around the table and represent dinner guests: two rows of four cards each, above and below the aces, and two columns of two cards each flanking the table. The four kings are placed at the four corners of the table. They, too, are part of the maneuver zone. Keep the talon face down.

Object

To complete four ascending suit sequences from ace to king.

Play

Available cards must be moved to their appropriate suit sequence in the foundation zone but cannot be transferred back to the maneuver zone. Consider Tableau 105: Move the 2 and 3 of diamonds onto the ace of diamonds immediately. In the maneuver zone, build descending suit sequences by moving each available card onto another of the same suit and next in rank. For example, move the queen of clubs onto the king of clubs. A card cannot be moved to a space other than that of a king. Vacant spaces are filled with cards from the talon.

After all the possible moves have been executed, deal another batch of 12 piles, one into each of the 12 spaces – filling vacancies or adding to existing piles – starting from the upper left and avoiding the four corners occupied by the kings and their suit sequences. During the deal, no card can be transferred to the foundation zone. Such transfers can be carried out only between deals.

If no "guests" remain after the entire talon has been turned up, proceed to invert the descending sequences and transfer the cards one by one onto the ascending sequences. If all the cards can be transferred, the game is successful. It fails if guests still remain in the tableau and no further moves are possible.

90. Neapolitan Solitaire

This game has its own twist. It requires a keen sense of anticipation in order to manage the reserve pile efficiently. The success rate is high for those able to think long-term. Grandmother once remarked that a friend had learned this game on a trip to Naples, hence its name.

Material
One deck of 52 cards.

Opening Tableau
Plan a foundation zone to host the four aces. In the maneuver zone, deal 48 cards face up in six overlapping rows of eight columns. Below the tableau, lay out the four remaining cards face up in a row; allow for four additional spaces next to this row for the remainder of the reserve.

Object
To complete four ascending suit sequences from ace to king.

Play
As aces become available, move them to the foundation zone so as to build ascending suit sequences. An available card may be transferred to its appropriate suit sequence in the foundation zone, but it may not be moved back to the maneuver zone. Within the maneuver zone, build descending suit sequences by moving one available card at a time onto another of the same suit and next in rank. You can also move an available card from the maneuver zone to the reserve so long as the latter doesn't hold more than eight cards. Cards are moved one at a time, and a vacant column can be filled only by a king. The game is successful when all four suit sequences from ace to king are complete.

Ascending Suit Sequences on the Ace – One-Deck Games

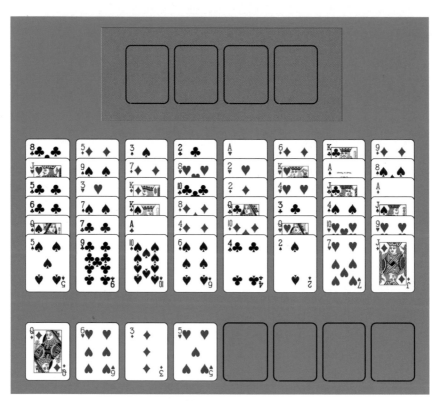

Tableau 106

Strategy

Often, a vacant column is less useful than a vacant space in the reserve because the latter can host any card, whereas the vacant column can only host a king. For example, if you wish to move the 4 and 5 of hearts, you may do so by transferring the 4 into an available space in the reserve, the 5 onto the 6 of hearts in the maneuver zone and, finally, the 4 from the reserve back onto the 5. It is unwise to use up all eight spaces in the reserve in order to, say, vacate a column in favor of a king, unless such a maneuver is necessary to unblock a serious impasse and you know you can free up one or two of the reserve spaces soon after. It's also important that you not build a lengthy suit sequence in a column that already holds a card of the same suit and lower rank, for such a sequence may prove impossible to undo later on.

91. Castle

This game resembles Beleaguered Castle *(no. 76), although the opening tableau has been slightly altered and play consists of building simple – rather than suit – sequences.*

Material
One deck of 52 cards.

Opening Tableau
The main features resemble those of *Beleaguered Castle* (no. 76) except for the following details: the aces are not removed from the deck and placed in the central column, or foundation zone, before play begins; and each wing of the maneuver zone has five rows of face-up cards – six cards in the first row and five cards each of the remaining four rows. In the left wing, each card slightly overlaps its neighbor to its right, whereas in the right wing, each card slightly overlaps its neighbor to its left.

Object
To complete four ascending suit sequences from ace to king.

Play
As aces become available, place them in the foundation column. An available card in the maneuver zone may be moved onto its appropriate suit sequence in the foundation column but may not be transferred back. In the maneuver zone, build ascending or descending suit sequences by moving one available card at a time onto another of the same suit that is either higher or lower in rank. You may change the direction of the sequences at will. Cards can be moved only one at a time, thus a sequence cannot be moved as a unit. A vacant row may host any card in the maneuver zone. The game is successful when all four suit sequences from ace to king are complete. It fails if the maneuver zone still contains cards that cannot be moved anywhere.

Ascending Suit Sequences on the Ace – One-Deck Games

Variant

The player has the option of choosing a foundation card other than an ace. Once all the cards are dealt, choose a foundation card that you deem most advantageous. The suit sequences to be built will therefore take the form of circular ascending sequences.

CHAPTER 9

Ascending Suit Sequences on the Ace – Two-Deck Games

92. Napoléon at St. Helena

Here is a great classic, judging from the impressive number of existing variants. The game requires concentration, calculation, a good memory and an especially keen sense of anticipation and combination. Grandmother was very fond of this game. As she played, she told me the story of the sad exile of a man whose name had once made all of Europe tremble. To overcome his boredom, he was reduced to spending long hours before an opening tableau, imagining that he was planning the strategy of his life on the battlefield.

Material
Two decks of 52 cards.

Opening Tableau
The foundation zone rests above the tableau, with eight spaces allotted for the aces on which you will build ascending suit sequences. To form the maneuver zone, deal 40 cards face up into four overlapping rows of 10 columns. Keep the talon face down, except for the top card, which is face up.

Object
To complete eight ascending suit sequences from ace to king.

Play
As aces become available, move them to the foundation. You may keep other available cards in the maneuver zone for as long as you think necessary to develop play. Once moved to the foundation zone, however, cards cannot be transferred back. In the maneuver zone, build descending suit sequences by moving one available card at a time onto another of the same suit and next-higher in rank. An already formed sequence cannot be moved as a unit. A vacant column may be filled by any available card from the tableau or from the discard pile.

Tableau 107

After all possible moves have been executed, draw cards from the talon one by one. Those that cannot be played are put in the discard pile, the top card of which is always available and may be reintroduced into play at the first opportunity. The game is successful when all eight ascending suit sequences are complete. It fails when the talon is exhausted and the tableau still contains cards.

Strategy

Vacate a column as soon as possible. Avoid blocking any column that you might consider vacating later and that might prove useful in accommodating a lengthy series of maneuvers.

Variants

1. Set up the opening tableau with three rows of 12 columns instead of four rows of 10 columns.
2. The opening tableau has three rows of 13 columns.
3. The opening tableau has four rows of nine columns.
4. The opening tableau has three rows of 10 columns.
5. The first two rows are face down, and the last two rows are face up.
6. The first three rows are face down, and the last one is face up.
7. The first row is face down, and the last three are face up.
8. Remove the eight aces and place them in the foundation zone before laying out the tableau.
9. In the maneuver zone, build descending sequences of alternating colors.
10. In the maneuver zone, build sequences regardless of color. However, you cannot place a card upon another of the same suit.
11. A sequence may be moved as a unit.

93. Miss Milligan

This game is another genuine classic whose success rate is rough-ly one in 50, according to Grandmother.

Material
Two decks of 52 cards.

Opening Tableau
Plan for a foundation zone that will hold the eight aces. In the maneuver zone, deal a row of eight face-up cards. Keep the talon face down.

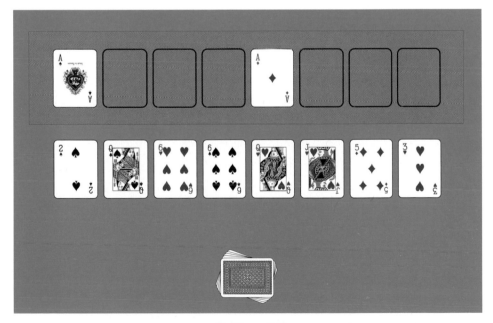

Tableau 108

Object

To complete eight ascending suit sequences from ace to king.

Play

Place aces in the foundation as they appear. An available card may be placed upon its appropriate suit sequence in the foundation zone but may not be transferred back. In the maneuver zone, build descending sequences of alternating colors by moving one available card at a time onto another of opposite color and that is next in rank. In Tableau 108, for example, move the 2 of spades onto the ace of spades, the jack of hearts onto the queen of spades and the 5 of diamonds onto the 6 of spades.

When all possible maneuvers have been executed, deal a second eight-card row, each card within it overlapping the one above it. Next, play all the new maneuvers made possible by this new deal. Continue in this manner until the talon is exhausted. A vacant column can be filled only by a king.

Once the entire talon has been dealt, place in the reserve an available card, or an already formed sequence as a unit, whose cards immediately become available for play. Carry out all new maneuvers made possible by this move. There's no limit to the number of cards you can put aside in the reserve, provided you use all of them before starting a new reserve. If this maneuver is not possible, the game fails. It is successful when all eight suit sequences are complete.

94. The Columns of Hercules

Grandmother said that this game was named after the columns in its opening tableau. Its low success rate and minimal space requirements make it an ideal travel companion. What's important is that you memorize the content of each column.

Material
Two decks of 52 cards.

Opening tableau
Deal eight cards into two columns set a distance apart (see Tableau 109). This is the maneuver zone. Plan a foundation zone between the two columns to hold the eight aces upon which you will build suit sequences. Keep the talon face down.

Object
To complete eight ascending suit sequences from ace to king.

Play
Move the eight aces, as they appear, to the foundation. For clarity, place them in the following order: spades, hearts, diamonds and clubs. An available card may be moved to its appropriate suit sequence in the foundation zone but may not be transferred back to the maneuver zone. On the other hand, you may keep cards in the maneuver zone for as long as you deem them useful to develop play.

Within the maneuver zone, build descending sequences by moving one available card at a time onto another that is next in rank, regardless of color. When all possible maneuvers have been executed, turn up cards from the talon one by one and place unplayable cards in the discard pile, the top card of which can be used at first opportunity. A vacant column must be filled at once with a card from the discard pile or, if there is none, from the talon. One deal is allowed per game. The game is successful when all eight ascending suit sequences are complete.

Ascending Suit Sequences on the Ace – Two-Deck Games

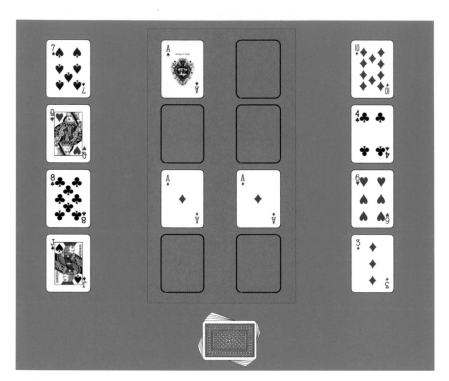

Tableau 109

Strategy

In the maneuver zone, it pays to build descending suit sequences that can easily be transferred to the foundation zone. For example, if you draw a 10 of clubs from the talon, place it upon a jack of clubs. In the meantime, if a 9 of clubs happens to be upon a 10 of hearts and an 8 of clubs upon a 9 of diamonds, it's better to move the 9 of clubs onto the 10 of clubs and the 8 of clubs onto the 9 of clubs. You will thus obtain a suit sequence, which you can then easily transfer onto an ascending suit sequence.

95. Diplomat

If you enjoy beating the odds, this is the game you've been wait-ing for. The success rate is low.

Material
Two decks of 52 cards.

Opening Tableau
Set up two columns of four cards each to host the eight aces on which you will build suit sequences. On each side of these foundation columns, deal four columns of four cards each, face up, with the outermost card slightly overlapping its neighbor and so on toward the center (see Tableau 109). Deal the cards by columns, alternating between the left and right sides of the foundation zone. Keep the talon face down.

Object
To complete eight ascending suit sequences from ace to king.

Play
Place the eight aces in the two foundation columns as they appear. For clarity, place same-suit aces in the same row. Available cards may be placed one at a time upon their appropriate suit sequence in the foundation zone but may not be transferred back. In the maneuver zone, build descending sequences by moving one available card at a time onto another of immediately higher rank, regardless of color. A vacant space may be filled by any available card in the maneuver zone, or from the discard pile or talon.

When all possible maneuvers have been executed, draw one card at a time from the talon, placing unplayable cards in the discard pile, the top card of which may be reintroduced into play at the first opportunity. One deal is allowed per game. The game is successful when all eight suit sequences are complete.

Ascending Suit Sequences on the Ace – Two-Deck Games

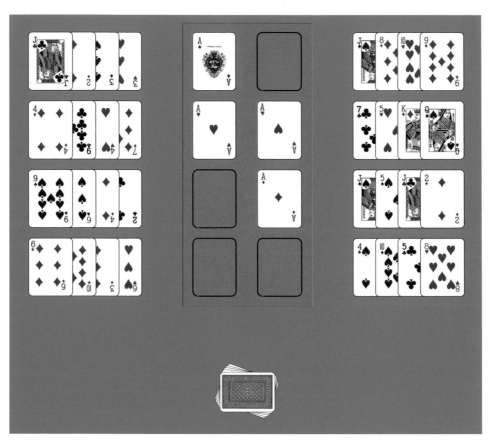

Tableau 110

96. Blockade

According to Grandmother, the blockade for which this game is named refers to the figurative "weapon" wielded by the luck of the draw to block all connections that a player may attempt to establish between various parts of the game.

Material

Two decks of 52 cards.

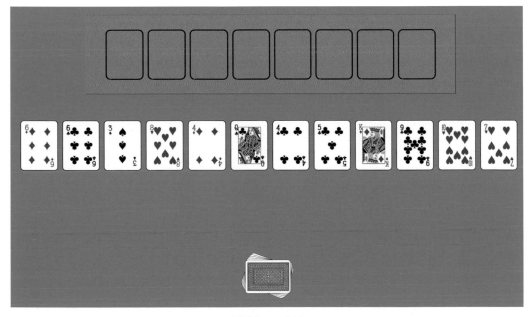

Tableau III

Opening Tableau

In the foundation zone, plan for eight spaces to host the aces on which you will build suit sequences. In the maneuver zone, deal out 12 cards face up in a horizontal line. Keep the talon face down.

Object

To complete eight ascending suit sequences from ace to king.

Play

As aces appear, place them in the foundation zone. An available card in the maneuver zone may be placed upon its appropriate suit sequence in the foundation zone but may not be transferred back. In the maneuver zone, move an available card or a sequence onto another available card of the same suit and next-higher in rank. In Tableau 111, for example, move the 7 of hearts onto the 8 of hearts, the 4 of clubs onto the 5 of clubs, and, finally, the duo of 4 and 5 of clubs onto the 6 of clubs. A vacant column may be filled by either an available card, an already formed sequence or a card from the talon. Whenever play is blocked, deal another 12-card row, but not before all the vacant columns have been filled. The game is successful when all eight suit sequences from ace are complete.

97. Fans

This game requires a large table to accommodate its uniquely colorful tableau. Its success rate is high, however.

Material
Two decks of 52 cards.

Opening Tableau
Plan the foundation zone by allowing eight spaces for the aces, on which you will build suit sequences. In the maneuver zone, deal out 54 cards face up in 18 fans of three cards; within each fan, the card farthest to the left overlaps the one in

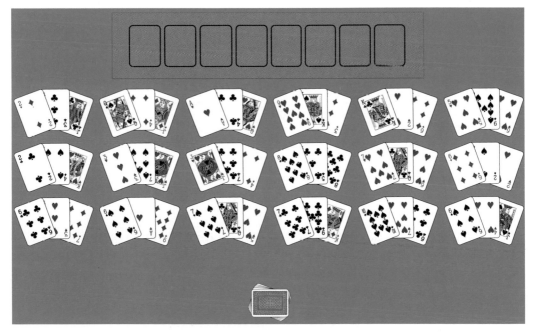

Tableau 112

Ascending Suit Sequences on the Ace – Two-Deck Games

the middle, while the latter overlaps its neighbor to the right. Keep the talon face down.

Object

To complete eight ascending suit sequences from ace to king.

Play

As they become available, move the aces to the foundation zone. An available card in a fan may be moved to its appropriate suit sequence in the foundation zone, but it may not be transferred back to the maneuver zone. Within the latter, build ascending or descending suit sequences by moving an available card from one fan to another, provided the contact card is of the same suit and next higher or lower in rank. Cards are moved one at a time. A sequence cannot be moved as a unit.

When two same-suit sequences meet, say, an ascending sequence to 7 and a descending sequence to 8, you may invert the ascending sequence onto the descending sequence, or vice versa, in order to unblock certain maneuvers. However, such inversion is allowed only in the maneuver zone, never in the foundation zone. In the maneuver zone, you may also change the direction of a sequence at will, from ascending to descending, and vice versa. For example, if you have a heart sequence of 9-8-7, you may invert the order and place upon the 7 of hearts an ascending sequence of 8, 9 and 10 of hearts. Circular sequences are not allowed, however. Only a queen may be placed upon a king, and only a 2 may cover an ace.

A vacant fan must be immediately replaced by another fan drawn from the talon. This is the only way to introduce cards from the talon into play. The last two cards may form a fan by themselves. Note that aces might still be in the talon and must be moved onto their appropriate rank in the fans. However, once they become available, they must be transferred to the foundation zone. One deal is allowed per game. The game is successful when all eight suit sequences are complete.

Strategy

In the maneuver zone, choose the highest-ranked cards on which to build descending sequences and the lowest-ranked cards on which to build ascending sequences. For example, if you have a jack, a 10, a 9 and an 8 of hearts – all available cards – move the 10 onto the jack first, then the 9 onto the 10, and finally the eight onto the nine. If you started by moving the eight onto the nine, you would have blocked the other two maneuvers.

It's important to empty fans at the start of the game in order to draw cards from the talon as soon as possible. Avoid rushing cards into the foundation zone. Instead, keep them in the maneuver zone for as long as necessary so as to build parallel suit sequences. When sequences of the same suit reach more or less the same level, ensure you can carry them both to their successful end before developing one ahead of the other.

Variants

1. In the opening tableau, deal out all the cards face up in 34 fans of three cards, and one fan of two cards. Proceed as in the original version.
2. Instead of eight ascending suit sequences from ace, build four ascending suit sequences from ace, and four descending suit sequences from king.

98. Carlton

Grandmother insisted on calling this game the Infernal Triangle, *due to the shape of its opening tableau and because of the cruel frustration she felt each time a new deal came along and messed up her cards. An inopportune appearance by a king or any other undesirable card may block a sequence about to emerge. "This is a game for experts who enjoy beating the odds," Grandmother sighed.*

Material
Two decks of 52 cards.

Opening Tableau
To form the maneuver zone, deal out 36 cards face up as follows: eight cards in row 1; overlap row 1 with a second row of seven cards, leaving the far-left card in row 1 uncovered; overlap row 2 with a third row of six cards, leaving the first card to the left of row 2 uncovered; and so on, until the tableau is completed (see Tableau 113). Above the triangle, in the foundation zone, set up eight spaces for the aces, on which you will build suit sequences. Keep the talon face down.

Object
To complete eight ascending suit sequences from ace to king.

Tableau 113

Play

The game rules are strict, and Grandmother permitted no departure from them. An available card from the maneuver zone must be immediately moved to the foundation zone and may not be transferred back. In the maneuver zone, build descending sequences by moving an available card onto another that is of opposite color and is next in rank. You may also move a sequence as a unit according to the same rules. A vacant column can only be filled by a king, alone or with its sequence. Whenever play is blocked, deal another batch of eight cards. The game fails when the talon is exhausted and play is blocked. To succeed, you must complete the eight suit sequences in the foundation zone.

Strategy
When you have a choice between two cards or two sequences, opt for the one that will generate the greatest number of subsequent moves.

Variants
1. The opening tableau contains nine, or even 10, columns.
2. Only the available cards at the bottom of columns are face up. All other cards in the opening tableau are face down. In this way, luck plays a dominant role since the player cannot guess what card will be turned up following a maneuver.
3. Instead of redeals of eight, nine or 10 cards, draw cards from the talon in groups of three, inserting into play any available card that's suitable. When the talon is exhausted, turn it over and, without shuffling the cards, continue drawing three cards at a time for as long as it takes, that is, until a new card can be introduced into play.
4. Draw one card at a time from the talon. However, only one deal is allowed per game.

99. Ascension

When Grandmother taught me this game, she used a metaphor to get her point across. "You cannot reach the top of the social ladder in a single bound," she said. " Like the cards in this game, you must raise your aspirations one step at a time. Little by little, the bird builds its nest," she concluded.

Material
Two decks of 52 cards.

Opening Tableau
Remove the eight aces from the deck and place them face up in a row. This is the foundation zone on which you will build suit sequences. In the maneuver zone, deal out 32 cards face up over four rows of eight columns. Keep the talon face down.

Object
To complete eight ascending suit sequences from ace to king.

Play
Only cards in the first row may be moved onto their appropriate suit sequences in the foundation zone. In Tableau 114, for example, you can only move the 2 of spades onto the ace of spades. In the first row, build descending sequences of alternating colors by using available cards in the first and second rows. Once again, consider Tableau 114: Move the queen of hearts onto the king of spades, the 7 of diamonds onto the 8 of spades, the 7 of clubs onto the 8 of hearts, and the 5 of diamonds onto the 6 of spades.

   A vacant space must be filled at once by a card in the row immediately below it, though not necessarily in the same column. For example, after moving the 2 of spades, fill the resulting vacant space with the 5 of spades, then move the 3 of diamonds into the second row and the 5 of spades into the third. The resulting

Ascending Suit Sequences on the Ace – Two-Deck Games

Tableau 114

vacant space in the fourth row will be filled by a card from the talon. Thus, vacant spaces are "moved down" toward the last row where they will be filled with cards from the talon. Cards are introduced into play at the bottom of the ladder, so to speak. They cannot be moved directly onto their appropriate suit sequence in the foundation zone but must move up row by row. The game is successful when all eight ascending suit sequences are complete. It fails if the talon still holds cards for which no spaces are available in the tableau.

Strategy

Try to vacate as many spaces as possible. Move up minor cards first, say, 2s, 3s and 4s. These can then be moved into the foundation zone to create yet more vacant spaces in the process. If, for some undetermined reason, minor cards cannot be transferred to the foundation zone, build long sequences in the upper row, starting with major cards, with a view to vacating as many spaces as possible and drawing more cards from the talon.

100. Napoléon's Square

This one has a considerable success rate: nine out of 10, said Grandmother, who claimed she could recognize the Emperor's battlefield maneuvers in this game.

Material
Two decks of 52 cards.

Opening Tableau
To form the maneuver zone, deal out 48 cards face up in 12 piles of four cards each, arranged along the three sides of a square, like an inverted U. Within the square is the foundation zone, which consists of two rows of four spaces each that hosts the aces on which you will build suit sequences. As the tableau is being

Tableau 115

laid out, when an ace appears, move it at once to the foundation zone. Keep the remaining cards in the talon face down.

Object

To complete eight ascending suit sequences from ace to king.

Play

An available card may be moved to its appropriate suit sequence in the foundation zone but may not be transferred back to the maneuver zone. Within the maneuver zone, you may move an available card upon another of the same suit and immediately higher rank so as to build descending suit sequences. You may also move an already formed sequence as a unit.

When all possible maneuvers have been executed, turn up one card at a time from the talon and place unplayable cards in the discard pile, the top card of which is always available and may be reintroduced into play at the first opportunity. A vacant space must be filled at once with a card from the discard pile or, if there is none, from the talon. One deal is allowed per game. The game is successful when all eight suit sequences are complete.

101. Octave

Grandmother baptized this Octave *because it consists of 13 deals of eight cards. The rules are the same as for* Carlton *(no. 98), but the opening tableau contains only one row of eight cards. There are three variants, which make the game much more flexible. "Those are wet-hen tricks," said my indignant grandmother.*

Material
Two decks of 52 cards.

Opening Tableau
Deal out eight cards in one row. Above this row is the foundation zone, with eight spaces available to host the eight aces on which you will build suit sequences. Keep the talon face down.

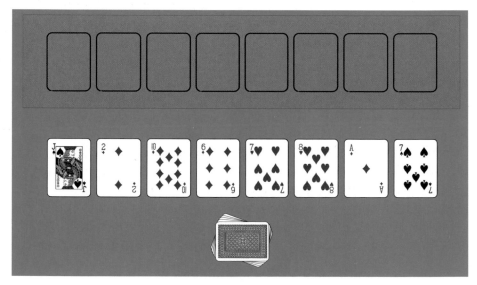

Tableau 116

Object
To complete eight ascending suit sequences from ace to king.

Play
If an available card fits in its appropriate suit sequence in the foundation zone, transfer it immediately. However, once a card is moved to the foundation zone, it cannot be returned to the maneuver zone. Consider Tableau 116: Move the ace and 2 of diamonds to the foundation zone. In the maneuver zone, build descending sequences of alternating colors by moving an available card onto another of immediately higher rank and opposite color. Cards may be moved one at a time or as a sequence. In Tableau 116, for example, move the 10 of diamonds onto the jack of spades, the 6 of diamonds onto the 7 of spades, and the 7 of spades and 6 of diamonds onto the 8 of hearts. A vacant column can only be filled by a king, alone or with its sequence. When play is blocked, deal another eight-card row onto the first row. The game fails if play is blocked after the talon has been exhausted, that is, after you have executed 12 redeals of eight cards each. To succeed, you must complete all eight suit sequences in the foundation zone.

Strategy
When you have a choice between two cards or two sequences, opt for the maneuver that will generate the greatest number of subsequent moves.

Variants
1. A vacant column may be filled not just by a king but by any card or sequence. This softening of the rule makes the game much more flexible.
2. The player is allowed to keep a card in the maneuver zone even when it fits in its appropriate suit sequence in the foundation zone.

102. Relay

Grandmother didn't play this game often. It takes up a lot of space, so don't try it if you don't have a big table. Its success rate is very high.

Material
Two decks of 52 cards.

Opening Tableau
Remove the eight aces from the decks and lay them out in a row to form the foundation zone. The maneuver zone contains three parts:
• Below the aces, deal a row of eight cards, face up, to start the reserve;
• To the left of the reserve, lay out four cards face up in a column to start a maneuver chamber;
• To the right of the reserve, set up four spaces in a column for the relay.
Keep the talon face down.

Object
To complete eight ascending suit sequences from ace to king.

Play
Move any card in the reserve to its appropriate suit sequence in the foundation zone. In Tableau 117, for example, move the 2s of spades and diamonds onto their respective aces. Next, move any card from the reserve onto any card in the left column, provided the latter is of the same suit and of next-higher rank so as to build descending suit sequences. In Tableau 117: Move the 8 of hearts onto the 9 of hearts, and the queen and jack of hearts onto the king of hearts.

When all possible maneuvers have been executed, deal another eight-card row neatly below the first row in the reserve zone. Deal all the cards from the

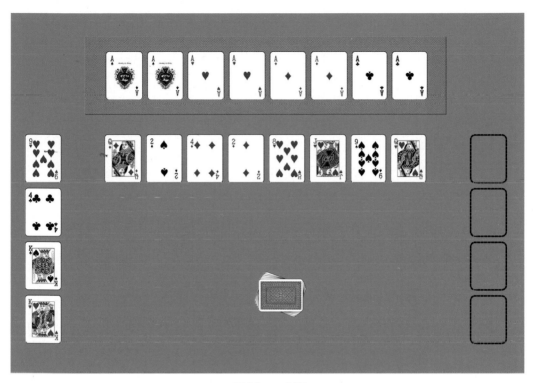

Tableau 117

talon in rows of eight cards, saving the last four cards. Move all possible cards onto their appropriate suit sequence in the foundation zone or onto descending suit sequences in the left column after each deal. Suppose that after four deals, Tableau 117 has been modified into Tableau 118.

Any available card in the reserve may be moved onto its appropriate suit sequence in the foundation zone or onto the left column of the maneuver zone. To be available, a card in the reserve must be either at the bottom of a column or directly above a vacant space so that its bottom is free. A vacant space in the reserve must remain vacant.

In the left column, you may move a card onto another of the same suit and next in rank. You may also move a sequence as a unit according to the same rules. For example, in Tableau 118, move the sequence from 9 to 4 of hearts onto the 10 of hearts, as well as any available card in the left column onto its appropriate suit sequence in the foundation zone. A vacant space here may be filled with any card from the reserve.

Tableau 118

The last four cards in the talon constitute the relay. Place them face up in the right-hand column. Once formed, the relay takes over from the left column. From now on, a card from the reserve can only be moved to the relay. Cards in the relay may be moved onto their appropriate suit sequence in the foundation zone. You may also build descending suit sequences and fill any vacant space with a card from the reserve. At this stage, the only movements allowed in the left column are transfers of cards from there to their appropriate place in the foundation zone.

103. Stage

This game is named after the shape of the opening tableau, which evokes a theater set, closed on three sides.

Material
Two decks of 52 cards.

Opening Tableau
Deal out the eight aces face up in two rows of four cards each. For clarity, place the same-suit aces in the same column. This is the foundation zone. To form the maneuver zone, deal 12 cards face up, with four cards arranged in a row above the foundation zone, and two columns of four cards each, one on each side of the foundation zone (see Tableau 119). Keep the talon face down.

Object
To complete eight ascending sequences from ace to king.

Play
An available card may be moved from the maneuver zone onto its appropriate suit sequence in the foundation zone but may not be transferred back. Within the maneuver zone, you may move any available card onto another of the same suit and next-higher in rank so as to build descending suit sequences. You may also move an already formed sequence as a unit or keep a card in the maneuver zone for as long as you deem it useful for developing play.

When no further maneuvers seem possible in the tableau, turn up one card at a time from the talon and place it either upon its appropriate suit sequence in the foundation zone or upon an available card of the same suit and immediately higher rank in the maneuver zone. Unplayable cards are placed onto the discard pile, the top card of which may be reintroduced into play at the first opportunity. A vacant space must be filled at once with a card from the discard pile or, if

Tableau 119

there is none, from the talon. The game is successful when all eight suit sequences are complete.

Variants

1. Instead of placing the aces in the foundation as you lay out the opening tableau, place them as they appear during the deal.
2. The stage is made of 10 cards instead of 12, four above the aces and three on each side.

104. Four Musketeers

This game closely resembles Relay *(no. 102), save for one essential element: the manner in which the reserve is handled. The success rate is very low – one in 100, according to Grandmother. She named the game for the last four cards, which pop up at the last moment to save the situation.*

Material
Two decks of 52 cards.

Opening Tableau
Remove the eight aces from the decks and lay them out in a row to form the foundation zone. In the maneuver zone, below the aces, deal out eight cards face up in a row to start the reserve. To the left of the reserve, deal out four cards face up in a column to form the maneuver chamber. To the right, set up four spaces for the four musketeers. Keep the talon face down.

Object
To complete eight ascending suit sequences from ace to king.

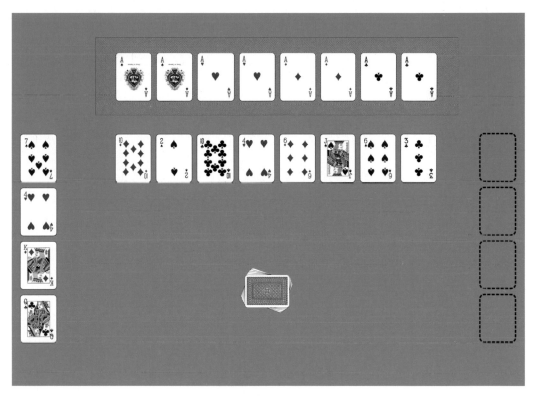

Tableau 120

Play

Any available card in the left column may be moved onto its appropriate suit sequence in the foundation zone but may not be transferred back to the maneuver zone. You may also move any available card in the left column onto another of the same suit and next-higher rank so as to build descending suit sequences. You may move a sequence as a unit according to the same rules. Note, however, that the left column is not terribly useful since it can only be replenished with cards from the talon, and, as such, one can hardly build any sort of sequence. A vacant column is filled at once with a card from the talon.

Any available card in the reserve may be moved onto its appropriate suit sequence in the foundation zone, but under no circumstances can you move a card from the reserve to the left column, nor from one space to another in the reserve. To be available, a card in the reserve must be at the bottom of a column. Any vacant space in the reserve must be filled by a card from the talon before a new deal is started. If this card can further a suit sequence in the foundation zone, it must be moved there at once and replaced with another card from the talon.

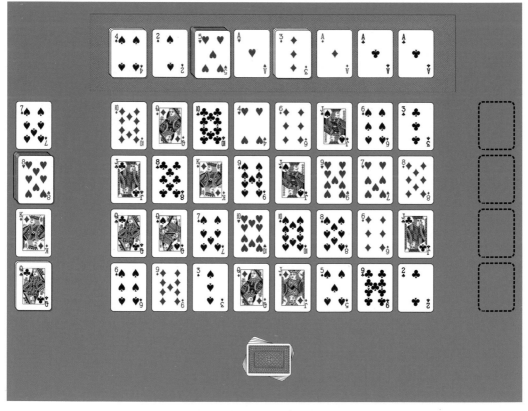

Tableau 121

When there is no more vacant space and no other card that can be transferred from the reserve to its foundation, deal a second row of eight cards below the first row. Next, move available cards, if any, onto their appropriate suit sequence in the foundation zone. Fill any newly created vacant spaces and deal yet another row of eight cards below the second row. Tableau 121 is the result of Tableau 120 after four redeals.

Move the 2 of clubs onto the ace of clubs, the 3 of spades onto the 2 of spades, the 5 and 6 of spades onto the 4 of spades, and the 7 of spades onto the 6 of spades. Fill the resulting vacant spaces and, if no cards drawn from the talon can be placed in the foundation zone, deal another row of eight cards. Thus, all the cards in the talon will have been dealt.

Once all the above maneuvers have been executed, if the reserve still contains cards, remove four of them, each of which may then be transferred to its foundation or to the left column. They are the four musketeers who spring up at the last moment to revive play. Vacant spaces that result from these latest removals will, in their turn, release cards in the upper spaces for play. It's at this point that you have an opportunity to put all your gifts for strategy into use: your keen sense of anticipation as well as your memory of any series of possible maneuvers. Once the musketeers have been used, if the reserve still holds cards and no further maneuver is possible, the game fails. It is successful when all eight suit sequences are complete.

105. Zigzags

This game is similar to Spider *(no. 107). Grandmother held them both in equal esteem. However, unlike* Spider, *this game calls for suit sequences to be built in the foundation zone and for simple sequences – rather than suit sequences – to be built in the maneuver zone. Zigzags requires sustained attention so as to avoid missing any maneuvers before proceeding to the next deal. Chance plays a dominant role. With a success rate rarely above one in 50, it's a connoisseur's favorite.*

Material
Two decks of 52 cards.

Opening Tableau
Deal out 55 cards, always left to right, as follows: a row of 10 cards, with the far-right card face up. Next, deal nine cards atop the first row, again leaving only the last card face up. The third row has eight cards; the fourth, seven cards; the fifth, six cards; the sixth, five cards; the seventh, four cards; the eighth, three cards; the nine, two cards and the tenth, one card. Thus, the resulting opening tableau contains a row of 10 piles, the first of which has 10 cards, the second, nine cards, the third, eight cards, and so on. Only the top cards are face up. (See Tableau 122.) Keep the remaining 49 cards in the talon face down. Above the tableau set up space in the foundation zone for the eight aces on which you will build suit sequences.

Object
To complete eight ascending suit sequences from ace to king.

Tableau 122

Play

As aces appear, move them to the foundation zone. In Tableau 122, for example, transfer the ace of spades to the foundation zone, a move which leaves the last column vacant. Any available card in the maneuver zone must be moved immediately to its appropriate suit sequence in the foundation zone but may not be transferred back. Within the maneuver zone, you may move any card, sequence or part of a sequence onto another available card of opposite color and that is next-higher in rank so as to build descending sequences of alternating colors. Thus, you may move the 10 of diamonds onto the jack of clubs, the 9 of spades onto the 10 of diamonds, and the trio of jack of clubs, 10 of diamonds and 9 of spades onto the queen of diamonds. Each time a new card is bared, turn it over at once.

Only a king, alone or with its sequence, can occupy a vacant column. In fact, a vacant column is the only destination for a king. What's more, once placed at the top of a column, a king can no longer be moved, except to complete a suit sequence in the foundation zone. A maneuver may be undone if no card has yet been turned up as a result. For example, if after moving the 9 of spades onto the

10 of diamonds in Tableau 122, you think that it would be more efficient to move the 9 of clubs instead, you may move the 9 of spades back to its original spot and place the 9 of clubs upon the 10 of diamonds, provided no face-down card has been turned up in the process and no further maneuver has been carried out. Note that you cannot undo more than two or more maneuvers in a row. ("What a cheat!" my grandmother exclaimed at my first attempt at this sort of tactic.)

Whenever play is blocked, draw cards from the talon and place them upon each column – the lower card slightly overlapping the one above it – skipping vacant columns or those containing a king, whether alone or with its sequence. Let's suppose that following a series of maneuvers, we arrive at Tableau 123.

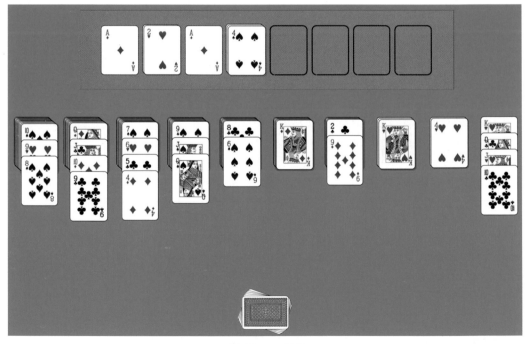

Tableau 123

Do not place cards upon the king of diamonds in the sixth column, nor the king of hearts in the eighth column, nor the 10 of clubs in the last column. And it's here that Grandmother's name for this game, *Zigzags*, originates: Each new deal may help advance play, but more often than not it introduces cumbersome elements into play. If the talon is exhausted and play is blocked, the game fails. It is successful when all eight suit sequences are complete.

Strategy

It is sometimes useful to split a sequence and move only a part of it onto another sequence so as to release a couple of cards that will help to build suit sequences in the foundation zone. For example, you may split a sequence, say, at the 5 of spades, and move the sequence beneath it onto the 5 of clubs, thus releasing the 5 of spades for transfer onto its suit sequence in the foundation zone. This maneuver will also free the 6 of spades, then the 8 of clubs (which, in turn, can be moved onto the 9 of diamonds) as well as a face-down card. Try also to vacate a few columns as soon as possible, so you can move the ever cumbersome kings.

106. Gargantua

This game is a two-deck variant of Gold Rush *(no. 63). It has the same rules, suitably adjusted to accommodate the extra material.*

Material
Two decks of 52 cards.

Opening Tableau
In the maneuver zone, deal out the cards from left to right in a row of nine columns, one card in the first column, two in the second column, three in the third, and so on, up to nine cards in the ninth column. The top card of each pile is face up. Above this tableau, reserve eight spaces for the eight aces on which you will build suit sequences. Keep the talon face down.

Object
To complete eight ascending suit sequences from ace to king.

Play
As they become available, move the aces to the foundation zone. The rules for *Gold Rush (no. 63)* apply in their entirety, except where the talon is concerned. In *Gargantua*, turn up one card at a time from the talon, placing unplayable ones in the discard pile. Two redeals are allowed per game. The game is successful when all eight suit sequences are complete. It fails if play is blocked after two redeals.

PART III

Suit Sequences and Other Runs

CHAPTER 10

Descending Suit Sequences

107. Spider

This game got its name from the eight suit sequences – resembling eight spider legs – that are to be built in the maneuver zone before being transferred, each as a unit, to the foundation zone. It's a very difficult game, to be sure, one that demands great attention, an innate sense of strategy and an ability to anticipate lengthy series of maneuvers. Luck also plays an important role. Some players put the success rate at two or three games out of 10, maintaining that ingenuity can win out over chance. All I can say is that Grandmother, a devotee if ever there was one, could only manage a single win out of roughly 30 attempts – without cheating, of course!

Material
Two decks of 52 cards.

Opening Tableau
Above the tableau, in the foundation zone, plan eight spaces for the eight suit sequences. To form the maneuver zone, deal 54 cards as follows:
- The first 40 cards face down on four overlapping rows of 10 columns;
- Add one card each, face down, to any four columns – usually the first four (although Grandmother preferred the first, fourth, seventh and tenth columns strictly for visual effect);
- Complete the tableau by placing a card, face up, at the bottom of each column (see Tableau 124).

Keep the talon face down.

Object
To complete eight descending suit sequences from king to ace.

Tableau 124

Play

Play proceeds exclusively in the maneuver zone. Suit sequences can be transferred to the foundation zone only after they have been built in the maneuver zone. Move an available card onto another next in rank, regardless of color. A jack can be moved onto any queen; a suit sequence of, say, 9, 8, 7 and 6 of hearts can be moved as a unit onto any 10; a duo of 7 and 6 of hearts can be moved as a unit onto an 8 of spades. A card that is overlapped by another card of a different suit cannot be moved until it has been bared. For example, you can move the 8 of spades only after the 7 and 6 of hearts have been removed. Note that while you can move a suit sequence as a unit, you can move a sequence or a run only one card at a time. For example, to transfer a sequence made of a club 9, a diamond 8, a spade 7 and a diamond 6, you must first move the 6, then the 7, followed by the 8 and, finally, the 9.

Once a face-down card is bared following a maneuver, turn it up immediately for play. A vacant column can be filled by any card, either single or with its suit sequence. A king, however, can only be moved to a vacant column, and, once there, it stays put until its own suit sequence is completed and the player wishes to transfer it to the foundation zone. You also have the option of keeping the completed suit sequence in the maneuver zone if you deem it useful. (There may be an advantage in breaking the suit sequence to aid in tableau manipulation.) Bear in mind, however, that hanging on to a suit sequence may prove cumbersome, and that, at times, it may be more advantageous to transfer it to its foundation, especially if this move enables you to clear a column or, better still, to unblock play. Once moved to its foundation, however, the suit sequence cannot be transferred back.

Whenever play is blocked, fill all vacant columns with cards from the talon before dealing a new batch of 10 cards, one to each column. Sometimes, these new cards may introduce inappropriate elements into play and thus are more of a burden than a help. If play is blocked after five rounds, the game fails. It is won when all eight suit sequences have been completed.

Strategy

Try to build sequences that can be split easily. For example, if the tableau offers two 8s and a 7, start by moving the 7 onto one of the two 8s; if necessary, you can always move that same 7 onto the other 8. Move same-suit cards first so as to build suit sequences that can eventually be moved as a unit. In Tableau 124, for example, move the 9 of diamonds onto the 10 of diamonds, then the 8 of spades onto the 9 of spades.

When faced with more than one maneuver, move the highest-ranked cards first. For example, in Tableau 124, move the jack of clubs onto the queen of diamonds before moving the 10 and 9 of diamonds onto the jack of clubs; in the same way, move the 3 of hearts onto the 4 of spades or diamonds before moving the 2 of diamonds onto the 3 of hearts. It is sometimes useful to split a suit sequence in order to place part of it upon another, more advanced, same-suit sequence. For example, you may want to break a 6-to-ace heart sequence at 4 in order to add it to a king-to-5 heart sequence.

The best way to maintain flexibility in the game is always to have a vacant column or two to help manipulate the tableau, say, splitting sequences in favor of suit sequences. Note, however, that all columns must contain at least one card before you can redeal.

Variants

1. Keep all eight suit sequences in the maneuver zone until the very end. "If you succeed with this virtuoso coup," said Grandmother sarcastically, "I'll award you the Patience Cross."
2. You can undo a maneuver, provided no new card has yet been turned up following this maneuver. For example, if you have carelessly moved a jack of hearts onto a queen of spades instead of the queen of hearts, you may make the switch before proceeding to any other maneuver. But you can't undo more than one maneuver. That's cheating!

108. Little Spider

As its name suggests, this game is a variant of the previous one.
In fact, the rules are the same but only one deck of cards is used.

Material
One deck of 52 cards.

Opening Tableau
Deal a row of seven columns. Each column contains three cards, two face down and one face up. The foundation zone has four vacant spaces to host suit sequences that will have been built in the maneuver zone. Keep the talon face down.

Object
To complete four descending suit sequences from king to ace.

Play
Play proceeds in the maneuver zone, as in *Spider*. Move an available card onto another next-higher in rank, regardless of color (although it is advantageous to build suit sequences whenever possible). Note that while you can move a suit sequence as a unit, you can move a sequence or a run only one card at a time. A king can only be moved to a vacant column. But a vacant column can be filled by any card, either single or with its suit sequence. When a face-down card is bared, it must be turned up immediately for play. When all possible moves have been made, fill every vacancy before dealing a new batch of seven cards, one in each column. Lay the last three cards over the first three columns. Suit sequences must be completed before they can be transferred to the foundation zone. The game is won when all four descending suit sequences from king to ace have been completed.

Variant

The opening tableau may be laid out as in *Gold Rush* (no. 63), that is, a row of seven columns, the first of which has one card, the second has two cards, the third has three cards, and so on; and only the top card of each column is face up.

109. Backbone

This game is named for the shape of its tableau. It requires a lot of space and is difficult to manipulate.

Material
Two decks of 52 cards.

Opening Tableau
As they appear, place the eight jacks in a column to start the foundation zone. As the kings and queens – called "dead cards" – appear, they are placed on an angle to each side of their matching jack (if the latter is already in its spot) so that, when completed, the column will resemble a backbone. This is the foundation zone.

In the maneuver zone, deal six cards face up in a row. Keep the talon face down.

Object
To complete eight descending suit sequences from jack to ace.

Play
Any available card may be moved onto its appropriate suit sequence in the foundation zone but may not be transferred back to the maneuver zone. Within the latter, build ascending suit sequences by moving an available card onto another of the same suit and of next-lower rank. You may also move an already formed suit sequence as a unit. A vacant column can only be filled with a card from the discard pile or the talon (if there's no discard pile) but never from another column.

Deal one card at a time from the talon, putting unplayable cards in the discard pile, the top card of which may be introduced into play at the first opportunity. Two rounds are allowed per game. The game is successful when all eight descending suit sequences from jack to ace have been completed.

Tableau 125

Descending Suit Sequences

110. Clans

This one is easy to play, although the success rate is very low.

Material

One deck of 52 cards.

Opening Tableau

Lay out the four kings in two rows, forming a square. This is the foundation zone. On each side of the square, deal a column of two face-up cards, forming the maneuver zone. Keep the talon face down.

Object

To complete four descending suit sequences from king to ace.

Tableau 126

Play

If the opening tableau contains a queen, move it at once onto its matching king. In Tableau 126, for example, move the queen of diamonds onto the king of diamonds before any other maneuver. If an available card fits into its suit sequence, transfer it at once to the foundation zone; once there, however, it cannot be moved back to the maneuver zone. Within the latter, place an available card onto another of the same suit and immediately lower rank so as to build segments of ascending runs. These segments will eventually be transferred onto descending suit sequences in the foundation zone.

When all possible moves have been executed, deal a new batch of four cards from the talon, filling vacancies or adding to columns in the maneuver zone. After each deal, transfer available cards onto their appropriate rank either in the foundation zone or the maneuver zone. A vacant space can be filled only at the next deal.

Whenever play is blocked, gather the four piles in the maneuver zone clockwise, starting with the top-left pile. Without shuffling, redeal in batches of four cards, as in the first deal. Two rounds are allowed per game. The game is successful when all four suit sequences have been completed.

111. Sycophants

This simple game has a high success rate and is popular with younger players.

Material
One deck of 52 cards.

Opening Tableau
Remove the four kings from the deck and lay them face up in a column. This is the foundation zone. It is flanked on both sides by the maneuver zone, comprising two columns of six face-up cards. Keep the talon face down.

Object
To complete four descending suit sequences from king to ace.

Play
Any suitable card in the maneuver zone must be transferred immediately over to its appropriate rank in the foundation zone but may not be moved back. In Tableau 127, for example, move the queen and jack of clubs onto the king of clubs. Within the maneuver zone, build ascending suit sequences by moving one available card at a time onto another of the same suit and next lower in rank. In Tableau 127, move the 7 of hearts onto the 6 of hearts. Fill vacant spaces with cards in the talon. Draw cards from the talon one by one, placing unplayable cards in the discard pile, the top card of which can be reintroduced into play at the first opportunity. Only one round is allowed per game. The game is won when all four descending suit sequences have been completed.

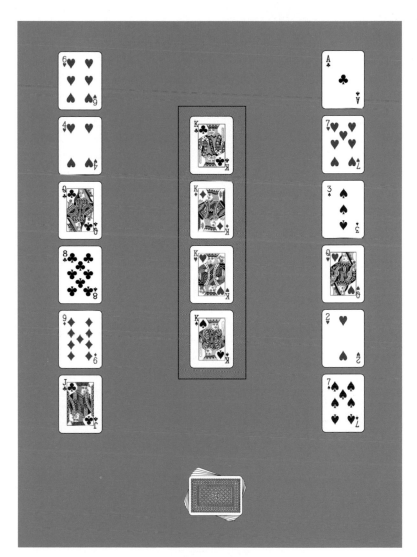

Tableau 127

112. L'Impériale

This game is also called Gaps. *Grandmother, who claimed to know Napoléon's life story better than anyone else in her township, said the Emperor was in the habit of playing this game on the eve of his military campaigns. It was his private crystal ball by which he could predict the outcome of the ensuing battle. L'Impériale is a complex solitaire, requiring keen concentration in order to anticipate the most efficient maneuvers. Chances of success are slim. It is a favorite among chess players.*

Material
One deck of 52 cards.

Opening Tableau
Spread all the cards face up over four rows of 13 columns. Remove the four aces. The resulting gaps will be used to manipulate the tableau.

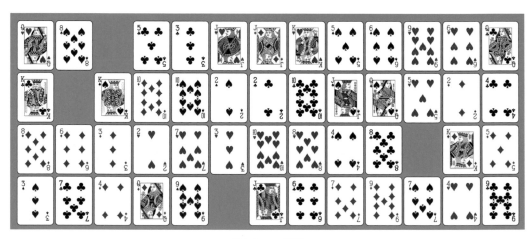

Tableau 128

Object

To complete four descending suit sequences from king to 2.

Play

Into each gap, move the card of the same suit and next-lower in rank to the card at left of the gap. Whenever a move vacates the first column of a row, fill it with a king, whose suit will dictate that of the rest of the row. A gap is closed for play if a 2 precedes it, since there is no card lower than 2. If all four gaps are preceded by 2s, the game fails.

Strategy

When filling the first column of a row, it's important to opt for the king that will generate the greatest number of subsequent maneuvers. It pays to anticipate as many moves as possible, as you would do in a game of chess.

Variants

This classic game has inspired a considerable number of variants. Some aim to make the game either easier or more difficult, while other variants are downright creative. Grandmother taught me the following six, which may be combined as you see fit:

1. The order of suits may be determined in advance: spades in the first row, hearts in the second row, diamonds in the third row and clubs in the fourth. Clearly, this variant doesn't simplify matters.
2. Some players distinguish between *La Grande Impériale* and *La Petite Impériale*. One round is allowed for the former, while three rounds are allowed for the latter. If all four gaps are preceded by 2s and play is thus blocked, gather all the cards – except aces and those already in their proper place – and shuffle them thoroughly. Redeal so as to complete the tableau, allowing a gap at the end of each already formed sequence. Continue play as before. If all four gaps are again preceded by 2s, gather the cards as before and deal again. Chances of success are increased with each deal; it's not unusual to win *La Petite Impériale*.

Descending Suit Sequences

3. Build ascending suit sequences from 2 to king. Thus, the card to be moved must be of the same suit and next higher in rank to the card immediately at left of the gap. If a gap is preceded by a king, play is blocked.
4. Remove the four aces and place them in the first column. The rows are arranged in the order of spades, hearts, diamonds and clubs. Build ascending suit sequences from ace to king. The opening tableau is thus made of four rows of 14 columns and four gaps. Play proceeds as in the original version.
5. To lay out the opening tableau, deal the cards in four rows of 14 columns, leaving the second column empty. These four gaps serve as starting points for maneuvers.
6. This variant is highly original: each gap can be filled either with a card of the same suit and next in rank to the card immediately at left, or a card of the same suit and next lower in rank to the card at right. This approach is certain to produce interesting maneuvers.

113. Martingale

This game has the same objective as L'Impériale *(no. 112), except for the opening and ending tableaux. The two extra gaps make* Martingale *a more flexible game. It was one of Grandmother's favourites.*

Material
One deck of 52 cards.

Opening Tableau
Remove the four aces from the deck. Deal the remaining cards face up in six rows of nine columns, providing space for six gaps: one each at the end of the first two rows and four others chosen randomly.

Object
To build descending suit sequences from king to 2, in a continuous line and in the order of spades, hearts, diamonds and clubs. The game is won when the end tableau shows the following:
- King of spades in row 1, column 1; and 2 of spades in row 2, column 4;
- King of hearts in row 2, column 5; and 2 of hearts in row 3, column 8;
- King of diamonds in row 4, column 1; and 2 of diamonds row 5, column 4;
- King of clubs in row 5, column 5; and 2 of clubs in the last row of the last column.

Play
Move any card into a gap, provided it is of the same suit and next lower in rank to the card at left of the gap, or next in rank to the card at right. For example, in Tableau 129, the gap between the 7 of diamonds and the 5 of spades may be filled with either the 6 of diamonds or the 6 of spades. In the same way, the gap

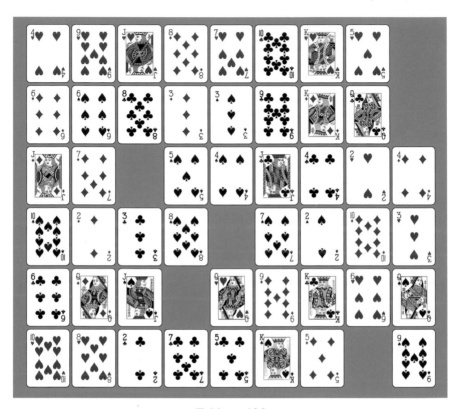

Tableau 129

between the 5 of diamonds and the 9 of spades may be filled either with the 4 of diamonds or the 10 of spades. Kings are not subject to this rule when they are placed in their appropriate spots; if they are moved elsewhere in the tableau, they, too, must conform to the "neighborhood" rule. The king of clubs may be moved onto its proper spot between the jack of spades and the queen of hearts, even though these two cards are not of the required suit or rank.

Since the object of the game is to complete suit sequences in a continuous line, gaps that happen to be at the start or end of a row are viewed as if they were, say, in the middle of a row. For example, the gap at the end of the first row may be filled with a 4 of hearts or a 7 of diamonds, since it can be considered to be between the 5 of hearts (in its own row) and the 6 of diamonds (in the following row). The game is won when all four suit sequences have been completed in a tableau of six rows and eight columns (the rows being arranged in a continuous line, in the order of spades, hearts, diamonds and clubs).

Strategy

It's advantageous to place kings in their proper space as soon as possible and to move cards in the descending order. Since each maneuver involves a choice, study the tableau carefully and opt for the most productive move. Avoid building too lengthy a suit sequence outside its own assigned zone, lest it be too cumbersome to move later on.

Variants

1. Instead of descending suit sequences, build ascending ones, from 2 to king. In this case the "neighborhood" rule is reversed: the card at right of the gap must be immediately higher in rank and the one at left, lower. This variant has no effect on the game's chances of success, however.
2. Instead of determining the direction of suit sequences in advance, the player can wait to see how the game plays out before making a decision.

114. Royal Audience

Grandmother used to tell me stories about upright and wicked rulers of ancient kingdoms. In those days, sovereigns used to grant audiences to their subjects in order to hear requests and dispense justice. A good king would listen attentively to his subjects and govern fairly. But there were bad kings too, utterly corrupt and oblivious to the concerns of their subjects. As far as my grandmother was concerned, it all boiled down to this: a successful game meant she had told a story of a good king. A failed game meant she had told one about a bad king.

Material
One deck of 52 cards.

Opening Tableau
The maneuver zone includes 16 face-up cards, arranged in a square with four cards on each side. That's the antechamber. Within the square is the audience hall – the foundation zone. The cards forming the square represent the subjects waiting for their turn to enter the audience hall. Keep the talon face down.

Object
Install the four royal couples on their thrones in the audience hall, and have the subjects, led by the four jacks, parade before their respective majesties, that is, four descending suit sequences from jack to ace.

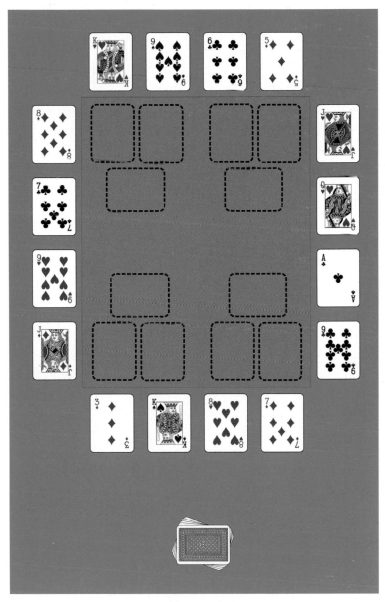

Tableau 130

Descending Suit Sequences

Play

To enter the audience hall, a royal couple – that is, any set of same-suit king and queen – must first be present in the antechamber. As shown in Tableau 130, both the king and queen of hearts are available and can thus occupy their thrones in the audience hall. Since the jack of hearts is also present in the antechamber, it, too, can enter the hall and will serve as the foundation upon which other cards will be piled (the so-called subjects to be brought before their matching king and queen) so as to build a descending suit sequence.

Back in the antechamber, the jack of diamonds must wait for his matching king and queen to turn up before he, too, can enter the audience hall. Fill the three vacant "seats" – left by the king, queen and jack of hearts – with cards from the talon. Suppose they are the 8 of clubs, the 3 of spades and the 9 of diamonds. We now arrive at Tableau 131.

Draw cards one by one from the talon, pausing to make whatever plays are possible. If a set of same-suit king and queen turns up, transfer them to the audience hall. If their matching jack turns up, transfer it as well.

In Tableau 131, no cards in the maneuver zone can be moved to the foundation zone. Suppose the next card drawn from the talon is a 4 of hearts; it can go directly onto the discard pile since it fits nowhere in the meantime – neither in the antechamber nor the audience hall. Suppose the next card from the talon is the 10 of hearts; it can be placed upon the jack of hearts in the audience hall. Fill gaps, if any, with cards from the discard pile or, in the absence of a discard pile, the talon. One deal is allowed per game. The game is won when all four royal couples are installed on their thrones and all their subjects succeed in coming before them – in other words, when all four descending suit sequences from jack to ace have been completed.

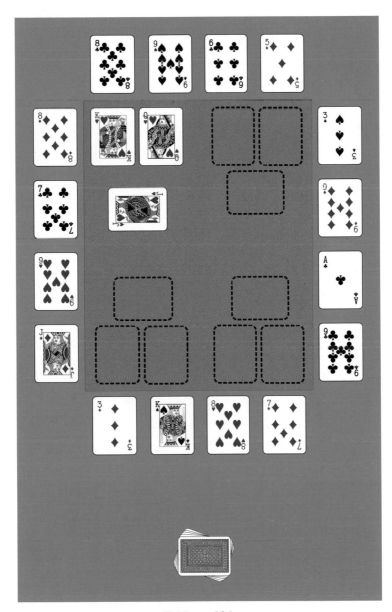

Tableau 131

<u>Descending Suit Sequences</u>

CHAPTER 11

Mixed Suit Sequences

115. Napoléon at Elba Island

According to Grandmother, this game was the favorite of all the great men: Napoléon Bonaparte, George Washington, Charles de Gaulle and Dwight D. Eisenhower, to name a few. Napoléon was believed to have practiced this game while in exile on the island of Elba, dreaming of future victories. Grandmother revered the game, which requires concentration, observation, memory and anticipation. The success rate is rather low.

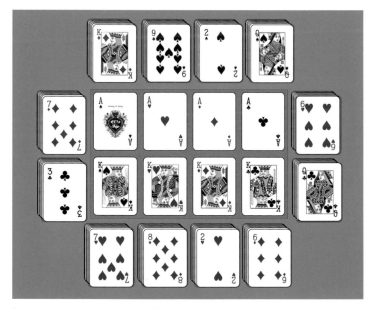

Tableau 132

Material

Two decks of 52 cards.

Opening Tableau

Remove aces and kings, one of each suit, and lay them out in two rows of four cards – aces in the first row and kings in the second. This is the foundation zone. To form the maneuver zone, deal the remaining cards in 12 piles – four piles each above and below the foundation zone, and two piles on each side of it. Deal clockwise, starting from top left.

Object

To complete four ascending suit sequences from ace to king and four descending suit sequences from king to ace.

Play

So as to build ascending or descending suit sequences, transfer available cards from the maneuver zone to the foundation zone as follows: Cards from the top row are placed on the kings, and those from the bottom row are placed on the aces. Cards on each side of the foundation zone may be moved onto either the kings or the aces, but once in the foundation zone, cards cannot be transferred back. In Tableau 132, for example, move the queen of spades onto the king of spades and the 2 of hearts onto the ace of hearts. However, the 2 of spades, which is located in the top row, may not be moved onto the ace of spades.

Whenever two suit sequences have been built up more or less to the meeting point, you may reverse one upon the other if this tactic helps advance play, except for the ace or king at the bottom.

In the maneuver zone, you may move an available card from one pile onto another, provided the contact card is next-higher or next-lower in rank, regardless of color. You may also reverse the order of a sequence in progress, except to form a circular sequence – since only a queen can be placed upon a king, and only a 2 can be placed upon an ace. Move only one card at a time. To move an entire sequence, reverse it upon another pile, again, one card at a time.

Mixed Suit Sequences

Three rounds are allowed per game. To start a new deal, pack the first pile in the maneuver zone atop the second, then the first and second piles atop the third, and so on, so as the last cards dealt out will be at the top of the new talon once it's turned over. Proceed as in the first deal. The game is successful when all eight suit sequences have been completed.

Strategy
In the maneuver zone, aim at moving cards onto piles on both sides of the foundation zone first, because once there, suitable cards can be moved onto any row in the foundation zone. For example, in Tableau 132, start by moving the 8 of diamonds onto the 7 of diamonds, the 7 of hearts onto the 8 of diamonds, then the 6 of diamonds onto the 7 hearts. Thus you will have added three cards onto a pile, which, in turn, can be transferred to any suit sequences in the foundation zone. Next, target the upper row in the foundation zone if you wish to build ascending sequences from ace, and the lower row if you wish to build descending sequences from king.

Variant
In the maneuver zone, build either ascending or descending suit sequences, instead of simple sequences.

116. Alhambra

This is a relatively simple game, but one with a low success rate.

Material

Two decks of 52 cards.

Play

Remove aces and kings, one of each suit, and lay them out in a row as shown in Tableau 133. This is the foundation zone. Next, deal eight piles of four face-up cards each and arrange them in a row. This is the reserve. Keep the talon face down.

Object

To complete four ascending suit sequences from ace to king and four descending suit sequences from king to ace.

Play

At the first opportunity, move any card in the reserve onto its appropriate suit sequence in the foundation zone. In Tableau 133, for example, move the queen of clubs onto the king of clubs and the 2 of hearts onto the ace of hearts. Whenever play is blocked, turn up cards from the talon one by one, placing unplayable cards in the discard pile. Following a maneuver, if the top card of the discard pile fits in a suit sequence in the foundation zone, transfer it there.

Move any card from the reserve onto the discard pile if the contact card is of the same suit and ranks immediately higher or lower. For example, if the top card of the discard pile is a 6 of diamonds, you may place upon it either a 5 of diamonds or a 7 followed by an 8 of diamonds. Three rounds are allowed per game. After each round, turn the discard pile over and, without shuffling, proceed to deal the cards one by one. The game is successful when all eight suit sequences have been completed.

Mixed Suit Sequences

Strategy

Since reserve cards are inert and don't advance play, aim at transferring them to the discard pile as soon as possible.

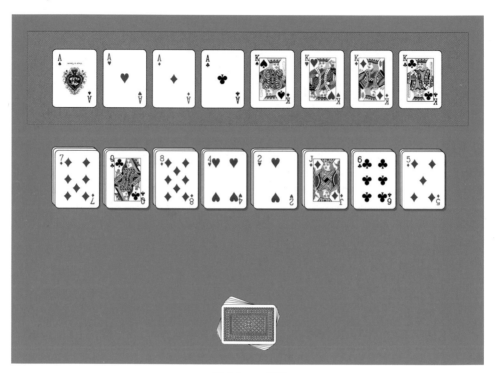

Tableau 133

117. La Nivernaise

Grandmother claimed she learned this one from a distant cousin who lived in Nevers, France.

Material
Two decks of 52 cards.

Opening Tableau
Set up eight spaces to host aces and kings, one of each suit, as they appear. These are foundations on which to build suit sequences. The maneuver zone is made up of two sections:
• The front, formed by four overlapping rows of six columns;
• The reserve, made of two columns of four cards, one on each side of the front.

Object
To complete four ascending suit sequences of ace to king and four descending suit sequences from king to ace.

Play
You may move any card from the reserve, or an available card from the front, onto its appropriate rank in the foundation zone. Once moved, though, this card cannot be transferred back. In Tableau 134, for example, move the 2 and 3 of hearts onto the ace of hearts. You will thus free up two spaces in the reserve, which may come in handy at some point later in the game. A gap in the reserve may be filled with an available card from the front, although you may want to wait for the right moment to do so.

An empty column, however, must be filled at once with four face-up cards drawn from the talon. In Tableau 134, the following maneuvers may be undertaken: the 10 of hearts onto the reserve; the jack of hearts onto the queen of

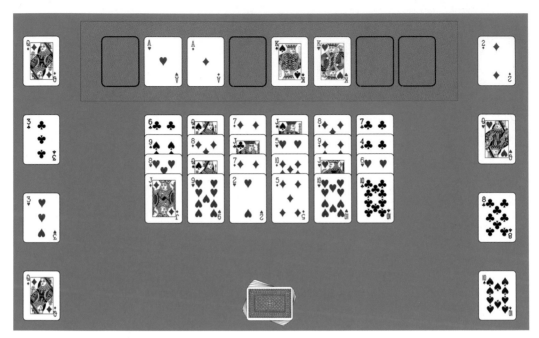

Tableau 134

hearts; the 10 onto the jack, and the 9 onto the 10; and the queen of spades onto the king of spades. Into the three gaps in the reserve move the 5 of diamonds, the 10 of diamonds and the 5 of hearts. Next, move the jack of spades onto the queen of spades. Draw four cards from the talon and place them, face up, in the newly vacant fourth column. Finally, move the 10 of spades onto the jack of spades so as to free up a space in the reserve.

Whenever play is blocked, start a new deal of 24 face-up cards – or whatever cards are left in the talon – in four overlapping rows of six columns. Deal the cards left to right, top to bottom. Move cards as in the previous round. Whenever two suit sequences meet in the foundation zone, reverse one onto the other, except for the ace and king at the bottom. Two rounds are allowed per game. To start a new round, gather the cards into one pile – the first column atop the second, then the combined pile atop the third column, and so on, so that the last column becomes first to be played once the talon is turned over.

The Complete Book of Patience

Strategy

Use gaps in the reserve sparingly, with the knowledge that you can free up another one before long, as in our earlier example concerning the 10 of hearts. In the same way, try not to fill gaps with cards that will be the last to be transferred onto suit sequences. Don't reverse a suit sequence just for fun. Rather, save this maneuver until it can help release a blocked card.

118. Parisian Solitaire

Also called The Isle of Capri, *the origin of this simple game is probably French. It depends almost entirely on luck, hence its low success rate.*

Material

Two decks of 52 cards.

Opening Tableau

Deal four cards face up in a row, and two cards face down to start the reserve. This is the maneuver zone. In the foundation zone, plan for eight spaces for aces and kings, one of each suit, as foundations on which to build suit sequences.

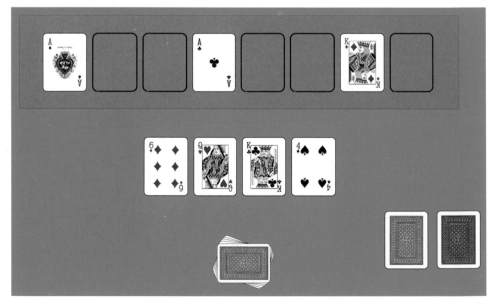

Tableau 135

Object

To complete four ascending suit sequences from ace to king and four descending sequences from king to ace.

Play

Move any card from the maneuver zone onto its appropriate rank in the foundation zone. Gaps will only be filled during the next deal (four cards, face up, in the tableau, and two cards, face down) in the reserve. Between deals, move any available card to its appropriate rank in the foundation zone. Do not build sequences of any kind in the maneuver zone. Cards are moved strictly from the maneuver zone to the foundation zone. Within the latter, suit sequences cannot be reversed. Whenever the talon is exhausted, turn up cards in the reserve and transfer all available cards, be they from the reserve or the tableau, to the foundation zone.

Three rounds are allowed per game. When the talon is exhausted for the first time, gather together all the cards in the maneuver zone in the opposite order of distribution so that the fourth column will be at the top of the new talon and the rest of the reserve underneath. Without shuffling, redeal as before – four cards face up and two face down. At third deal, however, do not place cards in the reserve. The game is successful when all eight suit sequences have been completed.

Variant

When laying the opening tableau, remove aces and kings, one of each suit, and lay them out in the foundation zone.

119. Colorado

This game is also known as Grand Canyon. *It is littered with pit-falls because cards are moved only from the maneuver zone to the foundation zone. Since every card placement has an impact on play, the player needs an adequate overview of the game, an acute sense of anticipation and, most especially, a constant attention to every detail. An error-free execution will almost certainly lead to success.*

Material
Two decks of 52 cards.

Opening Tableau
Plan for eight spaces in the foundation zone, in which you will build suit sequences. In the maneuver zone, deal 20 cards face up in two rows of 10 columns. Keep the talon face down.

Object
To complete four ascending suit sequences from ace to king and four descending suit sequences from king to ace.

Play
As the aces and kings of each suit appear, place them in the foundation zone. Draw cards from the talon one by one, placing suitable cards upon their appropriate rank in the foundation zone. Note that cards in the foundation zone may not be moved back to the maneuver zone. Cards from the talon that cannot be moved to the foundation zone may be placed upon any of the 20 cards in the maneuver zone, regardless of suit, color or rank. In fact, these 20 spaces serve as discard piles, the top cards of which may be moved onto their appropriate rank in the foundation zone at the first opportunity. A gap must be filled at once

with a card from the talon. One deal is allowed per game. The game is successful when all eight suit sequences in the foundation zone have been completed.

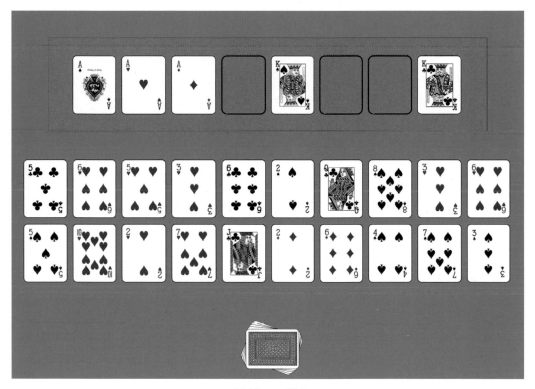

Tableau 136

Strategy
As you lay out cards in the maneuver zone, plan suit sequences and runs that you can easily transfer to the foundation zone. Pay special attention to impasses. For example, avoid placing a 4 of hearts upon a 5 of hearts if, in the foundation zone, the heart sequence has already been built past the 5-card. At this stage, the 4 and 5 of hearts in question can only be moved onto a descending suit sequence – that is, the 5 before the 4.

120. Whimsy

The name of this solitaire game derives from the fact that the player may switch the direction of suit sequences at will during the course of play. It has a low success rate.

Material
Two decks of 52 cards.

Object
In the foundation zone, place an ace and a king of each suit. In the maneuver zone, set up 12 spaces arranged in three rows of four columns in which to lay cards as the game progresses. Keep the talon face down.

Play
Turn up all the cards from the talon one by one and place them in the maneuver zone, left to right, top row to bottom row, pausing to place suitable cards in the foundation zone. During distribution, however, cards that have already been placed in the maneuver zone cannot be transferred back to the foundation zone. Tableau 137 represents the entire deck after the deal.

Once all the cards have been distributed, you may start moving cards about, either onto suit sequences in the foundation zone or onto other piles in the maneuver zone, provided the contact card is of the same suit and next-higher or next-lower in rank. The idea is to build ascending or descending suit sequences. In Tableau 137, for example, move the 8 of diamonds onto the 9 of diamonds in the foundation zone, and the 4 of spades onto the 3 of spades in the maneuver zone. You may change the direction of suit sequences at will, but you may not form a circular sequence such as placing an ace upon a king, or a king upon an ace. Only a queen may be placed upon a king, just as only a 2-card may be placed upon an ace.

Tableau 137

Three rounds are allowed per game. Whenever play is blocked, gather the remaining piles in the maneuver zone in the opposite order of distribution so that the last pile in the last row will be at the top of the new talon, and the first pile in the first row at the bottom. Redeal as before. The game is successful when all eight suit sequences have been completed.

121. Patriarchs

This fairly simple game has a rather low success rate. Since it depends almost entirely on chance, strategy is of secondary importance.

Material
Two decks of 52 cards.

Opening Tableau
The foundation zone is made up of two columns of four cards each. The left-hand column contains four aces, one of each suit; the right-hand column contains four kings, again, one of each suit. Between the two columns is the maneuver zone, which consists of three rows of three face-up cards. Keep the talon face down.

Object
To complete four ascending suit sequences from ace to king and four descending suit sequences from king to ace.

Play
Any card from the maneuver zone may be moved onto its appropriate rank in the foundation zone; once there, though, it may not be transferred back. Note that cards move in one direction only: from the maneuver zone to the foundation zone. In other words, no sequences of any kind are built in the maneuver zone. A vacant space must be filled immediately with a card from the discard pile, or, from the talon if there is no discard pile.

Turn up cards from the talon one by one, discarding those that cannot be used for building. The top card of the discard pile may be reintroduced into play at the first opportunity, either for building up the foundation zone or for filling a gap in the maneuver zone. Whenever two same-suit sequences have been built to the meeting point, you may reverse one upon the other, in whole or in part,

Tableau 138

except, of course, for the ace or king at the bottom. Two rounds are allowed per game. The game is successful when all eight suit sequences have been completed.

122. Corner Stones

This is an original and fascinating game. It requires an alert sense of anticipation and a phenomenal ability to remember the various aspects of the entire game. Grandmother played it occasionally.

Material
Two decks of 52 cards.

Opening Tableau
As they are turned up in dealing, place aces and kings of each suit in two foundation columns – the aces in the left-hand column and the kings in the right. The maneuver zone includes:

- Eight piles of face-up cards, arranged in two columns – one on each side of the foundation zone;
- Four piles of face-up cards, placed sideways at the four outer corners of the maneuver zone. These are corner stones, which will play a predominant role in the game.

To form the maneuver zone, deal all the cards from the talon, starting with the top left corner stone, moving on to the top right corner stone, down the right-hand column and continuing clockwise. During the distribution, pause to place suitable cards as they appear onto their appropriate rank in the foundation zone.

However, there is one important limitation: A card that would have gone onto one of the two columns in the maneuver zone may only be placed onto a foundation in the same row. On the other hand, cards that might land on corner-stones are playable on any foundation. For obvious reasons, this rule does not apply to the aces and kings serving as foundations. Whenever a card is placed upon its rank in the foundation zone, its space in the maneuver zone will be filled by the next card drawn from the talon. During dealing, however, no cards may be moved from the maneuver zone.

Object

To complete four ascending suit sequences from ace to king and four descending suit sequences from king to ace.

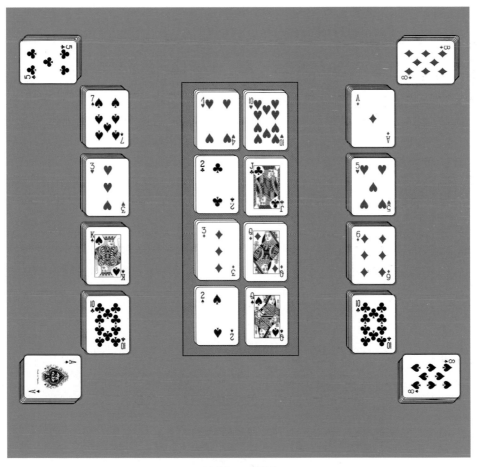

Tableau 139

Mixed Suit Sequences

Play

Any available card may be moved to its appropriate rank in the foundation zone but may not be transferred back. In the maneuver zone, you may move an available card onto another that is next-higher or next-lower in rank, regardless of color, so as to form ascending or descending sequences. You may move one card at a time but never a sequence as a unit. You may form circular sequences in the maneuver zone, such as moving an ace onto a king, or a 2-card onto an ace. The reverse, however, is not allowed. When two cards in two separate spaces rank next to each other, you may reverse a sequence upon the other at your discretion.

In tableau 139, you may not move the 10 of clubs onto the jack of clubs, nor the 5 of hearts onto the 4 of hearts, since neither of these cards are in the same row as their suit sequence. However, you may move the ace of diamonds onto the king of spades; the 7 of spades onto the 8 of spades; the 6 of diamonds onto the 7 of spades; the 5 of hearts onto the 6 of diamonds; and the 5 of hearts – which is now atop a cornerstone – onto the 4 of hearts; the 5 of clubs onto the 6 of diamonds; and so on. Only a vacant cornerstone may be filled by a card from the maneuver zone. Other gaps must remain as is. The game is successful when all eight suit sequences have been completed.

Strategy

While building sequences in the maneuver zone, aim at moving as many cards as possible onto the corner stones; from there they may be moved onto their appropriate suit sequence, regardless of where the suit sequence finds itself in the foundation zone. Thus, the five of hearts, at one point unplayable on its suit sequence because it was not in the same row, was eventually transferred after it was moved to a cornerstone. It's also better to build suit sequences in the maneuver zone since they may be transferred more easily to the foundation zone.

123. Face-to-Face

This is essentially a game of chance, hence its low success rate. Grandmother gladly played it whenever she felt in the mood.

Material

Two decks of 52 cards.

Opening Tableau

The entire tableau represents three sides of a rectangle. The foundation zone is made up of two columns of four cards each, placed a distance apart. The left-hand column contains one ace of each suit and the right-hand column, one king of each suit. These are foundations on which to build suit sequences. Between the

Tableau 140

two columns is the maneuver zone – a row of 10 face-up cards that lines up with the fourth row of the foundation columns. Keep the talon face down.

Object

To complete four ascending suit sequences from ace to king and four descending suit sequences from king to ace.

Play

Any card in the maneuver zone may be moved onto its appropriate suit sequence in the foundation zone, provided that there's no card above or below it. Once moved to the foundation zone, cards may not be transferred back. Note that cards are moved strictly from the maneuver zone to the foundation zone – no sequences of any kind are to be built in the maneuver zone.

Gaps resulting from a series of maneuvers must be filled simultaneously with cards drawn from the talon. In other words, you must wait until all the gaps are filled before proceeding to transfer suitable cards onto the foundation zone. Whenever play is blocked, deal a new row of 10 cards below the first row. Move cards as before, filling any newly created gaps with cards from the talon.

When no further maneuvers are possible, deal a third row of 10 cards below the second row. Start by moving cards that are placed in the first or third row. This, in turn, will free up spaces above or below cards in the second row, thus releasing them for play. Continue play in this manner – adding new rows of 10 cards to the tableau between rounds of maneuvers – until the talon is exhausted.

In general, only the card at the top or bottom of a column may be moved on to its foundation. Moving a card frees up a space for its upper or lower neighbor, thus releasing the neighbor for play. When two same-suit sequences have been built to the meeting point, you may reverse one upon the other, in whole or in part, except, of course, for the ace or king serving as the base card. Only one deal is allowed per game. The game is successful when all eight suit sequences have been completed.

124. Babette

This game requires a lot of space. Start playing only if you have a big table, otherwise you may not be able to finish the game. It wasn't among Grandmother's favorites because of the physical effort involved.

Material
Two decks of 52 cards.

Opening Tableau
Plan eight spaces in the foundation zone for the eight suit sequences. In the maneuver zone, deal eight cards face up in a row. Keep the talon face down. Bear in mind that, during the game, the maneuver zone will occupy an unwieldy space.

Object
To complete four ascending suit sequences from ace to king and four descending suit sequences from king to ace.

Play
As they appear, place aces and kings of each suit in the foundation zone. In the maneuver zone, deal eight cards into a second row, below the first. Any card with a gap or space beneath it may be transferred to its appropriate rank in the foundation zone. Gaps are not filled. Whenever play is blocked, deal a new row of eight cards. Suppose that, after seven redeals, we arrive at Tableau 141.

Since no further maneuver is possible, a new round is allowed. To form a new talon, gather the cards one column at a time, starting from the bottom card in the last column all the way to the top, then placing the pile thus formed upon the

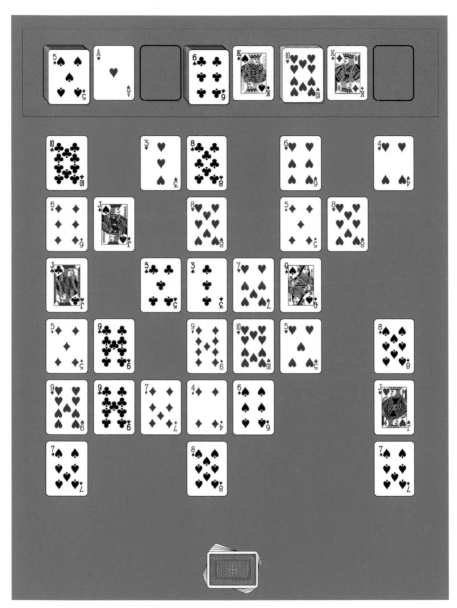

Tableau 141

bottom card in the seventh column, and so on, until you have reached the top card in the first column. Redeal a row of eight cards as before. The game is successful when all eight suit sequences have been completed.

125. Turkish Rug

Also called Crazy Quilt, *this colorful game requires a very large table. If you can muster up sustained concentration as well as an acute sense of anticipation and a good memory, you have an excellent chance of beating the odds. However, Grandmother found it cumbersome and seldom played it.*

Material
Two decks of 52 cards.

Opening Tableau
Remove an ace and a king of each suit from the deck and lay them face up in a row as foundations on which to build suit sequences. Below this row, in the maneuver zone, start a reserve of 64 face-up cards, arranged in eight rows of eight columns in a criss-cross pattern – like that of some intricate tapestry – alternating length and width (see Tableau 142). Keep the talon face down.

Object
To complete four ascending suit sequences from ace to king and four descending suit sequences from king to ace.

Play
Cards in the reserve may be moved, provided at least one of their narrower edges is free, i.e., there is a space or gap. Note that 16 cards (four on each side) of Tableau 142 are available: those placed vertically in the top and bottom rows, and those placed horizontally in the first and last columns. These cards – placed as they are on the perimeter of the tableau – are the first to be moved, just like a rug starting to fray at the edges. In turn, these maneuvers will release neighboring cards for play. In Tableau 142, for example, removing the 2 of spades and the queen of diamonds releases, respectively, the 7 of clubs and the 8 of spades on the one hand, and the 6 of diamonds on the other.

Tableau 142

Mixed Suit Sequences

Cards in the reserve may be moved onto their appropriate rank in the foundation zone, or to the discard pile, provided the contact card is next-higher or next-lower in rank, regardless of color. Form ascending or descending suit sequences, or even circular varieties, with, say, an ace resting upon a 2 or a king resting upon an ace.

When all possible maneuvers in the reserve have been executed, draw cards from the talon one by one, pausing to place them upon their appropriate rank in the foundation zone, or in the discard pile, so as to release still more cards from the reserve. Available cards from the discard pile, too, may be moved onto their appropriate rank in the foundation zone.

Two rounds are allowed. When the first round is done, turn over the discard pile and, without reshuffling, start the second deal. The game is successful when all eight suit sequences have been completed. It fails when after two rounds, cards that cannot move anywhere else still remain in the tableau.

Strategy

Study the tableau carefully and locate parallel or shadow cards that might be blocked inside the tableau, such as the two 4s of clubs in Tableau 142. It's important that you release these cards as soon as possible. Locate also groups of cards that are likely to create impasses. In Tableau 142, in the fourth row, the three heart cards – 4, jack and 8 – form such a group. If you build an ascending heart sequence up to the 8 before releasing the jack, for example, it will be impossible to build the descending heart sequence since the jack must be placed in its rank before the 8 and the 4. It's thus essential that you untie these knots before building suit sequences in the foundation zone.

During the first deal, try building sequences in the discard pile, all the while memorizing the ascending or descending order of these sequences for subsequent maneuvers during the second deal. For example, an ascending sequence of 7, 8 and 9 may be moved from the discard pile onto descending suit sequences in the foundation zone during the first deal, or onto ascending suit sequences during the second deal from the talon. But such a sequence will be doomed if the other 9-card and 7-card are buried deeper inside the discard pile.

126. L'Arlésienne

Grandmother claimed that her own grandmother had imported this game from the Provençal town of Arles, hence its name. It was one of her favorites, not just for sentimental reasons but also, I suspect, because of the game's intrinsic qualities. The unusual opening tableau – which depends entirely upon the luck of the draw – can be laid quickly and mechanically, while play unfolds in a slow, deliberate manner. Success depends largely on the talent of the player – his or her sustained concentration, attention to detail and phenomenal memory. Yet, even allowing for all these qualities, success may still be elusive....

Material
Two decks of 52 cards.

Opening Tableau
In the foundation zone, plan for a row of eight spaces to host an ace and a king of each suit on which you will build eight suit sequences. The maneuver zone includes:
- A first row of seven piles of face-up cards;
- A second row of seven piles, the fourth of which is the reserve, containing face-down cards. The cards in the remaining six piles are face up.

1	2	3	4	5	6	7
8	9	10	X	J	Q	K

To form the maneuver zone, deal cards from the talon one by one and place them face up in two rows, starting from the top left and skipping the reserve space. For each card that falls into its appropriate spot, add a card, face down, to the reserve pile. Suppose that following the first round, we arrive at Tableau 143. Since the jack of diamonds and the king of hearts fall into their appropriate spots, add two cards to the reserve pile. For each ace that turns up, regardless of

Mixed Suit Sequences

its position, add two cards to the reserve. Thus, add two cards for the ace of clubs. If an ace should fall into its own slot (column 1, row 1), add three cards – two because it's an ace, and the third one because it falls into its appropriate space. At the end of each deal, add three cards to the reserve.

Tableau 143

Now, start a new round according to the same rules, which will result, say, in Tableau 144. Since both the 9 of spades and the jack of clubs fall into their respective slots, add two cards to the reserve, followed by three others in order to close out the deal. Continue in this manner until all the cards have been dealt. The more cards there are in the reserve pile, the better the chance for success.

Tableau 144

Object

To complete four ascending suit sequences from ace to king and four descending suit sequences from king to ace.

Play

As soon as possible, move aces and kings, one of each suit, to the foundation zone. Suppose the completed tableau shows two aces of spades, an ace of diamonds, two kings of hearts and a king of spades. Move one of the two aces of spades, the ace of diamonds, one of the two kings of hearts as well as the king of spades to the foundation zone, followed by other suitable cards so as to build ascending or descending suit sequences.

When all conceivable moves have been made, turn up a card from the reserve pile and place it in its appropriate slot. If you turn up a jack, for example, place it in row 2, column 5; if you draw a 3, place it in row 1, column 3. Next, spread out all the cards in that same pile and, without disturbing the order of cards, proceed to transfer suitable ones over to the foundation zone. This done, place the pile back in its space. Turn up another card from the reserve pile and proceed in the same manner. Whenever all the cards in a particular pile have been used, its vacant space may be filled by an appropriate card if and when it's turned up from the reserve pile and provided it's not suitable for transfer to the foundation zone. Continue in this manner until all eight suit sequences have been completed. The game fails if play is irrevocably blocked.

Strategy

It's important to keep play as flexible as possible. For example, avoid completing a suit sequence too early, which would reduce subsequent card movements involving this suit. Try to memorize the contents of each pile in case you need to make a choice between, say, two same-rank cards. A good knowledge of the contents will help you select the card that will generate the greatest number of maneuvers or that will help advance, say, a long-blocked suit sequence.

When two same-suit sequences meet, you may reverse one upon the other, in whole or in part, in order to clear one or more cards from the tableau. Suppose that the ascending heart sequence has been built up to the 5-card, and the descending heart sequence to the 6-card, and that the tableau contains a queen, a jack, a 10 and a 9 of hearts. Reverse from the descending sequence the portion 6-to-queen upon the ascending sequence, thus allowing the queen, the jack, the 10 and the 9 of hearts to be moved onto the heart sequence from king.

Variant

Any completed suit sequence is normally off-limits, but a variant allows you to resort to a circular sequence in order to unblock play. Suppose the ascending heart sequence is complete and that the descending heart sequence has been built up to the jack. What's more, the tableau contains an ace, a 2 and and a 3 of hearts. You may mobilize these cards by forming a circular sequence, that is, by moving the ace onto the king, then the 2 and 3 of hearts onto the ace. In this way, both suit sequences are still active. Obviously, the cards must eventually be placed upon the descending heart sequence since the object of the game is to complete all eight suit sequences.

127. Fox

Just a modicum of attention will suffice to outsmart the vagaries of chance and win this game almost every time.

Material
Two decks of 52 cards.

Opening Tableau
The foundation zone is made up of two columns of four cards, placed a distance apart. The left-hand column contains one ace of each suit, and the right-hand column, one king of each suit. These are foundations on which to build suit sequences. Between the two columns is the maneuver zone – a reserve of 20 face-up cards, arranged in four rows of five columns. Keep the talon face down.

Object
To complete four ascending suit sequences from ace to king and four descending sequences from king to ace.

Play
Transfer suitable cards to their appropriate rank in the foundation zone, filling gaps with cards from the talon. Whenever there is no gap and play is blocked, turn up cards from the talon individually, placing suitable ones on their appropriate suit sequence, and also atop the 20 cards in the reserve.

Again, transfer suitable cards to the foundation zone. Note that cards are moved strictly from the reserve or maneuver zone to the foundation zone. In other words, you may not move a card from one pile to another in the reserve. Sequences of any kind are only built with cards from the talon.

When play is blocked again, deal another batch of 20 cards and continue in the same manner. Gaps may or may not be filled. They may be used to store unsuitable cards from the talon. In the foundation zone, suit sequences may not be reversed. One deal is allowed per game. The game is successful when all eight suit sequences have been completed.

Strategy

Avoid building identical suit sequences in the reserve, for example, two heart sequences of, say, 6-7-8. Build them instead in reverse order: 6-7-8, and 8-7-six. Avoid knots; for example, if you already have a 5 of spades on a 6 of hearts, avoid placing another 6 of hearts upon a 5 of spades. This sort of knot

Tableau 145

Mixed Suit Sequences

can usually be undone eventually, but it's better to prevent a problem than having to solve it. Keep a gap or two in the reserve for end-of-sequence cards, such as 2s, aces, kings and queens.

128. Weavers

This game involves complex maneuvers, hence its name. It demands due diligence and a good memory.

Material
Two decks of 52 cards.

Opening Tableau
Remove an ace and a king of each suit from the deck and place them in a row in the foundation zone. In the maneuver zone, lay all the cards face up in 13 piles, numbered one to 13. Ace counts as 1, jack as 11, queen as 12 and king as 13. When a card falls on the pile matching its own number, place it instead on a separate pile, called the "weavers," and deal the next card into the pile that would have hosted the rerouted card.

Object
To complete four ascending suit sequences from ace to king and four descending suit sequences from king to ace.

Play
Whenever play is blocked, turn up the top card of the weavers. If this card can be placed upon its appropriate rank in the foundation zone, it must be. Proceed to make all the resulting moves. Turn up the next weaver card. If it's not suitable for the foundation zone, place it at the bottom of the pile of its own number. For example, if it's a 4-card, slide it underneath the fourth pile; if it's a jack, place it under the 11th pile. Next, remove a card from this pile and slide it under the pile of its own number, and so on, until this process releases a card suitable for the foundation zone. After all the resulting moves have been made, start with another weaver card and proceed in the same manner.

Tableau 146

In the foundation zone, you may reverse a suit sequence upon another, except, of course, for the ace or king at the bottom. Whenever a king turns up, it automatically blocks play. To continue the game, put the king at the bottom of its pile – number 13 – and turn up another weaver card. If the weavers pile is empty, play is blocked. If it also turns out that the tableau piles contain only cards whose rank matches their own numbers, say, three 4-cards in the fourth pile, or five 7-cards in the seventh pile, there's nothing else you can do except start over or admit defeat.

Three rounds are allowed per game. To form the new talon, pack the first pile upon the second, then the combined pile upon the third, and so on, so that the

13th pile will be at the top of the new talon once it's turned over. Deal as before. The game is successful when all eight suit sequences have been completed.

129. Crescent

Like many others, this game is named after the shape of its open-ing tableau and requires a big table. You need to be constantly alert in order to overcome the luck of the draw. For those who are attentive and clear-sighted, the success rate is high.

Material
Two decks of 52 cards.

Opening Tableau
Lay an ace and a king of each suit over two rows of four columns. This is the foundation zone. Deal the remaining cards in 16 piles arranged in a semicircle to form the maneuver zone. The top card of each pile is face up, the other cards are face down.

Object
To complete four ascending suit sequences from ace to king and four descending suit sequences from king to ace.

Play
Any available card may be moved onto its appropriate rank in the foundation zone but may not be transferred back. In the maneuver zone, build either ascending or descending suit sequences by moving an available card onto another of the same suit and next higher in rank. In Tableau 147, move the queen and jack of diamonds onto the king of diamonds in the foundation zone; in the maneuver zone, move the 4 of hearts onto the 5 of hearts, the 8 of hearts onto the 9 of hearts, and the 8 of spades onto the 9 of spades. These moves release other cards that will, in turn, generate yet more maneuvers.

Tableau 147

You can move only one card at a time – a sequence may not be moved as a unit. In the foundation zone, whenever two same-suit sequences meet, you may reverse one upon the other, in whole or in part, except, of course, for the base

Mixed Suit Sequences

cards. Such reversal sometimes helps release one or more blocked cards in the maneuver zone. What's more, suit sequences may be circular – that is, with the 2-card resting upon the ace and the ace upon the king, if ascending, or with the ace resting upon the 2-card and the king upon the ace, if descending.

When a maneuver bares a face-down card, turn it up at once for play. A vacant space must remain as is. Whenever play is blocked, move the bottom card of each and every pile – including piles that no longer contain face-down cards (this may mess up already built suit sequences) – to the top, face up. Three such moves, from bottom to top, are permitted. The game is successful when all eight suit sequences have been completed. It fails when cards remain in the tableau and no further maneuver is possible.

Strategy

Reverse suit sequences before it's too late. For example, if you find yourself with two heart sequences of 7-8-9, take advantage of the presence of a 6-card to reverse the direction of one of these sequences. Although you cannot always avoid parallel suit sequences since they may be needed to release face-down cards, you must have the presence of mind to reverse them when the opportunity arises. In the maneuver zone, avoid switching the direction of a suit sequence if you don't think it can be split into two independent sequences.

Do not be in a rush to build suit sequences in the foundation zone unless the cards involved are no longer useful in the maneuver zone. You may also consider reversing one or more cards in the foundation zone if that will help unblock a card in the maneuver zone. It's important that same-suit sequences, whether in the foundation or maneuver zone, are maintained at the same level until you can be sure that the remaining portion can be transferred as is onto its foundation.

130. British Square

An error-free execution of this game practically guarantees success. It requires a meticulous attention and a keen sense of anticipation. It was one of Grandmother's favorites.

Material
Two decks of 52 cards.

Opening Tableau
To form the maneuver zone, deal 16 cards face up in four rows of four columns. In the foundation zone, plan for four spaces in which you will build four suit sequences. Keep the talon face down.

Object
To complete four double suit sequences, both ascending from ace to king and descending from the shadow king, i.e., the second same-suit king, to ace.

Play
As they appear, transfer one ace of each suit to the foundation zone. Cards from the maneuver zone may be moved to the foundation zone but may not be transferred back. However, you may keep them in the maneuver zone if you think they'll be useful. Cards are moved one at a time. To move a suit sequence, reverse it – one card at a time – upon another sequence.

In the maneuver zone, build ascending or descending sequences at will by moving any available card onto another of the same suit and next higher or lower in rank. However, once a card is laid upon another, it determines the building direction for that pile. For example, if you've already placed a 9 of hearts upon a 10 of hearts, you may not place the second 10 of hearts upon this 9, to be followed by, say, a jack and queen of hearts. A suit sequence, however, may be reversed upon another card or sequence. For example, to reverse an ascending suit

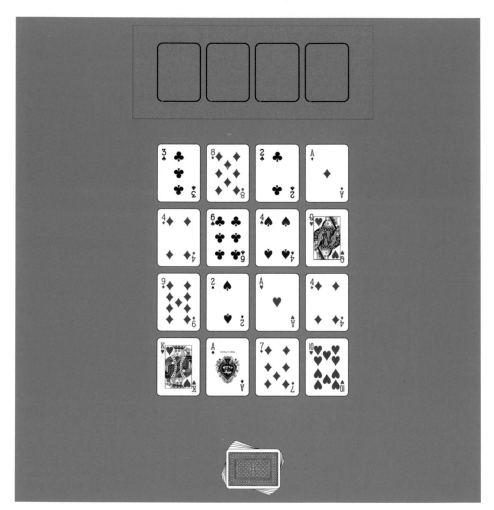

Tableau 148

sequence of 5-6-7 upon a descending suit sequence of 10-9-8, move the 7 onto the 8, then the 6 onto the 7, and, finally, the 5 onto the 6. Since a suit sequence must end either with a king or an ace, a circular sequence is not allowed – such as placing a king upon an ace in a descending suit sequence, or an ace upon a king in an ascending suit sequence.

When all possible maneuvers have been executed, turn up cards from the talon one by one, placing unplayable ones in the discard pile, the top card of which may be reintroduced into play at the first opportunity. A vacant space must be filled with a card from the discard pile, or the talon, if the discard pile is exhausted. Only one deal is allowed per game. The game is successful when all four double suit sequences have been completed.

Strategy

It's important that you fill a gap as soon as it's created with a card from the discard pile or the talon. If a new card sets off an entire series of moves, make sure you move higher-ranked cards first. For example, if the tableau offers a jack, a 10 and a 9 of spades, place the 10 upon the jack before tackling any other maneuver (if you start by placing the 9 upon the 10, you will not be able to place the 10 upon the jack). In the maneuver zone, it's better to build descending suit sequences first since they're usually the first to be reversed and transferred to the foundation zone. Once a shadow card turns up, you may safely use it to start building an ascending suit sequence. Avoid building parallel suit sequences – for example, two heart sequences of 7-6-5 – which often create awkward impasses.

It's better to keep a card in the discard pile that would otherwise have gone to the maneuver zone, especially if the card would block play. The following scenario will illustrate this point:

Suppose that the heart suit sequence in the foundation zone has been built to 9 and that the maneuver zone boasts a descending heart sequence from 7 to 5. To merge the latter with the former, you must wait for an 8 of hearts to turn up, which will be placed upon the 9. Next, the descending sequence 7-6-5 must be reversed upon another column in the maneuver zone before it can be transferred over to the foundation zone.

At this point, if you draw a 4 of hearts from the talon, it will be unwise to place it upon the 5 of hearts. Place it instead in the discard pile until you can transfer it back to a vacant column in the maneuver zone. You will then have a column headed by an available 4 of hearts upon which to reverse the descending heart sequence 7-6-5, making it ready for its eventual transfer to its final suit sequence in the foundation zone.

131. La Valaisanne

Grandmother said she learned this game from an elderly neighbor who hailed from the Swiss canton of Valais. The game is somewhat in the same vein as L'Arlésienne (no. 126), except for its opening tableau and the way it is played. Grandmother preferred L'Arlésienne to this game because she felt that its card manipulation was easier.

Material

Two decks of 52 cards.

Opening Tableau

The foundation zone is made up of two columns of four kings each upon which to build suit sequences – ascending in the left-hand column and descending in the right-hand column. The kings are arranged in the order of spades, hearts, diamonds and clubs.

Between the two columns is the maneuver zone. It is made of 12 spaces, arranged in four rows of three columns. Each space is assigned a rank: 1, 2 and 3 in the first row; 4, 5 and 6 in the second row; 7, 8 and 9 in the third row; 10, jack and queen in the fourth row. See Tableau 149.

To form the maneuver zone, fill the 12 spaces with face-up cards, pausing to place kings as they turn up in their assigned spots in the foundation zone. When a card falls in the space of its own rank, place it face up on a reserve pile instead and deal the next card into the space. For example, if you draw a 3 for the third space, place it on the reserve pile and deal the next card into the third space. Reserve cards will play a particular role in the game. At the end of each deal, add a card to the reserve pile and proceed to a new deal until the entire talon is exhausted. The more cards there are in the reserve, the better the chance of success.

Object

To complete four ascending suit sequences from king to queen and four descending suit sequences from king to ace.

Play

Move suitable cards onto their appropriate rank – in either ascending or descending sequences – in the foundation zone. Suppose that at the end of the

Tableau 149

card distribution, we arrive at Tableau 150. Move the ace, the 2 and the 3 of hearts onto the king of hearts in the left-hand column; the queen of clubs onto the king of clubs in the right-hand column; then the ace and the 2 of diamonds onto the king of diamonds in the left-hand column. If newly released cards can be moved onto their appropriate rank, they must be. Thus, if a 4 of hearts appears, place it upon the 3 of hearts, followed by the 5 of hearts (from either the eighth space or that assigned to queens).

When all possible moves have been made, choose a card from the reserve and place it in its corresponding space. Next, spread out all the cards from the pile in this space and transfer suitable ones over to the foundation zone. Note that

Tableau 150

sometimes a maneuver will set off an entire series of new moves. From Tableau 150, for example, suppose you pick the queen of spades. Place it upon the spade king, followed by the jack of spades. The removal of the latter releases another card that may be placed upon another suit sequence. In the same way, other cards underneath the spade queen may be transferred to their appropriate rank and release yet more cards for play.

Before returning a pile to its space, make sure that all possible maneuvers have been executed. A good memory will come in handy, allowing you to make a wise choice between, say, two same-rank cards, thus countering the vagaries of chance to some degree.

When all possibilities have been exhausted, choose another card from the reserve and proceed anew. Whenever all the cards in a pile have been used, fill the gap with a suitable card from the reserve; that is, a card that matches the rank assigned to said space and that is not playable to the foundation zone. The game is successful when all eight suit sequences have been completed. It fails if play is blocked before all the sequences can come out.

Strategy

The best strategy of all is memorizing the contents of each pile. It also pays to maintain play as flexible as possible. For example, avoid completing a suit sequence too early, which will reduce subsequent card movements involving this particular suit. Whenever you need to make a choice between two same-rank cards, opt for the card which will trigger the most maneuvers.

Give priority to any card that will reactivate a long-blocked suit sequence. When two same-suit sequences are separated by only one card, reversing one upon the other may release one or several cards in the tableau. For example, let's suppose that the descending heart sequence has been built to 7, the ascending heart sequence has been built to 6, and that an 8 of hearts is available in the maneuver zone. By transferring the 7 from the descending sequence over to the ascending one, you set the latter up to receive the 8 of hearts. Note that such reversal can be carried out successfully only once per suit. Thus, the removal of just one card can set off a productive series of maneuvers.

Mixed Suit Sequences

Variants

1. When laying out the opening tableau, remove the eight kings and place them in the two foundation columns. Start dealing the cards as in the original version.

2. A completed suit sequence is off-limits. However, you may resort to circular sequences to unblock play. For example, let's suppose that the ascending heart sequence is complete while the descending heart sequence has been built to the jack-card and that the tableau offers an ace, a 2 and a 3 of hearts. You may use these cards to form a circular sequence, placing the ace of hearts upon the king, followed by the 2 and 3 of hearts. In this way, both suit sequences remain active. It goes without saying that these circular cards will eventually be reversed upon the descending sequence so as to conform to the object of the game, which is to complete eight suit sequences.

3. Another variant allows two rounds per game. Whenever play is blocked, gather the cards in the maneuver zone, reshuffle and begin again according to the rules of the game. Some players even suggest adding a third round, a prospect that positively infuriated my grandmother.

132. Stag Party

This game is a variant of Babette *(no. 124) but with a much higher success rate, since its object is to build twice as many suit sequences. It is so named because all queen-cards are removed from play. "Solitaire for the macho," Grandmother remarked sarcastically.*

Material
Two decks of 52 cards.

Opening Tableau
The foundation zone consists of two columns of eight cards each, placed a distance apart. These are the foundations on which to build 16 suit sequences. Between the columns is the maneuver zone, consisting of a row of eight face-up cards. Keep the talon face down. Note that as play progresses, the maneuver zone will grow quite large.

Object
To complete eight ascending suit sequences from 6 to jack, and eight descending suit sequences from 5 to king.

Play
As they appear, place all the 6-cards in the left-hand foundation column and all the 5-cards in the right-hand foundation column. They are base cards upon which to build suit sequences. As they appear, remove queen-cards from play and put them in a waste pile. Transfer all suitable cards onto their appropriate rank in the foundation zone. Whenever play is blocked, draw eight new cards from the talon and deal them in a second row below the first row. If available cards fit in their suit sequences in the foundation zone, transfer them. (Available cards are those at the bottom row or those above a gap in the tableau). When all possible moves have been made, deal a new

Mixed Suit Sequences

batch of eight cards from the talon. Gaps are not filled. Tableau 151 shows a game in progress after, say, six deals.

Only one deal is allowed per game. The game is successful when all 16 suit sequences have been completed.

Tableau 151

133. Scarab

Grandmother enjoyed this game enormously. It requires an acute sense of anticipation, a prodigious memory and a watchfulness worthy of a Sioux warrior. It's one of only two one-pack games whose object is to build mixed sequences, the other being Quadrille (no. 134). Young players are drawn to the game's 50-50 success rate as well as its colorful tableau.

Material
One deck of 52 cards.

Opening Tableau
Remove two aces and two kings of opposite color, say, two red aces and two black kings, or two black aces and two red kings. Deal the four cards in a row – the kings on the left and the aces on the right. This is the foundation zone. To form the maneuver zone, deal the remaining cards face up in eight piles arranged in two rows, one each above and below the foundation zone. Thus the maneuver zone is split into two parts by the foundation zone.

Object
To complete two descending suit sequences from king to ace and two ascending suit sequences from ace to king.

Play
Any available card may be moved onto its appropriate rank in the foundation zone and may not be transferred back. Within the maneuver zone, build ascending or descending sequences by moving an available card onto another next higher or next-lower in rank, regardless of color. You can move only one card at a time. An already formed sequence may not be moved as a unit.

Mixed Suit Sequences

Tableau 152

You may, however, build circular sequences, say, by placing an ace upon a 2 or a king, and a king upon an ace or a queen. In instances such as this, a good memory of the content of various piles will help you select the most productive maneuvers. Gaps are not filled. The game is successful when all four suit sequences have been completed.

Strategy

Do not be in a rush to move cards over to their suit sequences in the foundation zone. Keep them instead in the maneuver zone for as long as possible so as to build ascending or descending sequences that you can then reverse and transfer over to the foundation zone. Since gaps are not filled, it is wise to keep as many "active" columns as possible in order to ensure flexibility in the maneuver zone.

Variant

To make this game more difficult, some players propose the following rules for moving cards to the foundation zone:

- Any card in the upper row may be moved, regardless of its column.
- A card in the lower row may be moved only if it is in the same column as its suit sequence in the foundation zone.

Thus, in Tableau 152, you can move the queen of diamonds onto the king of diamonds, but not the jack of diamonds onto the queen of diamonds, nor the 2 of spades upon the ace of spades, since these two cards are not in the same column as their suit sequence.

134. Quadrille

The final tableau of this game – assuming it's successful – represents one of the figures of an ancient quadrille, hence its name. Like Scarab *(no. 133), it's a one-pack game whose object is to complete mixed suit sequences.*

Material
One deck of 52 cards.

Opening Tableau
There's no opening tableau. As the game progresses, a tableau will emerge.

Object
To complete four ascending suit sequences from 6 to jack and four descending suit sequences from 5 to king.

Play
Draw cards one by one. As they appear, place the four queens on a pile in the middle of a "compass rose" made by alternating 5-cards and 6-cards. The 5s are placed at the North, South, East and West positions, with the 6s sitting at an angle between them.

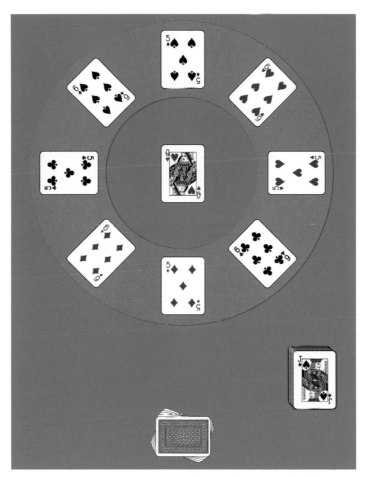

Tableau 153

Any face-up card from the talon must be placed immediately upon its appropriate rank, either on the 5s or the 6s, so as to build the following suit sequences: On the 5s, build down to aces followed by the kings. On the 6s, build up to jacks. Unplayable cards are put on a discard pile, the top card of which may be reintroduced into play at the first opportunity. Two rounds are allowed per game. Upon the second deal, turn over the discard pile and, without shuffling, redeal the cards one by one. You win the game by arriving at Tableau 154.

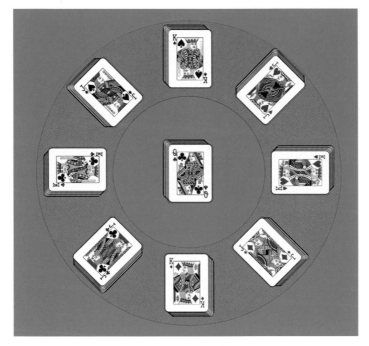

Tableau 154

When this game was successful for Grandmother, she called the figures in the quadrille "little hearts inside, with little devils outside marching all around them."

Variant

There's a two-deck variant, the object of which is to complete eight ascending suit sequences from 6 to jack, and 8 descending suit sequences from 5 to king. The game rules are the same, as is the layout of cards, except for an extra circle to accommodate the extra suit sequences. Tableau 155 shows a successful game.

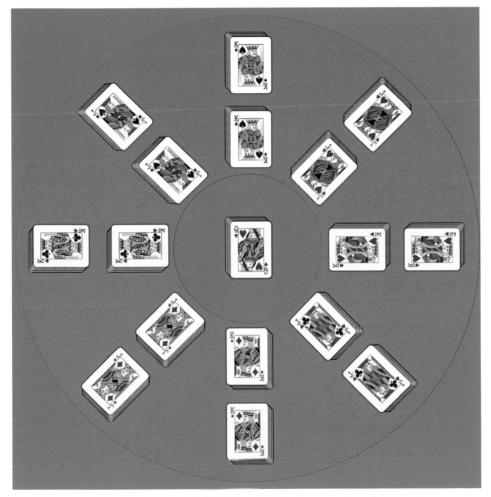

Tableau 155

Mixed Suit Sequences

CHAPTER 12

Circular Suit Sequences

135. Canfield

This great game is very popular and is considered a classic. Although the technique is simple and the card manipulation is manageable, this game has a very low success rate. Fortunately, variants abound to make it easier. I didn't even know how to read when Grandmother taught it to me. It requires a certain amount of attentiveness but not much calculation.

Material
One deck of 52 cards.

Opening Tableau
In the foundation zone, plan four bases upon which to build suit sequences. Draw a card from the talon and place it in the foundation zone; this card indicates the starting rank of the four bases. In the maneuver zone, set up a reserve pile – the bank – to the left. It contains 13 face-down cards. Underneath the foundation zone, deal a row of four face-up cards. Keep the talon face down.

Object
Starting from the rank of the first card in the foundation zone, build four ascending circular suit sequences: ace upon king, 2 upon ace, and so on. As per Tableau 156, the sequences will begin with 8-cards and complete circular suit sequences, ending with 7-cards.

Tableau 156

Play

As they appear, place base cards – whose rank was determined by the first card drawn from the talon – in the foundation zone. In Tableau 156, transfer the 8 of clubs immediately to the foundation zone, as it's the foundation for the club sequence. Any available card may be moved onto its appropriate rank in the foundation zone but may not be transferred back. Within the maneuver zone, move any available card onto another of opposite color and next higher in rank so as to build descending runs of alternating colors. Move the 10 of hearts onto the jack of clubs.

You may not deposit a card in the bank or reserve. On the contrary, it's advantageous to empty the reserve as soon as possible. An entire sequence may be moved as a unit, but it may not be broken and moved in part. For example, if you have a 9-to-3 descending sequence, you may not simply move the 6-5-4-3 sequence. A vacant column must be filled immediately with a card from the bank or reserve.

Suppose the first card from the bank is a 3 of diamonds. Place it upon the 4 of spades. If the next card from the talon is, say, the queen of spades, it may be placed in a vacant column. Suppose the next card from the talon is a 9 of clubs; it can go upon the 8 of clubs in the foundation zone. And if the next card is the 2 of hearts, place it in the second vacant column. We now arrive at Tableau 157.

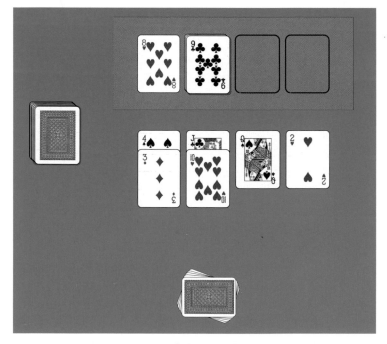

Tableau 157

When all possible moves have been made, turn the talon over and deal out packets of three cards face up onto a discard pile. If the top card of the packet can be placed upon its suit sequence in the foundation zone or upon a sequence in the maneuver zone, it must be moved. The same goes for the second and third cards in the packet. However, only the top card of the packet may be played. If the top card cannot be played, you must deal another packet of three cards; i.e., you may not play the other cards in the packet unless the top card is moved to the foundation zone or the maneuver zone. Redeal the talon as long as you can still draw and place cards upon their rank either in a suit sequence or a run in the maneuver zone. However, you may not shuffle the talon before each deal.

Continue to play as long as you can still transfer a card from the bank or the reserve pile onto a suit sequence in the foundation zone or onto a run in the maneuver zone. When the bank is empty, fill any vacant columns with the first available card in the discard pile. Sequences, as well as suit sequences in the foundation zone, are of the circular variety. The ace is placed upon the king in a suit sequence in the foundation zone, and upon the 2 in a run in the maneuver zone. The king is placed upon an ace in a run; however, this rule doesn't apply if the ace is the foundation of a suit sequence. The game is successful when all four suit sequences have been completed.

Variants

1. Choose base cards for suit sequences as follows: After counting 13 cards for the bank, deal five cards face up in a row, among which a base card is chosen, the four others serving as the start for runs.

2. Before starting, remove the four aces on which to build sequences.

3. Keep the bank open and place the top card upon a run or a suit sequence at the first opportunity. This will make play much easier.

4. Instead of drawing cards from the talon in groups of three for as long as it takes to move at least one card, draw them out one by one – in only one deal per game.

5. You may move only a part of a sequence onto another sequence. Keep in mind that a subtle move may lead to victory.

136. Round of Seven

This game is similar to Gold Rush *(no. 63), though not as popular. Nonetheless, Grandmother liked it, finding it more colorful and subtle.*

Material
One deck of 52 cards.

Tableau 158

Opening Tableau

Deal the first card face up above the tableau. This card will determine the rank upon which to build suit sequences in the foundation zone. Next, deal 28 cards in a row of seven columns – one card in the first column, two in the second, three in the third, and so on, as in *Gold Rush*. Only the top card of each pile is face up. Below this row, set up another row of seven spaces to start the reserve. Keep the talon face down.

Object

To complete four ascending circular suit sequences, starting from the rank determined by the first card.

Play

If an available card matches rank with the one already in the foundation zone, transfer it there at once. In the maneuver zone, build descending runs of alternating colors in accordance with the rules for *Gold Rush*, except for the following modifications:

Whenever a column becomes vacant, fill it only with a card (alone or with its sequence) next lower in rank than the base card. In Tableau 158, for example, only a 6-card, and its sequence if any, may fill a vacant column. When all possible maneuvers have been executed, instead of drawing cards from the talon in groups of three as in *Gold Rush*, deal seven cards face up into the reserve row, which you can use to build either suit sequences in the foundation zone or runs in the maneuver zone. Cards in the reserve row may not be moved from one column onto existing another. Gaps can only be filled at the next deal of seven cards.

Whenever play is blocked, deal a new batch of seven cards, filling vacancies or piling onto existing cards in the reserve row. You may use the last two cards from the talon without having to put them through the reserve. The game is successful when all four ascending circular suit sequences have been completed.

137. Eagle

This game, named for the shape of its opening tableau, is a tough one. It depends entirely on chance and demands just enough attention so as not to miss an opportunity.

Material
One deck of 52 cards.

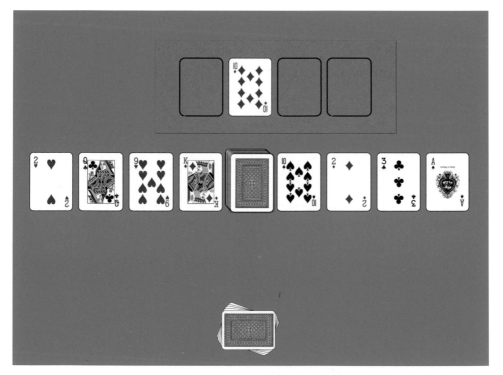

Tableau 159

Opening Tableau

Deal 13 cards face down to form the reserve pile. Next, deal out eight cards face up in row – four cards on each side of the reserve pile. This is the maneuver zone. For the foundation zone, place a card face up directly above the reserve pile. This card determines the rank upon which to build suit sequences. Keep the talon face down. The tableau thus resembles a "stylized" eagle with outspread wings.

Object

To complete four ascending circular suit sequences.

Play

As soon as a base card appears, place it in the foundation zone. In Tableau 159, move the 10 of spades next to the 10 of diamonds, and fill the gap with a card from the reserve. Turn up cards from the talon one by one, pausing to make whatever plays are possible and placing unplayable cards in a discard pile, the top card of which may be reintroduced into play at the first opportunity. The last card in the reserve pile is automatically available, that is, without having to be moved first onto a gap in the "wings." If the reserve is exhausted, fill gaps with cards from the discard pile or, if there is none, from the talon. Three rounds are allowed per game.

138. Magic Spell

The success rate for this game is low, even though play is simple.

Material
One deck of 52 cards.

Opening Tableau
In the maneuver zone, deal 12 cards face up in one row. Turn up the 13th card and place it in one of the four spaces set up to build suit sequences in the foundation zone. Keep the talon face down.

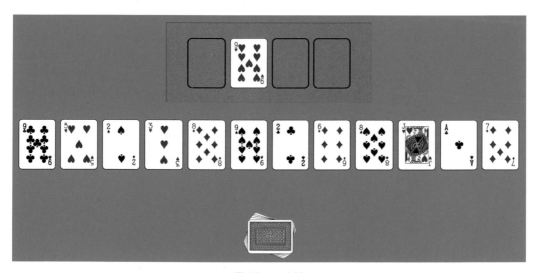

Tableau 160

Object
To complete four ascending circular suit sequences.

Play

Fill the remaining spaces in the foundation zone with suitable cards as they appear. In Tableau 160, for example, move the two 9s of clubs and spades to the foundation zone at once. Suitable cards, too, may be moved onto their appropriate rank but may not be transferred back to the maneuver zone. Build descending runs of alternating colors in the maneuver zone by overlapping an available card onto another of opposite color and next in rank. Runs may be developed in circular fashion, like placing a king upon an ace.

Cards are moved one at a time, and an already formed sequence cannot be moved as a unit. A gap may be filled with any card in the maneuver zone. When all possible maneuvers have been executed, turn up cards from the talon one by one, placing suitable ones upon their appropriate rank in the foundation zone, or upon a run or gap in the maneuver zone. Unplayable cards are placed in a discard pile, the top card of which may be reintroduced into play at any time. One deal is allowed per game. The game is successful when all four circular suit sequences have been completed.

Strategy

Use the discard pile as often as possible, for this is usually the source of the most serious problems a player may encounter.

139. Two Towers

This game is named for the characteristic shape of its opening tableau. Its high success rate makes it a favorite amongst beginners. In fact, a dash of attention will bring victory once every two games and, on lucky days, even two out of three. Grandmother found it too easy for her taste.

Material
One deck of 52 cards.

Opening Tableau
To form the maneuver zone, deal 10 cards face up in two columns of five cards each – the so-called "towers." Between them, place a card face up, which will determine the rank upon which to build suit sequences. This is the foundation zone. Keep the talon face down.

Object
To complete four ascending circular suit sequences starting from the rank determined by the card in the center.

Play
Fill the remaining spaces in the foundation zone with suitable cards from the two towers, followed by others that fit in the suit sequences. In Tableau 161, move the 5 of hearts below the 5 of clubs, then the 6 and 7 of hearts onto the 5 of hearts. Within the towers themselves, build ascending suit sequences by placing an available card, alone or with its own suit sequence, slightly atop another of the same suit and next lower in rank. Thus, in Tableau 161, move the king of spades onto the queen of spades, then the ace of spades onto the king of spades.

When no further maneuver is possible, fill the gaps in the towers with cards from the talon. In Tableau 161, you must draw five cards to fill the five vacancies created by the previous maneuvers. Suppose you draw the ace of hearts, the 9 and 5 of diamonds, and the 2 and ace of clubs. Place the 5 of diamonds below the 5 of clubs in the foundation zone, followed by the 6 of diamonds. Fill the two gaps thus created with cards from the talon, say, the 4 of clubs and the 10 of spades. Since another maneuver is impossible and there are no more gaps to fill, play is blocked. To continue, deal 10 new cards from the talon and place them slightly atop the 10 cards in the two towers, which brings us to Tableau 162.

Tableau 161

Continue to move cards according to the rules of the game – that is, one available card at a time, onto another of the same suit and next lower in rank. You may also transfer a suit sequence as a unit from a tower over to the foundation zone. When the talon is exhausted and no further maneuvers are possible, the game fails. It is successful when all four ascending circular suit sequences have been completed.

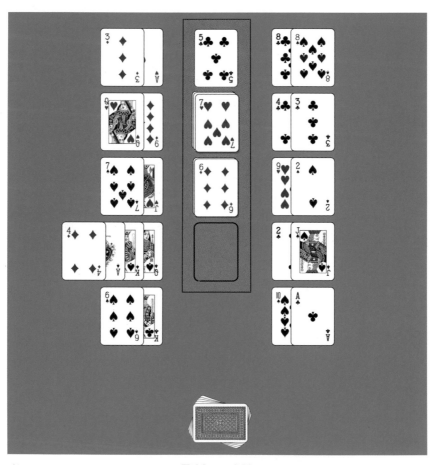

Tableau 162

140. Duchess

This lively game has a low success rate. Grandmother liked it.

Material
One deck of 52 cards.

Opening Tableau
In the foundation zone, set up four spaces on which you will build suit sequences. The maneuver zone is made up of a reserve and a maneuver chamber. To form the reserve, deal 12 cards face up in fans of three cards each. Within each fan, the card to the right overlaps that in the middle, which, in turn, overlaps the left-hand card. The four fans are arranged vertically to the left, below the foundation zone. To the right, deal a row of four cards, face up. This is the maneuver chamber. Keep the talon face down.

Object
To complete four ascending circular suit sequences.

Play
Choose any of the four available cards from the fans and place it in the foundation zone. This card will determine the rank of the four foundation cards upon which to build ascending suit sequences. As other foundation cards appear, place them in the remaining spaces. In Tableau 163, it seems useful to choose a 10-card as the base since there are two other 10s with which to fill the spaces in the foundation zone. You may move any available card from the reserve onto its appropriate suit sequence in the foundation zone, onto a run or into a gap. It's also advantageous to empty the reserve as soon as possible.

Cards from the maneuver zone may be moved onto their appropriate suit sequence in the foundation zone but may not be transferred back. Within the maneuver chamber, build descending runs of alternating colors by moving an

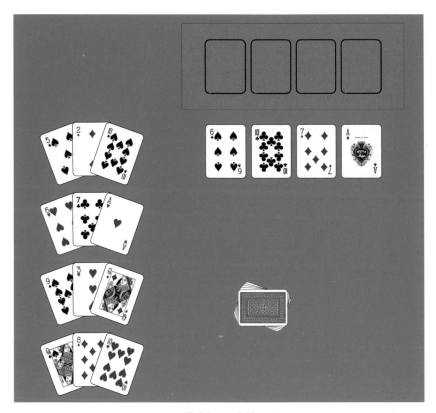

Tableau 163

available card onto another of opposite color and next in rank. You may also move an already formed run as a unit.

A vacant column must be filled by an available card from the reserve, or, if the reserve is exhausted, by a card or a sequence from another column, or, failing that, from the discard pile. When all possible maneuvers have been executed, turn up cards from the talon one by one, placing suitable cards upon their appropriate suit sequences or runs. Unplayable cards are placed in a discard pile, the top card of which may be reintroduced into play at the first opportunity. In general, a second deal is allowed. The game is successful when all four circular suit sequences have been completed.

141. The Birds

This game has everything that Grandmother enjoyed: complexity, unexpected developments and sudden twists and turns. It requires undivided attention. The success rate is relatively low.

Material
One deck of 52 cards.

Opening Tableau
In the maneuver zone, deal 24 cards in four groups to form the reserve. The six cards in each group are arranged in three rows, resembling a bird in full flight: the first row has three cards, the middle of which, called the "center-card," is face down and flanked by two face-up cards known as "wing-cards"; the second row contains two cards, which overlap the upper cards; and the third row has one card – the "beak" – overlapping the two cards in the second row. Above the four "birds" is the foundation row, where four spaces are set up to receive the center-cards as they become available. They are the foundation cards upon which to build ascending suit sequences. Keep the talon face down.

Object
To complete four ascending circular suit sequences.

Play
Turn up cards from the talon one by one and put them in a discard pile. Then, in order to get to the four center-cards in the reserve and transfer them to the foundation zone, move the available cards blocking them onto the discard pile, provided the contact card is next-higher or next-lower in rank, regardless of color. You may change the direction of these mini-sequences as you deem useful, or form circular runs by placing an ace upon a king or a 2. Obviously, the

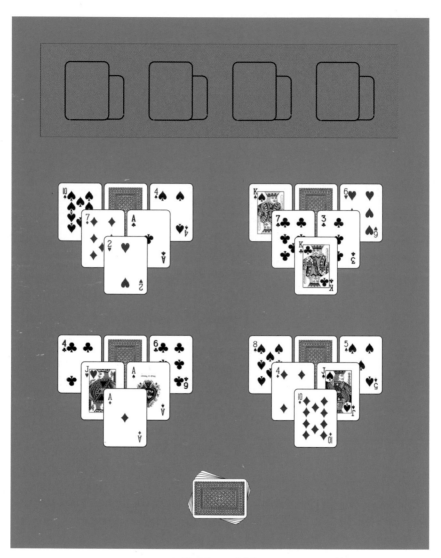

Tableau 164

first available cards in the reserve are the beaks, which, once removed, will bare others.

In Tableau 164, suppose the first turned-up card is the queen of hearts. Move the king of clubs onto this card, followed by the ace of diamonds, the 2 of hearts, and your choice between the ace of clubs, the ace of spades or the 3 of clubs.

As they become available, wing-cards are moved onto a separate row as foundations on which to build descending sequences. Suppose that during the previous maneuver, you opted to remove the ace of clubs, and the second card drawn from the talon was the 6 of diamonds. Place the 7 of diamonds upon the 6 of diamonds, and you'll bare a center-card for the foundation zone – say, the king of diamonds. Next, put the 10 and 4 of spades – the wing-cards – in the separate row. At this point, if the available wing-cards are of the same suit, you may start building descending suit sequences even though the four center-cards haven't yet been released for play.

It goes without saying that the center-cards may not necessarily represent the four suits, in which case you may want to build descending sequences for the missing suits in the maneuver zone, resorting, if necessary, to circular sequences. You can later reverse these suit sequences and transfer them to the foundation zone. If you have two same-suit sequences in the foundation zone, wait until they are built to the meeting point – say, a heart sequence running from 7 to 10 and another from 2 to 6 – so as to combine them. You may move any available card – either from the reserve, the discard pile or the talon – onto its appropriate rank in an ascending suit sequence. But once moved, this card may not be transferred back.

On the rare occasion when a suit or two are not represented by the center – or the wing-cards, the game automatically fails, and there's nothing you can do to revive it. Two rounds are allowed per game. The game is won when all four ascending circular suit sequences have been completed in the foundation zone.

Strategy

Unblock the centre- and wing-cards as soon as possible. In general, the opening tableau should be entirely turned up long before the first round is over. Make sure all possible maneuvers have been executed before drawing a new card from the talon. Use the discard pile only if necessary.

142. Cross

This deceptively simple game requires a good deal of attention, for success may come from several sources. It is named for the shape of the opening tableau.

Material
One deck of 52 cards.

Opening Tableau
Deal five cards face up in the form of a cross. This is the maneuver zone. Next, place another card face up at an angle between two of the cards. This card determines the rank on which to build ascending suit sequences. The four angles form the foundation zone. (See Tableau 165.)

Object
To complete four ascending circular suit sequences.

Play
Fill the other angles of the cross with suitable cards as they turn up. In Tableau 165, for example, move the 5 of clubs at once onto an angle. Any available card may be moved onto its appropriate rank in its suit sequence in the foundation zone but may not be transferred back to the maneuver zone. Within the cross itself, build descending sequences by moving an available card onto another next in rank, regardless of color. Sequences are built in a circular fashion – such as placing a king upon an ace – unless the ace constitutes the foundation of suit sequences in the foundation zone.

Move only one card at a time; an already formed sequence may not be moved as a unit. A gap may be filled with an available card from the cross or the top card of the discard pile or the talon. When all possible maneuvers have been executed, turn up cards from the talon one by one, placing suitable ones upon their appropriate rank in the foundation zone or upon sequences on the cross or in a gap. Unplayable cards are put on the discard pile, the top card of which may be reintroduced into play at any time. Only one deal is allowed per game. The game is won when all four circular suit sequences have been completed.

Strategy

Give priority to building descending sequences on the cross, for they may be transferred more easily to the foundation zone. Use cards in the discard pile as soon as possible, as the latter is a potential source of the most serious problems a player may encounter.

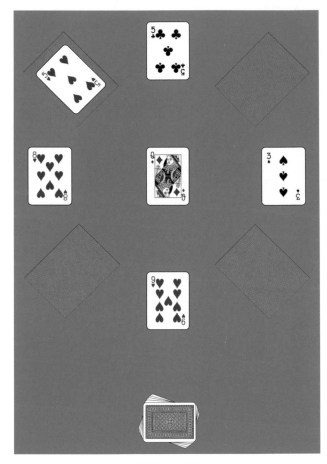

Tableau 165

143. Explosion

This game has all the elements one could hope for. As it's played out, the opening tableau "explodes" like fireworks in every direction: columns splitting, foundations proliferating, cards being matched and unmatched all over the place. This is what makes the game attractive, rather than its sky-high success rate, which becomes irrelevant in the final analysis. Nonetheless, Explosion *requires a keen sense of anticipation and unswerving attention, not to mention a very large table. It amused Grandmother to no end.*

Material
One deck of 52 cards.

Opening Tableau
Deal 49 cards face up in seven overlapping rows of seven columns to form the reserve. To the right is the depot – a column containing three cards and a vacant space. The foundation zone will emerge during the course of play.

Object
To complete four ascending circular suit sequences.

Play
As the first maneuver, move an available card from the reserve to the depot – either into its vacant space or onto one of its three cards, provided the contact card is of the same suit, regardless of rank. Thus, in Tableau 166, move the jack of diamonds from the fifth column of the reserve onto the queen of diamonds in the depot.

Once the jack of diamonds has been moved, divide the rest of the fifth column into two parts of three cards each – a maneuver that releases the 7 of clubs and the 4 of spades for play. An available card from the reserve may be used to

Tableau 166

fill the vacant space in the depot, or it may be moved onto any same-suit card there, regardless of rank. Thus, you can move the 4 of spades onto the 3 of spades.

Each time the available card in a three-card group is removed, separate the remaining two cards and place them at the bottom of the tableau, where each card becomes a foundation or base upon which to build an ascending or descending suit sequence. This is the foundation zone. Following the removal of the 4 of spades, for example, the 4 of clubs and the 6 of diamonds become foundation cards. In general, cards in the first, second, fourth and fifth rows of each column are susceptible to becoming foundation cards.

If you fill the vacant space in the depot with the jack of clubs, the seventh column may be split into two equal parts. You now have three groups of three cards each as well as two foundation cards. And if you move the 7 of clubs onto the jack of clubs, the 9 of diamonds and the 7 of spades will become two new bases. Next, transfer the 10 of diamonds onto the 9 of diamonds and separate the 5 of hearts and the king of hearts into yet two more bases, for a total of six bases.

Repeat the same maneuver in other columns and, as said earlier, the tableau explodes.

Only one card may be moved at a time; this universal rule applies to all maneuvers. As previously noted, an available card from the reserve may be moved onto a same-suit card or into the vacant spot in the depot. In their turn, available cards in the depot may be moved onto their appropriate rank in the foundation zone but not onto one another within the depot. While a card may be moved from one suit sequence onto another same-suit sequence in the foundation zone, it may not be transferred to the depot – this is tantamount to removing a card from the foundation zone and reintroducing it into the maneuver zone.

Strategy

Locate and memorize cards that may become foundation cards and anticipate how these new sequences may be merged. In the depot, keep a vacant space for as long as possible to maintain flexibility of play. Since cards may not be moved from one space to another within the depot, try to have as many suits as possible represented in there. For example, if the depot contains three heart cards, try to move two of them onto suit sequences so as to make room for other suits.

Even though the object of the game is to complete four ascending circular suit sequences, you may resort to temporary descending sequences to gain access to joint-cards, which will help merge sequences. In fact, a sequence may not be moved as a block onto another sequence, but only one card at a time in the reverse order, starting with the joint-card. You may not, for instance, move a 7-8-9 spade sequence onto a 4-5-6 spade sequence. However, let's suppose you have two other foundation cards, say, the 10 and jack of spades, in which case you must avoid the temptation of immediately placing the 10 upon the jack. Instead, transfer the 9 of spades onto the 10, then the 8 onto the 9. This maneuver releases the 7 of spades, which you may place upon the 6, thus setting off a new series of moves: 8 onto 7, 9 onto 8, 10 onto 9, and, finally, jack onto 10. The ascending spade sequence is thus on its way to completion. These same maneuvers may also be carried out if there is a vacant space in the depot or if one of the available cards is the 10 of spades.

The game is successful when all four ascending circular suit sequences are achieved, based as they are upon foundation cards of various ranks. Foundation cards obviously evolve as play progresses and are determined only at the very end. A final sequence may run from 4 to 3, another from jack to 10, the third one from 2 to ace, and so on. The game fails if no further possible maneuver can succeed in unblocking an impasse.

144. Grandfather's Clock

Despite its visual similarity to Clock *(no. 39), this infinitely more complex game proceeds in quite a different way. It needs little attention, and strategy has only a secondary role. Grandmother taught me this game on a Sunday afternoon, since we were alone and had a big table at our disposal.*

Material

One deck of 52 cards.

Opening Tableau

The foundation zone is shaped like the dial of a clock. Remove the following cards from the deck: 2, 6 and 10 of spades; 3, 7 and jack of hearts; 4, 8 and queen of clubs; and 5, 9 and king of diamonds. Spread these cards face up in a circle – the clock's dial – as follows:

- 2, 6 and 10 of spades at 5, 9 and 1 o'clock;
- 3, 7 and jack of hearts at 6, 10 and 2 o'clock;
- 4, 8 and queen of clubs at 7, 11 and 3 o'clock;
- 5, 9 and king of diamonds at 8, 12 and 4 o'clock;

In the maneuver zone, deal the remaining cards face up in five overlapping rows of eight columns. (See Tableau 167.)

Tableau 167

Object

To complete on each hour an ascending suit sequence, the last card of which shows the number appropriate to its position in the "clock." Ace counts as one, king as 13, queen as 12 and jack as 11. If necessary, sequences may be circular – that is, an ace may be placed upon a king, and a 2 may be placed upon an ace. Sequences built with any 10, jack, queen or king take four cards, while all the others take only three cards.

Play

Any available card from the maneuver zone may be moved to its appropriate rank in the foundation zone but may not be transferred back. Within the maneuver zone, build descending sequences by moving an available card upon another next in rank, regardless of color. Move only one card at a time. A gap may be filled with any available card. The game is successful when all the cards have been placed upon the dial and each top card shows the number appropriate to its position in the clock.

145. Nuptials at the Manor

This game calls for some degree of attentiveness, although play depends solely on the luck of the draw.

Material
Two decks of 52 cards.

Opening Tableau
Remove a queen and a jack of hearts from the decks and place them side by side as foundations upon which to build suit sequences. As the cards appear, complete the foundation zone with two jacks of diamonds and four black 10s. In the maneuver zone, deal 16 cards face up in two rows of eight columns. Keep the talon face down.

Object
To complete two heart sequences: one ascending from queen to jack and the other descending from jack to queen; two descending diamond sequences from jack to queen; and four descending black sequences from 10 to jack. Within the ascending circular sequence, place the ace upon the king, then the 2 upon the ace. Within the descending circular sequences, place the ace upon the 2 and the king upon the ace.

Play
Any available card in the maneuver zone must be moved immediately upon its appropriate rank in the foundation zone. In Tableau 168, for example, you must place the heart king upon the heart queen, and the 10 of hearts upon the jack of hearts, followed by the 9 and 8 of hearts. When no further moves are possible, deal 16 new cards face up, filling vacancies or adding to existing cards. Move cards as before onto the foundation zone. The last deal contains only six cards, which are placed upon the first six spaces of the top row. Vacancies are filled only at redeal.

Tableau 168

When the talon has been exhausted and no more cards can be transferred from the maneuver zone to the foundation zone, turn over the pile of cards in the 16th spot – that is, the last spot in the bottom row – and deal out the cards, starting with the 16th spot, then back to the first spot and going as far as the cards allow. Move cards as before onto the foundation zone, then proceed anew with the pile in the 15th spot, then those in the 14th spot, and so on, all the way to the first spot. When cards in the first spot have been redistributed and no further maneuver is possible, the game fails. It is won when all eight suit sequences have been completed in the foundation zone.

146. Sultan

This solitaire game its name from the final, winning tableau, which displays the sultan – the king of hearts – surrounded by his harem of eight queens. The success rate is high.

Material
Two decks of 52 cards.

Opening Tableau
To form the foundation zone, lay out the eight kings and the ace of hearts face up in three rows of three columns, with the middle column containing the two

Tableau 169

heart kings and the ace respectively. Flanking the foundation zone are two columns of four face-up cards each, forming the maneuver zone.

Object

To complete eight ascending suit sequences – seven sequences from king to queen, and one sequence from ace to queen. The heart king at the center of the foundation zone is a "dead" card, playing no role whatsoever.

Play

Any available card in the maneuver zone must be moved onto its appropriate rank in the foundation zone but may not be transferred back. No sequences of any kind are to be built in the maneuver zone. Cards can only be moved from the maneuver zone to the foundation zone.

Turn up cards from the talon one by one, putting those that do not fit the suit sequences in the foundation zone onto a discard pile. The top card of the discard pile may be transferred onto its appropriate rank in the foundation zone or used to fill a gap in the maneuver zone. Any vacancies must be filled immediately with cards from the discard pile or, if there is none, from the talon. Three rounds are allowed per game. The game is successful when all eight suit sequences have been completed.

147. Big Ben

This game presents a colorful and complex tableau. It requires an intense attention so you won't miss a single maneuver. Less mechanical than other "clock" games, Big Ben provides some opportunity for strategic reflection. Grandmother took immense pleasure playing the game.

Material

Two decks of 52 cards.

Opening Tableau

Remove the following cards from the deck: 2 of spades, 3 of hearts, 4 of clubs, 5 of diamonds, 6 of spades, 7 of hearts, 8 of clubs, 9 of diamonds, 10 of spades, jack of hearts, queen of clubs, king of diamonds. Place these cards face up in a circle – the clock's dial – starting with the two of spades at "9 o'clock" and continuing clockwise. This is the foundation zone. Around the dial, deal a fan of three cards opposite each "hour." These 12 fans form the maneuver zone. The remaining 56 cards are the talon, which is kept face down.

Object

To complete ascending circular sequences so that each top card shows the number appropriate to its position in the clock's dial. Note that the sequences at 9, 10, 11 and 12 o'clock each contain seven cards, while the other sequences have eight.

Tableau 170

Circular Suit Sequences

Play

In the maneuver zone, build descending suit sequences by moving an available card onto another of the same suit and next in rank. In the foundation zone, build ascending suit sequences by moving an available card from the maneuver zone onto any card in the clock's dial, provided it is of the same suit and next lower in rank. Sequences may be built around the ace, if necessary.

When all possible maneuvers have been executed, spaces (made by the removal of an entire fan) must be filled with cards from the talon, starting at 12 o'clock and moving clockwise to 11 o'clock. You may not fill these spaces with cards drawn from other fans nor with those from the discard pile. Next, turn up cards from the talon one by one, putting unplayable ones on the discard pile. At the first opportunity, the top card of the discard pile may be moved onto a suit sequence either in the foundation or maneuver zone, but it may not be used to fill a vacant space created by the removal of a fan. A card that has already been placed upon a suit sequence in the clock's dial may not be transferred back to a fan; this is tantamount to transferring a card from its foundation back to the maneuver zone.

Whenever play is blocked, start a new deal to fill the vacant fans. At the end of a redeal, each fan must contain at least three cards. One deal is allowed. The game is successful when each suit sequence shows the number appropriate to its position in the clock's dial.

Strategy

Resist the temptation to build suit sequences in the clock's dial too quickly. Keep cards in the maneuver zone for as long as they can be used to build suit sequences there. Aim at extricating cards that are blocked, especially by cards of the same suit and next in rank. When you have a choice, make sure you opt for the one that will prompt the most productive series of maneuvers.

CHAPTER 13

Skip Suits Sequences

148. Minuet

Also called Gavotte, *this game takes its name from the closing tableau, which depicts four queens facing their matching kings, as in a minuet. The success rate is high.*

Material
Two decks of 52 cards.

Opening Tableau
Deal two squares of 16 face-up cards each, arranged in four rows of four columns. These are the two wings of the maneuver zone. Between the wings, set up space for two foundation columns of 4 cards each: one column for aces, the other for 2-cards. Keep the talon face down.

Object
To complete eight suit sequences: four ascending sequences from ace to queen, and four descending sequences from 2 to king. Skip by two as follows:
- A, 3, 5, 7, 9, J, K, 2, 4, 6, 8, 10, Q;
- 2, 4, 6, 8, 10, Q, A, 3, 5, 7, 9, J, K.

Play
As they appear, place an ace and a two of each suit in the foundation zone. Within the right-hand wing, only the bottom card of a column may be moved and gaps are not filled. Within the left-hand wing, all cards are playable and gaps must be filled immediately with cards from the discard pile, or, if there are none, from the talon.

Turn up cards from the talon one by one, putting those that cannot be played to the foundation zone on the discard pile. The top card of the discard pile may be reintroduced into play at the first opportunity. The only card movement permitted is toward the foundation zone. In other words, no sequences of any kind

Tableau 171

are built in the maneuver zone. Two rounds are allowed. The game is successful when all eight suit sequences have been completed.

Strategy

Use cards in the right-hand wing as soon as possible. Use those in the left-hand wing mainly to extricate cards in the right-hand wing or to ensure a spot for a strategic card from the talon.

Variants

1. Switch the roles of the two wings.
2. After inspecting the opening tableau, determine the role that each wing will play.
3. Determine the rank of each of the foundation cards.

149. Olympia

Also known as Egyptian Campaign, *this game is named for the shape of its opening tableau – a mountain capped by a rainbow. According to Grandmother, it was one of the games favored by the Empress Josephine, who then introduced it to the Emperor. It's essentially a game of chance, leaving little room for strategy. Nevertheless, it requires close attention so as not to overlook any maneuvers that eventually might prove crucial. The success rate is very low.*

Material
Two decks of 52 cards.

Opening Tableau
To form the foundation zone, remove the eight aces and the eight 2-cards and arrange them – alternating in color – in an arc. The maneuver zone is a pyramid of 15 cards, arranged like a quincunx – one card in the top row, two in the second row, three in the third row, four in the fourth row and five in the fifth row (see Tableau 172). Keep the talon face down.

Object
To complete 16 suit sequences: eight sequences from ace to king, and eight sequences from 2 to queen. Note that sequences on the ace contain cards in odd ranks; those on the 2 contain cards in even ranks. Skip by two as follows:
- A, 3, 5, 7, 9, J, K;
- 2, 4, 6, 8, 10, Q.

Play
Any available card in the maneuver zone may be moved onto its appropriate suit sequence in the foundation zone but may not be transferred back. A card is said

Tableau 172

Skip Suits Sequences

423

to be available when its lower narrow side is entirely bared. Within the maneuver zone, build ascending suit sequences by moving any available card onto another of the same suit and higher by two in rank – for example, a 6 of hearts onto an 8 of hearts, or a 3 of clubs onto a 5 of clubs. An already formed sequence may be moved as a unit. A gap must be filled at once with a card from the talon.

When there are no more possible maneuvers, start a new deal, placing cards in a quincuncial fashion below the last row and adding a card to each new row. Note that all gaps must be filled before the redeal. As you transfer cards and suit sequences over to the foundation zone, the pyramid may be truncated beyond its original shape, say, at the third row. In this case, the new row – the fourth on the pyramid – will contain only four cards.

It's when you begin drawing cards from the talon that you tempt fate. An untimely card might turn up and block a good suit sequence that you have been carefully building. Or it might create an impasse, the kind that happens when you draw, say, a king of hearts as the card to be placed upon a 9-7-5 heart sequence, especially when the other heart sequence on the ace has already been completed. One round is allowed per game. The game is successful when all eight suit sequences have been completed.

150. Cavalcade

Grandmother found this game very pleasant because it demands all the attributes of a good strategist: clarity of execution, a keen sense of anticipation, strictness of order, a memory for various series of maneuvers, the courage for calculated risk and the cunning of a fox. When the game is successful, the closing tableau looks impressive: All the jacks are in the first row, all the queens in the second and all the kings in the third – a superb parade.

Material
Two decks of 52 cards.

Opening Tableau
To form the maneuver zone, deal 24 cards face up in three rows of eight columns. Below this tableau, deal another row of eight cards to form the reserve. Keep the talon face down. As play progresses, the maneuver zone will evolve into the foundation zone.

Object
To complete the following suit sequences, skipping by three:
- Eight ascending suit sequences from 2 to jack: 2, 5, 8, J;
- Eight ascending suit sequences from 3 to queen: 3, 6, 9, Q;
- Eight ascending suit sequences from 4 to king: 4, 7, 10, K.

Play
Remove all the aces, which are dead cards, as they appear. In Tableau 173, remove the aces of spades and clubs and replace them with two cards from the talon. If an ace falls into the reserve during the deal, it, too, must be removed. The 2-cards must ultimately be in the first row, 3-cards in the second row and 4-cards in the third row. If any of these foundation cards is not in its appropriate

Tableau 173

row, it may switch rows with another so as both will be in their respective rows. For example, in Tableau 173, you may switch the 2 of spades in the second row with the 3 of spades in the first row; the 4 of spades in the first row with the 2 of diamonds in the third row; and the 3 of spades in the third row with the 4 of diamonds in the second row.

You can start building a suit sequence only after the relevant foundation card is in its appropriate row. For instance, you may not start a sequence on a 2-card if it's in the third row, or on a 3-card if it's in the first row. A card may be moved onto its appropriate rank in its sequence provided the vacancy its creates may be filled at once with an appropriate foundation card from another row or from the reserve. In Tableau 173, you may move the 6 of spades from the third row onto the 3 of spades in the second row and fill the vacancy (left by the 6 of spades) with the 4 of hearts from the reserve.

In the same way, you may move the 5 of spades onto the 2 of spades in the first row and fill the vacancy with the 2 of diamonds from the reserve. However, you may not move the 9 of spades from the third row onto the 6 of spades in the second row since there is no longer a 4-card with which to fill the resulting gap. Any other card in the tableau, but not the reserve, may be used to fill a vacancy, provided the gap created by its own removal can be filled by a foundation card from another row or the reserve. Thus, you may move the 8 of spades onto the 5 of spades in the first row and fill the vacancy with the queen of clubs, provided there's a 3 of diamonds in the reserve with which to fill the gap left by the queen of clubs.

When all possible maneuvers have been executed, draw eight new cards from the talon and place them face up upon the eight columns in the reserve. At the first opportunity, an available card from the reserve may be moved onto its appropriate rank in a suit sequence. A foundation card from the reserve – a 2, a 3 or a 4 – may only be used to fill a vacancy in its appropriate row. A gap in the reserve may only be filled during a redeal. Only one round is allowed. The game is successful when all 24 suit sequences have been completed.

Strategy

Whenever you can, avoid placing foundation cards in an irretrievable position in the reserve; as they appear, make sure they are placed so as to be available to fill vacancies. Switching foundation cards is not always an efficient maneuver, for a foundation card that is in a row other than its own may be useful for extricating another foundation card from the reserve. In Tableau 173, although the first row offers scores of easy maneuvers in order to make room for 2-cards – for example, by stacking the 5, 8 and jack of spades, and by moving the 7 and 10 of hearts onto the 4 of hearts in the third row (a maneuver made possible after the 4 of hearts has been transferred from the reserve to take the place of the 6 of spades) – the second row offers no such immediate possibilities. Thus, it is wise to delay transferring the 2 of hearts in the second row onto the first row until a 3-card turns up in the reserve with which to fill the gap left by the 2 of hearts. When that moment arrives, create a vacancy for the 2 of hearts in the first row by moving the 5 of spades onto the 2 of spades, or the 7 of hearts onto the 4 of hearts, then move the 2 of hearts into the space thus created and fill the gap in the second row with the 3-card from the reserve.

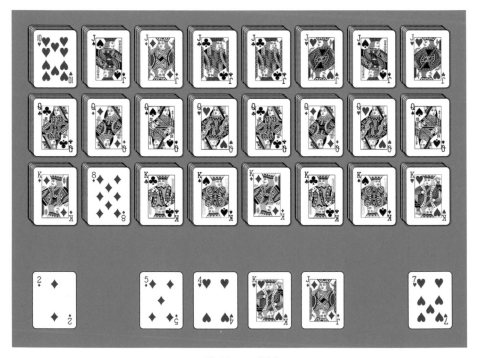

Tableau 174

Use cards from the reserve as soon as possible. For example, before starting a new deal, move the 7 and 10 of spades onto the 4 of spades, and the 7 of diamonds onto the 4 of diamonds. Watch out for reversals, or situations in which a card finds itself covering another card of the same suit and lower-ranked. Try also to avoid "mutual impasses" in which two cards block each other. Tableau 174 shows a game brought to an end by such an impasse, formed by the 10 of hearts and the 8 of diamonds. Faced with such an impasse, the only thing you can do is admit defeat.

Variant

Remove a 2, a 3 and a 4 of different suits and place them in a column. To the right of the column, deal 21 cards face up in three rows of seven columns. Play proceeds as in the original version.

151. Alternation

This uncomplicated game has a low success rate. It and Minuet *(no. 148) share the same objective, but* Alternation's *more restricted maneuver zone makes play more difficult.*

Material
Two decks of 52 cards.

Opening Tableau
In the foundation zone, set up eight spaces for an ace and a 2 of each suit as foundations on which to build suit sequences. In the maneuver zone, deal nine cards face up in three rows of three columns. Keep the talon face down.

Object
To complete eight ascending suit sequences: four on the ace and four on the 2-card. Skip by two as follows:
- A, 3, 5, 7, 9, K, J, 2, 4, 6, 8, 10, Q;
- 2, 4, 6, 8, 10, Q, A, 3, 5, 7, 9, J, K.

Play
Any available card in the maneuver zone may be moved onto its appropriate rank in the foundation zone but may not be transferred back. Turn up cards from the talon one by one, placing unplayable ones on a discard pile. A gap must be filled at once with a card from the discard pile, or, if there is none, from the talon. The top card of the discard pile must be reintroduced into play at the first opportunity. Two rounds are allowed. The game is successful when all eight suit sequences have been completed.

152. Royal Cotillion

This game is named for the closing tableau, when princes and princesses come together in great pomp and circumstance. It requires a high level of concentration so as to keep track of the various suit sequences that need to be built.

Material
Two decks of 52 cards.

Opening Tableau
To form the foundation zone, remove the eight aces from the decks and place them in two rows, each row containing all four suits. Next, remove a 2-card of each suit and place two of them at each end of the second row. In the maneuver zone, deal a reserve of 16 cards face up in two rows of eight columns. Keep the talon face down.

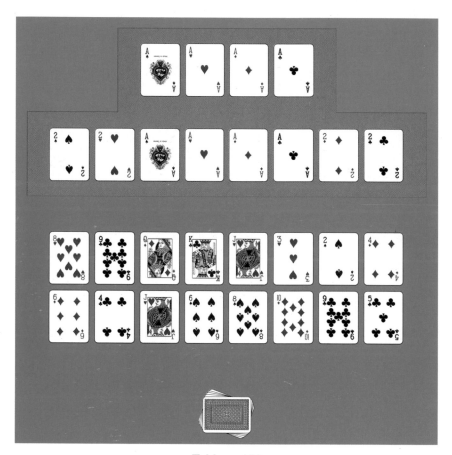

Tableau 175

Object

To complete four ascending suit sequences from ace to queen in the first row of the foundation rows: A, 2, 3, 4, 5, 6, 7, 8, 9, 10, J, Q. To complete four ascending suit sequences on the ace (up to king), in the second row, skipping by two as follows: A, 3, 5, 7, 9, J, K; and four ascending suit sequences on the 2-card (up to queen), again, skipping by two: 2, 4, 6, 8, 10, Q. The remaining four kings – called widower kings – will be distributed on each side of the four aces in the first row. Tableau 176 shows the final layout.

Tableau 176

Play

Any card in the reserve may be moved onto its appropriate rank in the foundation zone. In Tableau 175, for example, you may move the 2 of spades onto the ace of spades in the first row; the 3 of hearts onto the ace of hearts in the second row; the 4 of clubs onto the 2 of clubs; and the 4 of diamonds onto the 2 of diamonds, followed by the 6 of diamonds. A vacancy in the reserve must be filled at once with a card from the discard pile, or, if there is none, from the talon. Turn up cards from the talon one by one, placing unplayable cards upon a discard pile, the top card of which may be moved onto its appropriate rank at the first opportunity. One round is allowed per game. The remaining four kings, or widower kings, may be placed on each side of the aces in the first row in the foundation zone, but only after their counterparts have been placed upon their appropriate suit sequence in the second row. The game is successful when all 12 sequences have been completed and the four widower kings are properly placed on each side of the aces in the first row.

153. Pendulum

This game requires sustained attention, an exceptional sense of anticipation – especially when choosing the interval for building sequences – and a complete grasp of the tableau so as not to miss possible maneuvers. The game's complexity and low success rate make it a favorite of connoisseurs. Grandmother sat for hours on end in front of this curious tableau that swings constantly, leaving behind an ever changing configuration.

Material
One deck of 52 cards.

Opening Tableau
Deal four aces in a row, face up. They are the foundations upon which to build ascending suit sequences. In the maneuver zone, deal the remaining cards face up in six rows of eight columns.

Object
To complete four ascending suit sequences. You may choose whatever interval of build you wish after seeing the tableau.

Play
After inspecting the tableau, choose the interval that most favors the progression of sequences. The chosen interval must apply to all four suit sequences. As far as Tableau 177 is concerned, building by three seems to be the logical choice. Thus, the sequences will be built as follows: A, 4, 7, 10, K, 3, 6, 9, Q, 2, 5, 8, J. Only the bottom card of each column is available for play, and you may place it upon a suit sequence in the foundation zone as per the chosen interval. For example, in Tableau 177, you may move the 4 of diamonds onto the ace of diamonds, then the 4 of spades onto the ace of spades. You may also move a card onto the one

Tableau 177

directly above it in the column, provided the latter is of the same suit and three above in rank. In other words, you may build descending suit sequences as per the same chosen interval. Back to Tableau 177: You may move the 6 of spades onto the 9 of spades.

Skip Suits Sequences

You may also move a bottom card onto the card occupying either the upper left or upper right corner of the tableau, provided the contact card is of the same suit and appropriate rank. Thus, you may move the 10 of hearts onto the king of hearts in the upper left corner. Furthermore, an already formed suit sequence may be moved as a unit onto the card directly above it in the column, or onto either end card of the top row, according to the same rules regarding suit and interval. A vacant column must be filled as soon as possible and only by a bottom card of the same suit and rank as the last-wanted card in a suit sequence. In our example, since all sequences must end with a jack, only a jack can fill a vacant column.

Whenever play is blocked, swing the pendulum. The first movement must be from left to right. It consists in sliding all the cards – in rows where there are vacant spaces, and without disturbing their order – toward the right so as to leave all the vacant spaces on the opposite side, in this case, the left. The top row is not affected by the pendulum swing, since any gaps there are immediately filled. Swing to each side alternately. When all the rows have been consolidated, proceed to carry out the maneuvers made possible by the pendulum swing. (Each swing must be completed before you can tackle a new maneuver.) There's no limit to the number of swings. The game is successful when all four ascending suit sequences have been completed in the foundation zone. It fails if the pendulum swing fails to create new possibilities.

Here are some examples of the opening maneuvers for Tableau 177:
- 4 of diamonds onto ace of diamonds;
- 4 of spades onto ace of spades;
- 6 of spades onto 9 of spades;
- 10 of hearts onto king of hearts;
- 7 of diamonds onto 4 of diamonds;
- 10 of diamonds onto 7 of diamonds;
- Pendulum swing toward the right;
- 4 of hearts onto ace of hearts;
- 7 of spades onto 4 of spades;
- 10 of spades onto 7 of spades;

- King of spades onto 0 of spades;
- 7 of hearts onto 4 of hearts;
- Pendulum swing toward the left.

After six pendulum swings – three toward the right, and three toward the left – we arrive at Tableau 178.

Move the 2 and 5 of spades onto the spade sequence and swing the pendulum toward the right. Continue in this manner until the game is won or play is blocked. The game is won when all four suit sequences have been completed.

Tableau 178

Skip Suits Sequences

Strategy

Delay transferring a card to the foundation zone if you think it will be useful for advancing play in the maneuver zone. Wherever you can, avoid maneuvers that might result in two rows containing the same number of cards, for in that situation the flexibility of the pendulum swings will be sharply reduced.

CHAPTER 14

Suit Sequences With Abridged Decks

154. Jacob's Ladder

This relatively simple game has so low a success rate that only the most persistent will ever be successful.

Material

Thirteen cards of the same suit.

Opening Tableau

There's no opening tableau.

Object

To complete an ascending suit sequence from ace to king.

Play

Hold the cards face down. Turn up the first card. If it's not an ace, there's no need to go further because the game is already lost. If the first card is an ace, slide the second card beneath the packet and turn up the third card, which must be a 2. If it's not, the game fails. Continue by alternating between turning up a card and sliding the next one underneath the packet. If the sequence is broken, the game fails.

Variant

After inspecting the first card, you may decide on what kind of sequence to build: ascending or descending. Chances of success will be slightly greater as a result.

155. Royal Flushes

This game is purely a game of chance and requires little manipulation. The success rate is low, however. Still, Grandmother found it reasonably charming.

Material
A deck of 24 major cards, from 10 to ace.

Opening Tableau
Deal the cards face down in four rows of five columns. Turn up the top-right and bottom-right cards.

Tableau 179

Object

To form four royal flushes.

Play

The game is successful when you will have completed, from left to right, four ascending suit sequences from 10 to ace in the following order: spades in the first row, hearts in the second row, diamonds in the third row and clubs in the fourth row.

Select one of the two face-up cards and transfer it onto its appropriate flush. In Tableau 179, suppose we start with the jack of hearts, which we move to its appropriate place – at row 2, column 2. We then turn up the card at that spot, let's say it's a 10 of clubs, which we then move to its own space – row 4, column 1. Continue in this manner until the game is won or play is blocked.

Various scenarios may present themselves:

1. If the two face-up cards in the opening tableau are the ace of spades in the first row and the ace of clubs in the fourth row, the game fails right from the start since no other maneuver is possible.

2. Play is blocked right from the start if, as the first maneuver, you turn up the ace of spades in the first row or the ace of clubs in the last row. However, you have a second chance with the second face-up card, which, according to Tableau 179, is the king of spades.

3. Chances are you may turn up an ace, which must then go into the space occupied by the second face-up card in the opening tableau. In this case, this second face-up card is considered as any other face-down card and played accordingly. In Tableau 179, if you turn up an ace of clubs, put it in the space of the king of spades and continue play with the latter. The inconvenience is that you no longer have a second chance to continue if you bump into an impasse.

If play is blocked again and no further maneuver is available, deal the cards again, face down. This time, perhaps each card will be in its appropriate place. But that's wishful thinking, if you ask me.

156. Amazons

This patience depends entirely on chance, and as such is unappealing. It requires a great deal of manipulation, but little else.

Material

A deck of 52 cards, stripped of kings, 2s, 3s, 4s and 5s.

Opening Tableau

Plan a row of four spaces in the foundation zone. In the maneuver zone, deal four cards face up to form the reserve. Keep the talon face down.

Object

To complete four suit sequences from 6 to queen.

Play

As 6-cards appear, move them to the foundation zone, from left to right. Turn up four cards from the talon and place them atop the four cards in the reserve. Any available card in the reserve may be moved onto its appropriate rank in the foundation zone, provided it's in the same column as its suit sequence. This rule does not apply to queen-cards, which may go onto their appropriate sequence, regardless of their column. After each deal of four cards, move available cards onto their suitable rank in the foundation zone. Whenever play is blocked, deal a new batch of four cards and continue building sequences in this manner. Gaps in the reserve are filled only at redeal time.

Here are the seven deals during a hypothetical round:

First deal: 7 of spades, queen of clubs, 8 of hearts, 9 of diamonds, no 6-card: play is blocked.

Second deal: 10 of diamonds, queen of hearts, queen of diamonds, 10 of spades: play is blocked.

Third deal: 8 of spades, jack of spades, queen of spades, 8 of diamonds: play is blocked.

Fourth deal: 6 of clubs, 6 of hearts, 9 of hearts, 7 of diamonds: place the 6 of clubs in the first column and the 6 of hearts in the second column.

Fifth deal: 6 of diamonds, jack of clubs, 6 of spades, jack of hearts: place the 6 of diamonds in the third column and the 6 of spades in the fourth column.

Sixth deal: 7 of clubs, 10 of clubs, 9 of spades, 9 of clubs: place the 7 of clubs upon the 6 of clubs since it's in the same column.

Seventh deal: 10 of hearts, 8 of clubs, jack of diamonds, 7 of hearts: you cannot place the 8 of clubs upon the 7 of clubs, nor the 7 of hearts upon the 6 of hearts, since neither cards are in the same column as their foundation.

To proceed to a new round, stack the cards in the fourth column onto those in the third column, then this pile onto the cards in the second column, and finally the entire pile onto the cards in the first column. Turn the pack over and deal again in batches of four cards. There's no limit to the number of rounds. The game fails when an entire round goes by without producing a single possible maneuver. It is successful when all four suit sequences from 6 to queen have been completed.

157. Shadows

Complex rules and surprising combinations are what attracts afi-cionados to this game. Its success rate is very low: once out of every 50 attempts, according to Grandmother. No matter how attentive you may be or how carefully you plan your moves, chance still takes a hand in this game, as in all of them, and often plays havoc with the tableau.

Material
Two decks of 52 cards.

Opening Tableau
Deal 32 cards face up in four rows of eight columns. Keep the talon face down. The foundation and maneuver zones are one.

Object
To complete four ascending suit sequences from 6 to king.

Play
Remove from the tableau all same-suit pairs of minor cards – aces to 5s – and discard them. Note that ace counts as one. Thus, in Tableau 180, discard the 3s of hearts, 4s of clubs and aces of spades. In the tableau, cards higher than 5 are moved strictly onto their appropriate rank in a suit sequence – their one and only destination. Suit sequences are built from left to right – the 6s occu-pying the first column, and the kings, the last column. Should you stumble upon the "shadow," or double, of a card that has already been placed in its suit sequence, put the shadow card in the discard pile. For example, in Tableau 180, if you decide to fill the gap created by the removal of the 3 of hearts with the 10 of spades in the second row, discard its shadow – that is, the other 10 of spades in the fourth row.

Suit Sequences With Abridged Decks

Tableau 180

You must determine the suit for each row. This choice is of paramount importance since it often influences the outcome. In order to make a wise decision, inspect the tableau carefully and locate cards that happen to be in their appropriate column. In Tableau 180, the 7 and 8 of diamonds are in the second and third columns of the fourth row, making it logical to "assign" the diamond suit to this row. This choice may not necessarily be the best, for other considerations may impose a different option – the potential of a mutual impasse, for example.

After removing the 10 of spades, fill the resulting gap with the 9 of spades. This maneuver creates a gap at row 2, column 1, which may be filled by the 6 of spades, making it logical to assign the spade suit to the second row. Now that you've got two suits assigned, it's important to note that if you decide to assign the heart suit to the third row, you will create a mutual impasse between the 10 of diamonds at row 3, column 2, and the 7 of hearts at row 4, column 5, for each currently occupies the other's supposed space and a switch is virtually impossible. And so the heart suit must go to the first row, and the club suit to the third row. Thus the final suit arrangement is: hearts in the first row, spades in the second, clubs in the third and diamonds in the fourth. You will note that sometimes it's better to wait until the game is played out somewhat before assigning a suit to each row.

When all possible maneuvers have been executed, fill all the gaps with cards from the talon and proceed to move cards as before. If the tableau contains no other available cards, turn up a card from the talon. If the latter is a shadow of a minor card in the tableau, discard both. If it's a shadow of a major card that has already been placed in its appropriate spot, discard this shadow too. However, if a major card turns up from the talon whose double hasn't yet reached its final destination in the tableau, put this card in a discard pile for the time being. (It may be reintroduced into play at the first opportunity.)

Whenever a maneuver results in a gap, fill it with the top card from the discard pile, or, if there is none, from the talon. Only one round is allowed per game. The game is successful when all four ascending suit sequences from 6 to king have been completed. Chances are the game will be won before all the cards from the talon are turned up, although usually the last card is the one that decides the outcome.

158. Boomerang

This game is worthy of its name: Suit sequences change direction and return to their point of departure. The game requires careful attention and a keen sense of anticipation.

Material
Two decks of 52 cards, stripped of 2s, 3s, 4s, 5s and 6s.

Opening Tableau
The foundation zone comprises four spaces in which to build four suit sequences. In the maneuver zone, deal 12 cards face up in three rows of four columns. Keep the talon face down.

Object
To complete four double suit sequences in the following order: 7, 8, 9, 10, J, Q, K, A, K, Q, J, 10, 9, 8, 7, A.

Play
Move a 7-card of each suit, as they appear, to the foundation zone. Any available card in the maneuver zone may be moved onto its appropriate rank in the foundation zone, but once moved, it may not be transferred back. In the maneuver zone, build ascending or descending suit sequences by moving an available card onto another of the same suit and next-higher or next-lower in rank. However, the direction of a sequence must be maintained until it is moved out of its space.

You can move only one card at a time. An already formed suit sequence may not be moved as a unit. Given the prescribed direction of suit sequences, an ace may be moved onto a king or a 7 of the same suit, but only a king may be placed upon an ace. A vacant space must be filled immediately by a card from the talon, never one from another space. Draw cards from the talon one by one, filling vacancies or placing suitable cards upon their appropriate sequence – either in the foundation or maneuver zone. The game fails when cards can no longer be played. It is won when all four suit sequences in the foundation zone have been completed.

Strategy

It's important to create as many vacancies as possible. To this end, start with the highest-ranked cards when building down, and with the lowest-ranked cards when building up. For example, if the tableau offers a jack, a 10, a 9 and an 8 of hearts, cover the jack with the 10, then the 10 with the 9, then the 9 with the 8. If you started by covering the 9 with the 8, you would be able to vacate only one space instead of three. You must always start with descending sequences, for they are the first to go up – by inversion – to the foundation zone. In a given space, the best way to start a suit sequence is by placing a king upon an ace. Once a particular card has been placed upon a sequence, regardless of the zone, you may safely start an ascending sequence with its shadow card.

Avoid building "shadow" or identical sequences for they may create inextricable impasses. Instead, use shadow cards to build reverse sequences. Sometimes, though, the tableau is such that you must build temporary shadow sequences just to advance play. In this case, watch the movement of the cards carefully so as to spot the right moment to reverse the sequences.

Variant

Strip the decks of all cards from 2 to 8, inclusively. Build suit sequences in the following order: 9, 10, J, Q, K, A, K, Q, J, 10, 9, A. Deal 10 cards in two rows of five columns. Play proceeds according to the same rules.

159. Czarina

Czarina boasts a colorful and grandiose tableau. I saw Grandmother play this game only once, on a Sunday afternoon after she had commandeered the long kitchen table. As the entire family looked on, Grandmother's sense of drama got the best of her and she put on quite a show. Unless you own a very big table, don't even contemplate this one.

Material

Four decks of 52 cards.

Opening Tableau

To form the foundation zone, put all the eight black queens in a pile, topped by the queen of clubs – the "czarina." Place the eight red jacks in a circle around the czarina. Those are her "bodyguards." Both queens and jacks are dead cards – figureheads really, with no role whatsoever during play. On the jacks' periphery, place the eight black aces, and on the aces' periphery, place the eight red kings. These aces and kings are foundation cards upon which to build suit sequences.

The maneuver zone comprises four rows of 12 cards each, face up. Form the first two rows with only red cards, placing the black cards in a discard pile, then form the next two rows with only black cards, placing the red ones in a second discard pile. The red rows represent the marine, the black rows, the army. Keep the talon face down.

Object

To complete eight ascending black suit sequences from ace to king (on the inner circle), and eight descending red suit sequences from king to ace (on the outer circle). Since the black queens and red jacks (placed in the core of the tableau) have been discarded from play, the ascending suit sequences skip from jack to king, and the descending suit sequences skip from queen to the 10-card.

Tableau 181

<u>Suit Sequences With Abridged Decks</u>

- Black suit sequences: A, 2, 3, 4, 5, 6, 7, 8, 9, 10, J, K.
- Red suit sequences: K, Q, 10, 9, 8, 7, 6, 5, 4, 3, 2, A.

Play

Move suitable cards from the maneuver zone over to the foundation zone. Cards are moved by mixed couples as defined above: black 2 (onto the inner circle) with red queen (onto the outer circle): black 3 with red 10; black 4 with red 9, and so on. As gaps are created, fill them with respective cards from the two discard piles, or the talon, if the discard piles are exhausted: red cards in the red rows, and black cards in the black rows. If cards in the maneuver zone can no longer be played to the foundation zone, form mixed couples within the maneuver zone by moving cards onto one another, according to the same rule cited above: black 10 onto red 3, or black jack onto red 2, and so on. These couples will eventually be moved onto their respective suit sequences in the foundation zone.

When all possible maneuvers have been executed, draw cards from the talon one by one, placing them upon their respective discard piles: black cards on the black pile, and red cards on the red pile. These cards become available for play only after they have been moved into vacancies in the maneuver zone: red cards in the so-called marine, and black cards in the army. The game is successful when all eight ascending black suit sequences and eight descending red suit sequences have been completed. It fails when vacancies can no longer be created in either the army or the marine. Tableau 182 shows a successful game.

Strategy

When matching mixed couples for later use, make sure you maintain some balance between the army and the marine by alternating between black-upon-red and red-upon-black maneuvers. Whenever a particular suit sequence is blocked, give priority to cards of that suit. For example, if a diamond sequence is blocked and you have a choice of placing a 5 of diamonds upon an 8 of clubs, or the 8 of clubs upon the 5 of diamonds, opt for the former maneuver. Also, avoid matching same-suit cards: say, if you match three 9s of spades with three 4s of

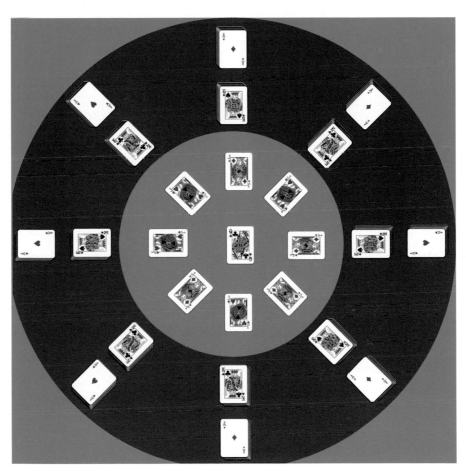

Tableau 182

hearts, you risk blocking the game by depriving the diamond and club cards of their eventual partners. A better approach is to reserve a 9 of spades for a 4 of diamonds, or a 4 of hearts for a 9 of clubs.

160. Eugenia

The secret of this game lies in the art of stalling. You must learn to bide your time patiently while preparing various routes through the maneuver zone for the eventual "conquest" of the foundation zone.

Material
Four decks of 52 cards, stripped of 2s, 3s, 4s, 5s and 6s.

Opening Tableau
In the maneuver zone, deal 49 cards in seven rows of seven columns. Cards in odd rows – that is, 1, 3, 5, 7 – are face up, the others are face down. To form the foundation zone, remove the 7-cards as they appear and place them in two columns, one on each side of the maneuver zone. They are the foundation cards upon which to build ascending suit sequences. Keep the talon face down.

Object
To complete 16 ascending suit sequences from 7 to ace.

Play
In the maneuver zone, build descending runs of alternating colors by moving a face-up card onto another of opposite color and next in rank. An already formed run may be moved as a unit. Only a bottom card may be moved onto its suit sequence in the foundation zone. When a face-down card finds itself at the bottom of a column, turn it up for play.

Draw cards from the talon one by one, putting those that do not fit in the maneuver zone onto the discard pile. Except for 7s, cards from the talon may not be played directly to the foundation zone but must first go through the maneuver zone. A vacant column may only be filled by an ace at the bottom of a col-

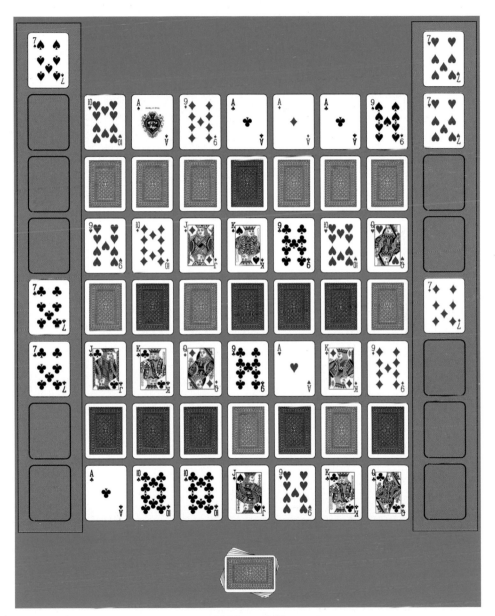

Tableau 183

Suit Sequences With Abridged Decks

umn, or an available ace from the discard pile. The game is won when all 16 suit sequences have been completed.

Strategy

Give priority to runs in the maneuver zone. Build suit sequences in the foundation zone strictly as a means to unblock a game. Aim at creating vacant columns so as to move any aces – single or along with their runs – that may block other cards in a column, or in the discard pile. Wherever possible, avoid blocking lower-ranked cards in the discard pile. This may be achieved by retaining middle-ranked cards in the maneuver onto which to transfer those lower-ranked cards. Since only a bottom card may be moved to the foundation zone, it's preferable to build sequences at the bottom of columns.

CHAPTER 15

Various Runs and Sequences

161. Four Cantons

This game gets its name from the opening tableau. Though simple, it takes an acute memory to remember the order of cards in the discard pile.

Material
One deck of 52 cards.

Opening Tableau
Remove the four aces from the deck and place them in a square. They are the foundations upon which to build ascending sequences of the same color, red upon red, black upon black, regardless of suit. Place a card at each of the four corners of the square, to start the four discard piles. Keep the talon face down.

Object
To complete four ascending same-color sequences.

Play
Turn up cards from the talon four at a time, placing them atop each of the four discard piles. After each deal, move suitable cards from the discard pile onto their appropriate sequence in the foundation zone. You're allowed two rounds per game. When the first round is over, gather all the discard piles and reshuffle the cards to form a new talon. Deal cards in batches of four as before. The game is won when all four ascending sequences have been completed. It fails if after two rounds, one or more cards still remain in the discard piles.

Tableau 184

Strategy

Wherever possible, place a discarded card upon a higher-ranked card. If this maneuver is not feasible, avoid placing a card in a pile that already contains another card of the same rank. If you unwittingly block four same-rank cards with a higher-ranked one, the game is doomed.

Various Runs and Sequences

162. Pons Asinorum

This is a rather routine game with a fairly high success rate. Of interest only to beginners.

Material

One deck of 52 cards.

Opening Tableau

Deal 30 cards in a row of 10 columns. Only the top card of each column is face up. Keep the talon face down.

Object

To complete four descending runs of alternating colors from king to ace.

Play

Play proceeds strictly in the maneuver zone. An available card may be moved onto another next in rank and of opposite color, red on black, or black on red. You may also move an already formed run. A vacant column may only be filled by a king, single or with its sequence. A king may not be placed upon an ace. When a face-down card is bared, turn it up at once for play. Whenever play is blocked, draw cards from the talon one by one, placing those that are unplayable in the discard pile, the top card of which may be reintroduced into play at the first opportunity. Only one round is allowed per game. The game is won when all four descending runs have been completed.

163. Red and Black

The high success rate of this easy game will certainly appeal to beginners.

Material

Two decks of 52 cards.

Opening Tableau

Remove the eight aces from the decks and lay them in a row in the foundation zone. In the maneuver zone, lay a row of eight face-up cards. Keep the talon face down.

Object

To complete eight ascending runs of alternating colors from ace to king.

Play

An available card in the maneuver zone may be moved onto its appropriate rank in the foundation zone but may not be transferred back. You may also overlap an available card with another, provided the contact card is of alternate color and next in rank. Only one card at a time may be moved. An already formed run cannot be moved as a unit. Draw cards from the talon one by one, placing unplayable ones in a discard pile, the top card of which may be reintroduced into play at the first opportunity. A vacant column in the maneuver zone must be filled at once by a card from the discard pile, or from the talon if there's no discard pile. Only one round is allowed per game. The game is won when all eight runs have been completed.

164. Blondes and Brunettes

This game is named for the alternating color sequences to be built: red on black, black on red. It calls for great concentration, as well as a keen sense of anticipation, a phenomenal memory and an eerie flair so as to beat all odds. It was one of Grandmother's favourites.

Material
Two decks of 52 cards.

Opening Tableau
Set up eight spaces for foundation cards upon which to build sequences. In the maneuver zone, deal a row of 10 face-up cards to form the reserve. These cards are overlapped so that the last one to the right is the first available for play. Below the reserve, deal three cards face up, to start the maneuver zone. Keep the talon face down.

Object
To complete eight ascending sequences of alternating colors (circular, if necessary).

Play
Among the three face-up cards, choose one (or two, if both are of the same rank) that will determine the rank upon which to build the eight sequences. Transfer this card to the foundation zone. In Tableau 185, for example, let's choose the king of hearts. Don't select the queen of hearts because two other queen-cards are buried deep in the reserve; nor the 5 of diamonds, which, as the foundation card, would block the reserve for an indeterminate length of time since the first available card for play in the reserve – the 4 of clubs – will become the last card needed in a sequence in the foundation zone. Draw seven new cards from the talon and place them, face up, next to the two remaining cards. We now arrive at Tableau 186.

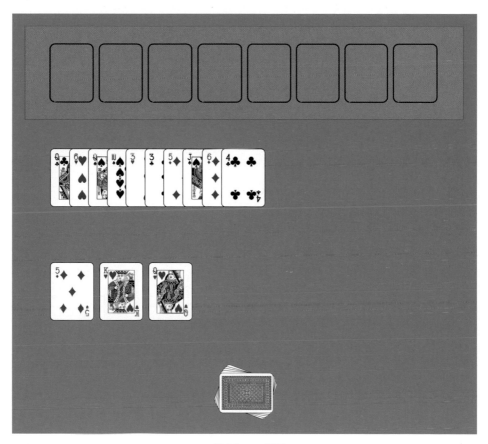

Tableau 185

As they appear, place the remaining foundation cards in the foundation zone. Cards from the reserve can only be played – one at a time – onto their appropriate rank in the foundation zone. Within the maneuver zone, build descending sequences by moving an available card onto another of opposite color and next in rank, the lower card slighly overlapping its upper neighbor. Available cards in the maneuver zone, too, may be moved onto their appropriate rank, alternating in color, in the foundation zone. Cards may be moved only one at a time. An already formed sequence may not be moved as a unit.

Various Runs and Sequences

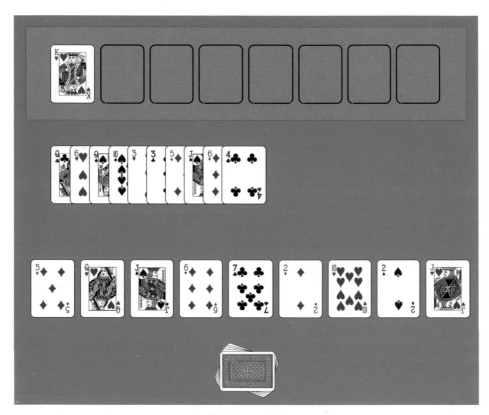

Tableau 186

A vacant column may only be filled by a card from the discard pile or the talon, and never by a card from the reserve or from another column. Turn up cards from the talon one by one, placing unplayable ones in the discard pile, the top card of which is always available and may be introduced into play at the first opportunity. One round is allowed per game. After 12 maneuvers, we arrive at Tableau 187.

The game is won when all eight ascending sequences have been completed. It fails if play is irrevocably blocked, which happens most often at the very end of a game.

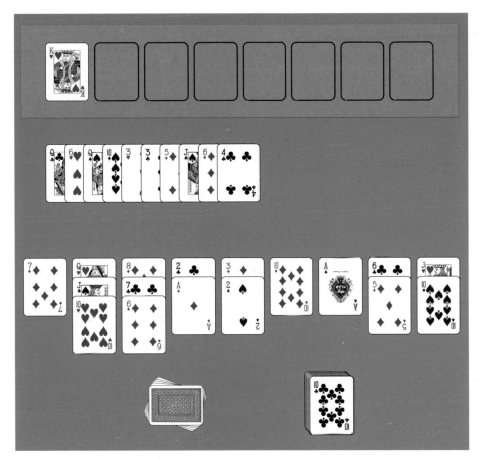

Tableau 187

Strategy

The selection of the foundation card is, without a doubt, the most important maneuver. When choosing among the three face-up cards, consider the two following factors:

1. Avoid choosing a rank whose cards are buried deep in the reserve. For example, don't choose a 6 when other 6-cards are blocked by, say, an 8, a 10 and a jack in the reserve.

2. Choose a rank that will help extricate cards from the reserve in reverse sequence – a situation that occurs when one or several lower-ranked cards block the one first needed to build a sequence. Suppose a red jack is buried under five other cards in the reserve, including a black 8. If your foundation card is a red 9, you will need the red jack before the black 8. Most of the time, a subtle strategy can help form an inverted sequence, thus solving the problem.

It's important to empty the reserve as soon as possible. Build sequences in the foundation zone only as a means of releasing cards from the reserve. In particular, try to save or create vacancies for cards that may block other cards for any length of time in the reserve. When building descending sequences, consider the following strategies:

- Wherever possible, start with the end-of-sequence cards;
- Avoid blocking cards that you will need almost right away;
- Envisage various moves for available cards;
- Avoid long sequences;
- Vacate columns in order to reintroduce cards in the discard pile into play.

165. British Solitaire

This colorful game calls for an acute sense of anticipation, as well as absolute attention and a keen memory. The success rate is relatively high, making the game a favorite among amateurs. Grandmother liked it.

Material
One deck of 52 cards.

Opening Tableau
Set up four spaces in the foundation zone for sequences. In the maneuver zone, deal 24 cards face up in eight fans of three cards each. Within each fan, the right-hand card overlaps the one in the center, the latter, in turn, overlaps the left-hand card. If a king turns up, slide it underneath the other two cards. Below the eight fans, deal three cards face up as the reserve. Keep the talon face down.

Object
To complete four ascending sequences from ace to king.

Play
As they appear, move the aces onto the foundation zone. For example, in Tableau 188, transfer the aces of diamonds and hearts. Any available card must be moved onto its appropriate rank in the foundation zone and may not be transferred back. Here, move the 2 of hearts onto an ace, followed by the 3 of diamonds. Cards are moved only one at a time. In the maneuver zone, you may build descending sequences by moving an available card onto another next lower in rank, regardless of suit or color. However, a fan can never contain more than three cards.

Thus, in Tableau 188, with the aces freed, the jack of hearts cannot be moved onto the queen of clubs, but the 10 of spades can go onto the jack of hearts. Since

Various Runs and Sequences

Tableau 188

suitable cards must be transferred to the foundation zone, proceed with the following moves: 3 of diamonds onto 2 of hearts; 6 of hearts onto 7 of clubs; 4 and 5 of clubs onto 3 of diamonds, followed by 6 of hearts, then 7 and 8 of clubs; 9 of clubs from the reserve onto 8 of clubs, followed by 10 of spades, jack of hearts and queen of clubs; 2 of diamonds onto an ace, followed by 3 of hearts. We have now exhausted both the reserve and a fan. You may reconstitute the exhausted fan, although it's more useful to empty the reserve.

The reserve comprises three columns. Any available card at the bottom of a column may be moved onto a sequence in the foundation zone, or onto a fan in the maneuver zone, provided the contact card is next in rank. However, a card from a fan may not be moved onto a card in the reserve. Within the reserve, you may not move a card from one column onto another. When all possible maneuvers have been executed, draw three cards from the talon and place them upon each of the three columns in the reserve. Carry out maneuvers between these three-card deals so as to keep the reserve to a minimum of cards, especially if king-cards are yet to turn up. A vacant column is filled only at redeal time. Only one round is allowed per game. The game is won when all four ascending sequences have been completed.

Strategy

Right from the start, inspect the opening tableau and locate all inverted sequences, that is, situations where a minor card finds itself blocked by higher-ranked cards, and anticipate ways to clear these impasses. Sometimes, it's imperative to build a sequence in the foundation zone as soon as possible in order to remove a major card that stands in the way of a minor card. When you have a choice between a card from a fan and another from the reserve, it's preferable to opt for the latter, unless you need to extricate a minor card from the fan. If you must choose between two fans, choose the one that will help clear an impasse or that will set off the longest series of maneuvers.

166. Quadriga

This game is another of those classics so favored by experienced players. It requires a keen memory for the position of various cards in the discard piles, and some degree of foresight so you can place cards in such a way as to be easily retrievable for subsequent play. Needless to say, the success rate is low.

Material
One deck of 52 cards.

Opening Tableau
Remove the four aces and place them in the foundation zone. Deal a row of four cards to start four discard piles. Keep the talon face down.

Object
To complete four ascending sequences from ace to king.

Play
Draw four cards at a time from the talon, placing them upon each of the four discard piles in any order you choose. Keep in mind that it's here that chance may play tricks on you. Suppose that the maneuver zone starts with the jack of diamonds, the 3 of clubs, the queen of spades and the 8 of hearts. And suppose that the next deal produces a 10-card, which you place upon the jack; a 5, which you place upon the 8; a 9, which goes onto the queen; and, finally, a king – a card you might need before long – which has nowhere else to go but onto the 3. After each four-card deal, proceed to move all available cards onto their appropriate rank in the foundation zone. Cards may not be moved from one discard pile onto another. The game is won when all four sequences have been completed.

Strategy

When putting cards on the discard piles, aim at placing them atop higher-ranked cards. Avoid placing two same-rank cards in the same discard pile. Particularly, avoid blocking several cards of the same rank under a higher-ranked card. Bear in mind that chance has a hand in this game, as in all others, and that the afore-mentioned precautions are not always possible.

Variant

As they appear, deposit the aces in the foundation zone. This will make the game more difficult to play.

167. Lord Whittle

Grandmother claimed to have inherited this game from an old aunt who immigrated to England to marry a certain Lord Whittle with whom she had fallen madly in love. The game depends almost entirely on chance. Only rarely does the player feel the need to resort to strategy; for example, when he or she has a choice between two or three same-rank cards to move from the maneuver zone to the foundation zone. The game's low success rate – once every 50 attempts, according to Grandmother – is what makes it appealing to players who like beating the odds.

Material
One deck of 52 cards.

Opening Tableau
Remove the four aces from the deck and place them face up as foundations on which to build sequences. In the maneuver zone, deal four cards face up in a row. Keep the talon face down.

Object
To complete four ascending sequences from ace to king.

Play
Any available card must be moved onto its appropriate rank in the foundation zone; once moved it may not be transferred back. The only card movement is that from the maneuver zone to the foundation zone. No sequence of any kind is to be built in the maneuver zone. When cards can no longer be played to the foundation zone, deal four new cards, placing them in each of the four columns. Do not interrupt a deal in order to trans-

fer cards to the foundation zone – these maneuvers can only be carried out between deals.

If the entire talon has been dealt and cards remain the maneuver zone – which is often the case – choose a pile and deal its cards, three at a time, onto the three remaining piles. Between deals, transfer cards to the foundation zone as before. Repeat with a second discard pile, then with a third. In the end, there will remain only the last-chance pile. The game fails if you cannot play all the cards to the foundation zone. It is won when all four sequences have been completed.

168. Tree Frog

Play requires sustained attention and a sharp sense of anticipation. Unfortunately, chance often has the nasty habit of turning the best thought-out plans upside down. Success is, therefore, difficult to come by.

Material
Two decks of 52 cards.

Opening Tableau
Plan eight spaces for the aces, on which you will build sequences. In the maneuver zone, set up a reserve pile of 13 cards, the top card of which is face up. Set up a row of five spaces for discard piles. Keep the talon face down. As the game unfolds, the tableau will slowly take shape.

Object
To complete eight ascending sequences from ace to king.

Play
Build ascending sequences in the foundation zone with available cards from the reserve or the discard piles, regardless of color. Turn up cards from the talon one by one, placing those that cannot be played to the foundation zone upon each of the five discard columns. Tableau 189 shows a game in progress, after some 10 cards have been drawn from the talon. Only one round is allowed per game. The game is won when all eight sequences have been completed.

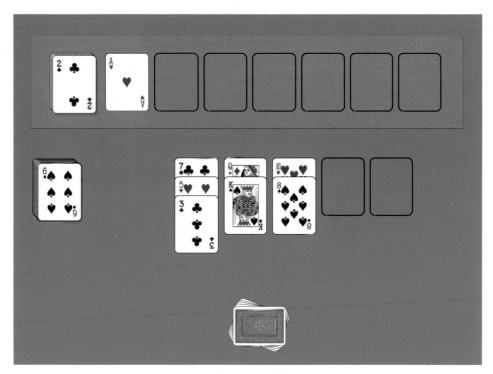

Tableau 189

Strategy

Reserve at least one discard column for court cards (kings, queens and jacks), which are among the last-wanted cards in a sequence. Within the discard columns, build as many descending sequences as possible, for they are easily transferrable over to the foundation zone. Avoid piling same-rank cards in the same column. Due to an unlucky draw, suppose you have no choice but to cover a 5-card with a 9-card. Later, it will certainly be risky to place a 4-card upon this 9-card, especially if you don't know the position of the other 4-cards in the talon. And it will be sheer madness to pile all 4-cards in the same column.

Various Runs and Sequences

Variants

1. Limit the number of cards in the reserve to 12, instead of 13.
2. Another variant allows you to transfer at least one ace of your choice onto the foundation zone during a redeal. If no ace turns up, choose one from the talon.

169. Courtesans

The name Courtesans *refers to the queen-cards, which play a leading role in this game. You need to pay close attention so as not to miss opportunities. Its success rate, fairly high in the original version, diminishes considerably in the variants.*

Material
Two decks of 52 cards.

Opening Tableau
To form the foundation zone, set up eight spaces for 6-cards and eight spaces for 5-cards. These are the foundations on which to build sequences. To form the maneuver zone, deal a queen-card, face up. This zone will slowly take shape as play unfolds.

Object
To complete eight ascending sequences from 6 to jack, and eight descending sequences from 5 to king.

Play
Turn up cards from the talon one by one and place them upon the queen-card to start a column – the lower card overlapping its upper neighbor. As they appear, remove the 5s and 6s. Each time a new queen-card turns up, use it to start a new column. Any available card in the maneuver zone may be played to its appropriate rank in the foundation zone, regardless of color, either upon an ascending sequence on the 6 or a descending sequence on the 5. For example, if a 5-card is already in the foundation zone, you may place a 4-card on top of it. However, you may also decide to keep that 4 in the maneuver zone for as long as you deem it useful. When a queen-card becomes available, you may place upon it any available card you choose from the maneuver zone. You may move only one card at

Various Runs and Sequences

a time. Tableau 190 shows a game in progress after some 20 cards have been drawn from the talon.

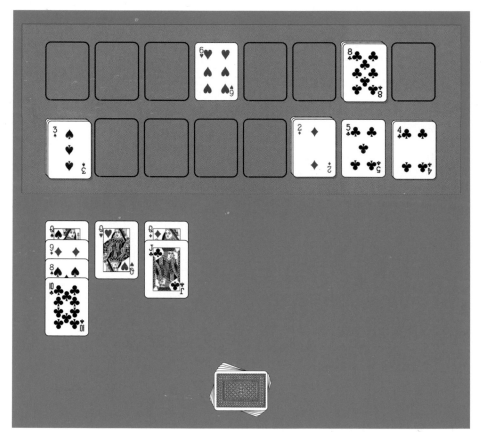

Tableau 190

The queen of hearts has just been uncovered by the removal of the 8 of clubs. You may thus transfer the 10 of clubs there in order to release the 8 and 9 cards that precede it. When the talon has been exhausted, continue to transfer cards over to the foundation zone. Only one round is allowed per game. The game is won when all 16 sequences have been completed.

Variants

1. You may only place as many 5s and 6s in the foundation zone as there are queens in the maneuver zone. For example, if the fourth 5-card appears and so far only three queens have turned up, you must keep this 5-card in the maneuver zone and place it in the column started by the first queen to turn up in the maneuver zone.

2. Another variant makes things even more difficult, suggesting that any 5 and 6 be placed in the foundation zone only after its same-suit queen has turned up in the maneuver zone. For example, if you draw a 5 of clubs from the talon, and the queen of clubs hasn't yet appeared, you must place this 5 of clubs in the column started by the last queen to turn up in the maneuver zone. These cards will be easily retrievable if the game unfolds favorably.

170. Precedence

Grandmother claimed that she invented this game. It requires a fair amount of attention so as not to miss opportunities. But since it's essentially a game of chance, Precedence *calls for neither calculation nor farsightedness.*

Material
Two decks of 52 cards.

Opening Tableau
Remove any king and place it in the foundation zone. Set up seven other spaces for other foundation cards on which to build sequences. Keep the talon face down. Note that the tableau will slowly take shape as play unfolds.

Object
To complete eight descending circular sequences – ace on 2 and king on ace – based on eight selected foundations, regardless of suit: from king to ace, queen to king, jack to queen, 10 to jack, 9 to 10, 8 to 9, 7 to 8, and 6 to 7.

Play
Turn up cards from the talon one by one. To the right of the king-card, on the same row, place the remaining seven foundation cards as they turn up. The basic rule of the game is that no sequence may be built faster than the one preceding it. The first card to be placed is a queen, which goes onto the king. You must wait for the second queen to turn up to start the second sequence. Then you must wait for enough jacks to turn up to build on both the king's and queen's sequences before starting a sequence on the jack; then for enough 10s to appear for the sequences on the king, queen and jack before starting the sequence on the 10, and so on.

It's in your interest to build the sequence on the king as far down as possible because it opens up the way for later sequences. Thus, bring this sequence to, say, the 7-card before starting the sequence on the queen, which you may also consider building to 7. Suits and colors are irrelevant. Unplayable cards from the talon are put in a discard pile, the top card of which may be introduced into play at the first opportunity. Tableau 191 shows a game in progress after some 20 cards have been drawn from the talon.

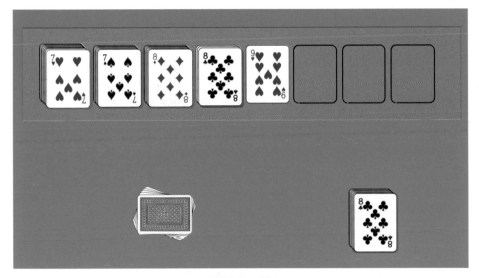

Tableau 191

As you can see, the sequences on the king and queen have been built to 7, those on the jack and 10 to 8, and that on the 9-card has just been started. You may now move the 8 of clubs from the discard pile onto the 9 of hearts and, when the next 8-card turns up, use it to start the sequence on the 8. Three rounds are allowed per game. At each new round, take the discard pile in hand, and, without shuffling the cards, turn them over and draw cards one by one. The game is won when all eight sequences have been completed.

Various Runs and Sequences

171. Stratagem

This one is custom-made for sly foxes. Grandmother gladly took it on anytime. Success depends more on proven flair than skillful calculation.

Material
Two decks of 52 cards.

Opening Tableau
The foundation zone is comprised of two separated columns of four spaces each, on which you will build sequences. Place a card face up in the first space of the left-hand column. This card determines the rank of all eight foundation cards. Between the two columns is the maneuver zone, which comprises a chamber of 12 face-up cards – arranged in three rows of four columns – and a reserve pile of 13 cards. The top card of the reserve pile is face up, the others are face down. Keep the talon face down.

Object
To complete eight ascending circular sequences – ace on king, 2 on ace, and so on. As per Tableau 192, suit sequences will run from 5 to 4.

Play
You must wait until the first sequence is completed before placing the second foundation card upon its base. Only then can other foundation cards be transferred to the foundation zone from the maneuver zone, the discard pile or the talon. To fill the third base, however, you need not wait until the second sequence is completed; this rule only applies to the first sequence. Note that the top card of the reserve pile may be moved onto a sequence in the foundation zone and replaced by the card directly underneath.

In the maneuver zone, build descending sequences by moving an available card onto another next in rank, regardless of color. You may move only one card

Tableau 192

at a time. An already formed sequence may not be moved as a unit. If a foundation card turns up before the first sequence is completed, it may be used to fill a vacant space, although it may not host another card. If there is no vacant space, the card goes to the discard pile. In other words, a foundation card cannot be used for building sequences in the maneuver zone.

So long as the first sequence is not completed, a vacant space can only be filled by a foundation card drawn from the discard pile or the talon. Once the sequence is completed, it can be filled by any card from the discard pile or the talon but never by a card from the maneuver zone.

Draw cards from the talon one by one, placing suitable ones either in the foundation zone or the maneuver zone. Unplayable cards are put in the discard pile, the top card of which may be reintroduced into play at the first opportunity. Only one round is allowed per game. The game is won when all eight sequences have been completed.

Strategy

It's obvious that the sooner you complete the first sequence the better, since it's the only way you can start building other sequences. Use the reserve as much as possible, for crucial cards may be locked in there. You don't have to fill vacancies at once, so wait instead for a soon-to-be-useful card to turn up.

172. Propeller

Named for the shape of the opening tableau, Propeller *requires a fair amount of attention and a keen sense of anticipation. The success rate is relatively low. It's also called* Windmill.

Material
Two decks of 52 cards.

Opening Tableau
Remove any ace from the deck and place it in the center of the tableau. This is the first foundation. Draw eight face-up cards, placing two each above and below the ace, forming a column, and two cards on each side of the ace, forming a row. The perpendicular lines represent the propeller's blades – the maneuver zone. Move any four kings as they turn up, regardless of color, into the angles between the blades. The kings, along with the ace in the center, are the five foundations on which to build sequences. Keep the talon face down.

Object
To complete an ascending circular sequence of 52 cards – starting from the ace – and four descending sequences from king to ace.

Play
All cards in the blades may be moved onto their appropriate rank in the foundation zone. Turn up cards from the talon one by one, putting unplayable ones in a discard pile, the top card of which may be played on a sequence at the first opportunity. You may reverse a card from a king-sequence onto the ace-sequence, but not an entire sequence, for the next card on the ace-sequence must come from elsewhere. It's obvious that a foundation-king cannot be transferred onto the ace-sequence. A vacant space in the blades must be filled at once by a card from the discard pile, or from the talon if there is no discard pile. Only one

Various Runs and Sequences

round is allowed per game. The game is won when all five sequences have been completed.

Strategy

Give priority to building the ace-sequence, at the expense of king-sequences, and wait for problem cards to turn up from the discard pile. Try to maintain as great a variety of cards as possible in the blades and the king-sequences with which to feed the ace-sequence. To this end, delay creating vacancies in the blades when you know you can only fill them with same-rank cards.

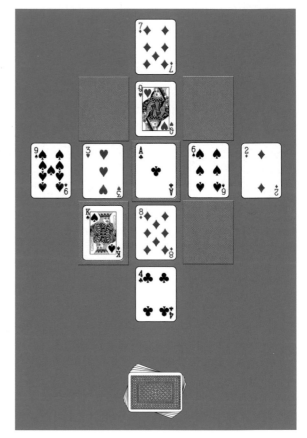

Tableau 193

173. Stalagmites

Despite its apparent simplicity, Stalagmites *requires an acute sense of anticipation and a good memory. Even before play starts, you must plan, and remember, a whole series of complex maneuvers in order to make wise choices about sequence intervals and what cards to put in the reserve. If you give the game the attention it deserves, success will not be far off.*

Material
One deck of 52 cards.

Opening Tableau
To form the foundation zone, deal four cards face up in a row on which to build ascending sequences. These foundation cards must remain visible at all times. In the maneuver zone, deal the remaining cards, face up, in six overlapping rows of eight columns.

Object
To build up four different circular sequences.

Play
Inspect the opening tableau and decide whether to build the sequences by one or by two. This decision will apply to all four sequences. Build them by moving any available card, regardless of color, onto a suit sequence whose last card is lower in rank – by one or by two, as per the chosen interval of build. Each completed sequence must contain 13 cards. Cards are moved one at a time, strictly from the maneuver zone to the foundation zone. Cards in the maneuver zone cannot be moved from one column to another. A vacant column must remain so. You may, however, remove any two available cards to form a reserve with which to build

sequences. The reserve may be renewed, but it can never contain more than two cards. The game is won when all four sequences have been completed.

174. Chameleon

This game is called Chameleon *because cards are considered strictly on the basis of their rank, regardless of color. Like a chameleon changes its color to suit its environment, sequences may be built in whatever color is dictated by the situation at hand. The high success rate makes this game a favorite among young players.*

Material
One deck of 52 cards.

Opening Tableau
In the maneuver zone, form a reserve pile of 12 cards, the top card of which is face up. To the right of this pile, deal a row of three face-up cards. Above the

Tableau 194

Various Runs and Sequences

row, place a face-up card in the foundation zone. The latter will determine the rank upon which to build ascending sequences. Keep the talon face down.

Object

To complete four ascending circular sequences, the base of which is determined by the luck of the draw.

Play

Any available card may be moved onto its appropriate rank in the foundation zone but may not be transferred back. Thus, in Tableau 194, move the 5 of hearts onto its base, then the 6 of diamonds onto either the 5 of spades or of hearts. Within the maneuver zone, build descending sequences by moving an available card onto another next in rank, regardless of color. Turn up cards from the talon one by one, placing unplayable ones in a discard pile. Note that the top card of the discard pile may be reintroduced into play at the first opportunity. A vacant column is filled by a card from the reserve, or from the discard pile if the reserve is empty, or from the talon if there's no discard pile. Only one round is allowed per game. The game is won when all four sequences have been completed.

175. Pascal

This is a game that requires sustained attention, unswerving concentration and a rare aptitude for arithmetic. Card manipulation plays only a secondary role. In other words, it's a game for the experts. Grandmother named it Pascal, *after the French mathematician who, in 1642, invented his famous calculating machine, the ancestor of today's calculators and computers. She never played this one with me, saying she needed to be alone so that she could concentrate properly. Indeed, Grandmother spent many a sleepless night playing* Pascal *and did win more than once, or so it seemed.*

Material
One deck of 52 cards.

Opening Tableau
In the foundation zone, place from left to right an ace, a 2, a 3 and a 4, regardless of suit or color. These are foundation cards on which to build ascending sequences. The maneuver zone is comprised of four discard columns that will store temporarily unplayable cards. Keep the talon face down.

Object
To complete four ascending sequences according to the following intervals of build:
- On the ace-sequence, build by ones: A, 2, 3, 4, 5, 6, 7, 8, 9, 10, J, Q, K;
- On the 2-card, build by twos: 2, 4, 6, 8, 10, Q, A, 3, 5, 7, 9, J, K;
- On the 3-card, build by threes: 3, 6, 9, Q, 2, 5, 8, J, A, 4, 7, 10, K;
- On the 4-card, build by fours: 4, 8, Q, 3, 7, J, 2, 6, 10, A, 5, 9, K.

Various Runs and Sequences

Play

Ace counts as one, jack as 11, queen as 12 and king as 13. Turn up cards from the talon one by one. If an available card can help build up a sequence in the foundation zone, transfer it. If not, place it face up on the table to start one of the four discard columns. Cards that cannot be played to the foundation zone are put into a discard column of your choice. This is where calculation is important, for cards must be placed in such an order as to be retrievable when they're most needed for building sequences. For example, if you manage to establish a discard column made up of a jack, an 8, a 5 and a 2 – useful for building the sequence by threes – avoid adding an ace onto the 2, lest you block the sequence for a long time.

If an ace turns up, place it upon the 3-card in the third discard column – useful for building the sequence by twos – and leave the first column vacant. If a

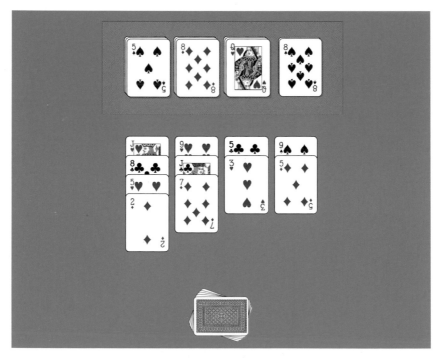

Tableau 195

The Complete Book of Solitaire

card is suitable for play on more than one sequence, inspect the tableau's configuration carefully to see which sequence will be more productive. Note, however, that to be able to see all available possibilities, one would need no less than a computer! And there's also the random character of chance to contend with. Only one round is allowed per game. The game is won when all four ascending sequences have been completed.

Strategy
Maintain a discard column for king-cards as long as possible. Unblock any stagnant sequence as soon as you can. When faced with a choice between two sequences, opt for the one that will help extricate the most cards from the discard columns.

Variant
Instead of four discard columns, pack all unplayable cards into one discard pile. Needless to say, this will make the game infinitely more difficult. Two rounds are allowed per game, instead of one. The downside is that this variant greatly diminishes the role of calculation, a key attraction of the game.

176. Gradation

Grandmother said this game came to her in a dream. Similar to Pascal (no. 175), sequences are built as per four different intervals, but the resemblance stops there. Gradation is a good candidate for young players. It requires a good dose of attention and memory but little calculation.

Material

One deck of 52 cards.

Opening Tableau

Remove the four aces and lay them face up in a row. Keep the 48-card talon face down.

Object

To complete four ascending sequences, from ace to king, as follows:

- The first sequence by ones: A, 2, 3, 4, 5, 6, 7, 8, 9, 10, J, Q, K;
- The second sequence by twos: A, 3, 5, 7, 9, Q, K;
- The third sequence by threes: A, 4, 7, 10, K;
- The fourth sequence by fours: A, 5, 9, K.

Note that if the game is successful, 23 unused cards will remain.

Play

Turn up cards from the talon one by one, placing suitable ones onto sequences in the foundation zone. Unplayable cards are placed face up in a discard pile, the top card of which may be moved onto a sequence at the first opportunity. One round is permitted per game. The game is won when all four sequences have been completed.

Strategy

When you have a choice between two sequences upon which to place a card, the general rule of thumb is to go for the more advanced sequence. However, your choice must also be guided by the kinds of cards that have already been played, as well as whatever stagnant sequences there might be in the tableau.

177. Bohemian

Grandmother said she learned this game from a transient beggar, hence its name.

Material

Two decks of 52 cards, stripped of 2s, 3s, 4s, 5s and 6s.

Opening Tableau

To form the foundation zone, set up eight spaces on which to build sequences. Remove any 7-card from the decks and place it in one of the spaces. To form the maneuver zone, turn up cards from the talon one by one, arranging them in a column below the 7 – the lower card overlapping its upper neighbor. Whenever the second 7-card turns up, place it to the right of the first 7 in the foundation zone and start a second column below the second 7. Continue in this manner until you will have set up the eighth column below the eighth 7-card.

During distribution, pause to place any 8s and 9s that turn up upon their suit sequences in the foundation zone. No other cards may be transferred, especially not those already placed in a column. A column may be very long, another may contain two or three cards, or no card at all, should two 7s turn up consecutively.

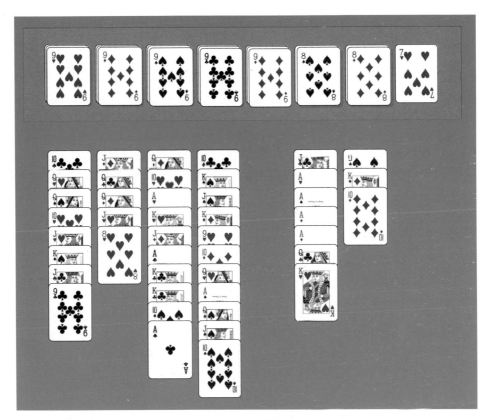

Tableau 196

Object

To complete eight ascending sequences from seven to ace.

Play

Any available card in the maneuver zone must be moved onto its appropriate rank in the foundation zone and may not be transferred back. No sequences of any kind are to be built in the maneuver zone. The only allowed card movement is that from the maneuver zone to the foundation zone. A vacant column may be filled by any available card in the maneuver zone. The game is won when all eight sequences have been completed.

Variants

1. Remove all cards between 2s and 8s inclusively. Thus, 9s become the foundation cards. No card may be placed upon its base during distribution.

2. Instead of sequences, build runs in alternating colors in the foundation zone. You will note that the success rate will decrease accordingly.

3. To make the game still more difficult to play, some players suggest building suit sequences instead of ordinary sequences.

178. Snake

The object of this game is to complete one continuous, circular sequence, not unlike a snake curling up in the grass. The game's unusual and original tableau sets it apart, and the spectacular developments that crop up during play motivate the player to win. Snake requires a natural head for figures and a good dash of attention in order to remember the various sequence intervals. Grandmother gladly took it on anytime, "Just to keep myself alert," she said.

Material

One deck of 52 cards.

Opening Tableau

Deal nine cards face up in three rows of three columns. The card in the center constitutes the foundation zone, the only base on which to build the sequence. The cards around it form the maneuver zone. Keep the talon face down.

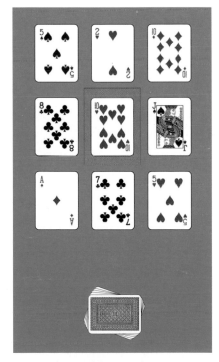

Tableau 197

Object

Build only one ascending sequence in the following order: A, 2, 4, 8, 3, 6, Q, J, 9, 5, 10, 7. Repeat this order four times. Note that the order of this sequence is arrived at by doubling each step, then deducting 13 from any total exceeding 12. To this effect, ace counts as 1, jack as 11, queen as 12 and king as 13. The calculation is as follows:

1 (ace) x 2 = **2**; 2 x 2 = **4**; 4 x 2 = **8**; 8 x 2 = 16 (- 13) = **3**; 3 x 2 = **6**; 6 x 2 = **12**; 12 x 2 = 24 (- 13) = **11**; 11 x 2 = 22 (- 13) = **9**; 9 x 2 = 18 (- 13) = **5**; 5 x 2 = **10**; 10 x 2 = 20 (- 13) = **7**; 7 x 2 = 14 (- 13) = **1**; 1 x 2 = **2**; and so on, the first round to be repeated four times. Note that kings have no place in the sequence. They are considered "dead cards."

Play

The card in the center of the opening tableau indicates the point of departure for the sequence, say the 10 of hearts (as per Tableau 197). Thus, you may move the 7 of clubs onto the 10 of hearts (10 x 2 = 20 – 13 = 7), then the ace of diamonds onto the 7 of clubs (7 x 2 = 14 – 13 = 1), then the 2 of hearts onto the ace of diamonds (1 x 2 = **2**). When all possible maneuvers have been executed, turn up cards from the talon one by one, pausing to transfer suitable cards onto the sequence. Unplayable cards are used to fill vacant spaces in the tableau, with the rest going to the discard pile, the top card of which may be reintroduced into play at the first opportunity. Whenever a king turns up, it must be placed in a vacant space from which it cannot be removed and in which it will stay for the length of the game. If there are no vacancies in the tableau, the king-card will go to the discard pile, to be transferred to a vacancy if one should present itself. Only one round is allowed per game. The game is won when all the cards have been placed onto the sequence, that is, except for the four kings, which cannot move from their spaces. It fails when cards remain in the maneuver zone or the discard pile.

179. Salic Law

In France, Salic law stipulated that women had no right of succession to the throne. This game gets its name from the fact that queens play no role in the game.

Material
Two decks of 52 cards.

Opening Tableau
In the foundation zone, set up eight spaces for the aces on which to build sequences. In the maneuver zone, place any king-card. Keep the talon face down.

Object
To complete eight ascending sequences from ace to jack.

Play
On the king, place all cards, as they are dealt, in a overlapping column. As aces appear, place them upon their bases in the foundation zone. Discard all the queens. With each king, start a new column. Any available card in the maneuver zone must be placed upon its appropriate rank in the foundation zone, regardless of color. For example, if a 5 of clubs is already in the foundation zone and you draw a 6 of hearts from the talon, you must place the latter at once upon the 5 of clubs. You can move only one card at a time.

The only allowed card movement is that from the maneuver zone to the foundation zone. You cannot move a card from a column onto another in the maneuver zone with a view to build a sequence. It's only when a king becomes available that an available card may be moved onto it in the maneuver zone. Tableau 198 shows a game in progress, after some 20 cards have been drawn from the talon.

As you can see, the king of hearts has been bared following the removal of the 3 of clubs. You may thus move the 10 of hearts upon the king so as to release the minor cards preceding the 10-card. When the talon is exhausted, continue to

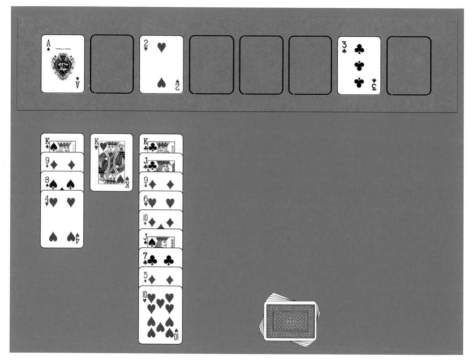

Tableau 198

move cards to the foundation zone. The game is won when all eight sequences have been completed.

CLUES

No. 12: Decimal (p. 50)

If you add up all 52 cards in a deck, counting court cards as 10 each and the ace as one, you will arrive at a total multiple of 10, namely: $(4 \times 1 = 4) + (4 \times 2 = 8) + (4 \times 3 = 12) + (4 \times 4 = 16) + (4 \times 5 = 20) + (4 \times 6 = 24) + (4 \times 7 = 28) + (4 \times 8 = 32) + (4 \times 9 = 36) + (4 \times 10 = 40) + (4 \times 3 \times 10 = 120) = 340$. Grandmother was right: *Decimal* is not a real game of solitaire.

No. 52: Mixed Pairs (p. 145)

A quick glance at the opening tableau will usually tell you whether or not the game can be won. If the tableau displays any of the following combinations: a four-of-a-kind, a proil, two red aces, two black kings or two black queens, the game automatically fails. Otherwise, success is a sure thing.

No. 59: Knight (p. 163)

The following tableau constitutes a solution:

13	22	9	30	3	24	7	32
10	29	12	23	8	31	2	17
21	14	27	4	19	16	25	6
28	11	20	15	26	5	18	1

There are at least three other solutions. Can you find them? If not, consider the mirror effect. What does it tell you?

BIBLIOGRAPHY

Bezanovska, Maria and Kitchevats, Paul. *Le Livre des patiences*, Montreal, Les Éditions de l'Homme, 1987.

Cadogan, Lady Adelaide. *Illustrated Games of Patience*, circa 1870.

Dick & Fitzgerald. *Dick's Games of Patience*, New York, 1883 series and 1898 series.

Henshaw, Annie B. *Amusements for Invalids*, Boston, 1870.

Loréac-Ammoun, Frank. *Tous les jeux de cartes. Règles, techniques, conseils*, Solar, 1987. With the collaboration of Olivier Meyer.

Morehead, Albert H., and Mott-Smith, Geoffrey. *The Complete Book of Solitaire and Patience Games*, 1949.

Pelter, David. *The Penguin Book of Patience*, 1960.

Phillips, H. *The Pan Book of Card Games*, 1960.

Phillips, H. & Westall, B.C. *The Complete Book of Card Games*, 1939.

Raymond, Richard. *Règles des jeux de cartes et des patiences*, Vol. 2, Les Éditions Quebecor, 1997.

Romano, Pasqual. *Réussites et patiences. Jeux de cartes en solitaire*, Marabout, 1998.

Sciuto, Giovanni. *Le Guide des réussites*, Paris, Jacques Grancher, 1987. Reprinted by Éditions du Club de France Loisirs, 1989.

INDEX